Chicken Soup
for the Soul.

My Very Good, Very Bad Dog

Chicken Soup for the Soul: My Very Good, Very Bad Dog
101 Heartwarming Stories about Our Happy, Heroic & Hilarious Pets
Amy Newmark. Foreword by Robin Ganzert.

Published by Chicken Soup for the Soul Publishing, LLC www.chickensoup.com
Copyright ©2016 by Chicken Soup for the Soul Publishing, LLC. All Rights Reserved.

The publisher gratefully acknowledges the many publishers and individuals who
granted Chicken Soup for the Soul permission to reprint the cited material.

Front cover artwork courtesy of iStockphoto.com/ Igorri1 (©Igorri1)
Back cover photo of puppy courtesy of iStockphoto.com/WebSubstance (©WebSubstance)
Back cover photo of dog with tilted head courtesy of iStockphoto.com/dhotard (©dhotard)
Interior dog illustrations courtesy of iStockphoto.com/AdrianHillman (©AdrianHillman)
Interior photos of dogs courtesy of Chicken Soup for the Soul employees
Photo of Amy Newmark courtesy of Susan Morrow at SwickPix
Photo of Robin Ganzert courtesy of Anne Grant

Cover and Interior by Daniel Zaccari

Distributed to the booktrade by Simon & Schuster. SAN: 200-2442

Publisher's Cataloging-In-Publication Data
(Prepared by The Donohue Group, Inc.)

Chicken soup for the soul : my very good, very bad dog : 101 heartwarming stories
about our happy, heroic & hilarious pets / [compiled by] Amy Newmark ; foreword by
Robin Ganzert.

   pages : illustrations ; cm

   ISBN: 978-1-61159-956-5

   1. Dogs--Behavior--Literary collections. 2. Dogs--Behavior--
Anecdotes. 3. Dog owners--Literary collections. 4. Dog owners--
Anecdotes. 5. Human-animal relationships--Literary collections. 6.
Human-animal relationships--Anecdotes. 7. Anecdotes. I. Newmark, Amy.
II. Ganzert, Robin. III. Title: My very good, very bad dog : 101
heartwarming stories about our happy, heroic & hilarious pets

SF426.2 .C45 2016
636.7/02   2015956064

PRINTED IN THE UNITED STATES OF AMERICA
on acid∞free paper

21 20 19 18 17 16   03 04 05 06 07

Chicken Soup for the Soul

My Very Good, Very Bad Dog

101 Heartwarming Stories
about Our Happy, Heroic
& Hilarious Pets

Amy Newmark

Foreword by Robin Ganzert
President and CEO, American Humane Association

Chicken Soup for the Soul Publishing, LLC
Cos Cob, CT

Chicken Soup
for the Soul

Changing the world one story at a time®
www.chickensoup.com

Contents

❸
~My Therapeutic Dog~

❹
~My Naughty but Nice Dog~

❺
~My Heroic Dog~

❻

~My Inspiring Dog~

❼

~My Clever Dog~

❽

~My Protective Dog~

❾

~My Working Dog~

❿

~My Intuitive Dog~

Foreword

Our best friends are miraculous, therapeutic, sometimes goofy, and often heroic. They can be naughty but nice, clever, inspiring, protective and intuitive. And they work to make our lives better. How did humans get so lucky to have dogs as our best friends?

Dogs throughout history have gone above and beyond the call of duty for us humans, saving lives on the battlefield and here at home, comforting the ill, aged and afflicted, bringing hope to those who have lost it, and reminding us of the powerful, age-old bond between dogs and people.

And the bond with our best friends inspires us to change the world through compassion, hope and kindness.

These amazing stories will warm your heart, make you laugh and giggle out loud, and perhaps shed a few tears. And I hope the stories will encourage you to open your heart and home to adopt a new best friend from your local animal shelter or rescue group. There are millions of animals right now waiting for a forever loving home and a second chance at life. And if you can't adopt a new best friend right now, please consider volunteering at an area shelter. Dog walkers are always needed!

In the case of my rescue dog, Daisy, she was waiting not for her second chance *but for her third chance* when our family came along. As they say, the third time's a charm, as Daisy brings us joy, humor, and unconditional love every day.

Speaking of humor, you will be highly entertained by this new volume from Chicken Soup for the Soul. For example, can you imagine going into a coffee shop while leaving your two pups outside tied to a metal table, and then looking up to see the table bouncing down the road? That's what happened in "The Great Table Caper" when Tyler and Zoe were left outside a café while their mom went in for just a minute. Thanks to the kindness of a stranger, danger was averted and the dogs, with a banged up table, were safe and sound after running several blocks. I can still picture Tyler and Zoe running down the street with the table chasing them... their middle-aged mom racing behind them.

In "The Birthday Miracle," a boy wants a puppy for his birthday but his single mother can't afford one. He has already picked out a name for his dog—Rusty. But miracles do happen, as do second chances for forever loving homes! When the mom and son go to the store to get a birthday donut, which is all she can afford to give him for his birthday, a stranger approaches and gives them a precious puppy, already named Rusty. Devon and Rusty were truly meant for each other.

Being that Daisy is a little white dog, I couldn't wait to read "Little White Dog," the story of newlyweds who rescue a little dog who ends up holding their marriage together while they go through the upheaval of moving to a new state early in their marriage. That little white dog keeps them all bonded, dishing up her daily doses of inspiration.

I'm sure you've heard about dogs who love doing their daily yoga stretches. After all, they don't call it the Downward Dog pose for no reason. In "Yoga Spirit," an adorable pup named Spirit likes his daily yoga practice, but not for the sake of exercise. He knows that as soon as the meditation begins, he gets to steal his mom's cucumber slices right off her closed eyes!

Nothing is more heartwarming about the power of the bond than when dogs are real heroes. In "Dynamic Duo," a Great Dane named Komomai and his owner rescue a drowning swimmer in the ocean off a Kauai beach. Courage comes in the form of four legs, fur and a wagging tail. And the dog didn't even know that he had done something heroic.

Now who doesn't love cheese? I know I do, as does Wolfie in "Working for Cheese." Wolfie's owner found him abandoned in a riverbed. She adopted him, and worked with him to become a search-and-rescue dog. But Wolfie wasn't in it for the glory. Turns out he was in it for the cheese, which he proceeded to swipe from the rescuers' backpacks one day during a practice session while they were helping the "victim" he had skillfully found for them.

And I adore the story of Tater, a senior dog living in a shelter who finds a forever loving home with a widow in "Meant for Each Other." I can't emphasize enough the tremendous value that senior dogs add to people's lives... and they are too often left behind at the shelters.

While this book features 101 heartwarming and hilarious stories about our best friends, there are at least a million doggone good reasons to consider adopting a dog. Each year, an estimated three to four million animals are waiting in shelters for someone to give them a safe, forever loving home. Too many never find a hero to adopt them.

If you're thinking about getting a dog, be a hero and consider adopting a dog from your local shelter or rescue group. You'll be saving a life and greatly improving yours! Dogs are amazing, supportive and heroic companions who can make a huge difference in your world as a best friend, an exercise buddy, or simply as a furry face eager to greet you when you come home after a hard day.

Your local shelter is the perfect place to find dogs of every type, size, age and personality — all waiting for a loving home. Or if you prefer a particular breed that isn't at your local shelter, go online to find a legitimate breed-specific rescue group in need of adopters like you.

If you're thinking about bringing an adopted dog into your family, here are some things to consider:

- Like children, dogs are completely dependent on their owners for all their needs—food, water, medical attention, exercise, shelter and, most important, companionship.
- But unlike children, dogs will never learn to pour themselves a drink, fix breakfast or take their own bath.
- Dogs never learn to look both ways before crossing a street and they can't stop and ask for directions.

Opening your home to a dog can be highly rewarding, as long

as you understand and accept the daily responsibilities and routines that come with owning a dog. For many, the years of companionship and unconditional love and devotion they receive from their dog far outweigh the daily responsibilities.

You may be the perfect dog owner if you…

- Believe caring for a dog for fifteen years does not seem like a lifetime.
- Look forward to big wet kisses when you come home each day.
- Like sharing your house with someone who sheds, occasionally tracks in dirt, and possibly drools.
- Don't mind sharing your house with someone who will never clean up after him or herself.
- Want to take care of someone every day.
- Love a playmate who likes to chase balls and drag off shoes.
- Don't mind a playmate who likes to slobber on balls and toys.
- Would like to spend your extra money on pet food, toys, veterinary care, chew bones and more chew bones.
- Want someone to adore you even on a bad hair day.
- Believe that spaying and neutering pets will help solve the pet overpopulation problem.
- Can't imagine leaving your devoted pet behind when you move.
- Want to keep an ID tag on your pets, so they can always get back to you no matter what.
- Enjoy unconditional love and constant companionship.

As you make your way through this wonderful collection, be sure to look at the photos at the beginning of each chapter. You'll meet ten soulful dogs who are part of the Chicken Soup for the Soul family — each one rescued off the streets or adopted from a shelter.

And if inspiration strikes after enjoying these stories and looking at the photos, please visit your local shelter to adopt a new best friend. There is no greater love than that of a dog. And remember that the qualities and personality you want in a dog are more important than size and appearance. For example, an older Shepherd mix might do better than an energetic Terrier in an apartment or with an older person.

Chicken Soup for the Soul talks about how their books are "changing the world one story at a time" and we appreciate that very much at American Humane Association. Not only does this book advocate for all the wonderful dogs who are waiting to give back to their adoptive families, but the royalties from this book will help support the work that we are doing at AHA to promote dog adoption and animal welfare. It's the right thing to do for Man's best friend.

~Robin Ganzert, President and CEO, American Humane Association

Rocky

My Very Good, Very Bad Dog

My Goofy Dog

Fun fact: The cartoon dog Goofy was created by Walt Disney Productions in 1932. His original name was Dippy Dawg.

The Great Table Caper

Fun fact: In most U.S. cities, to protect both people and dogs, "leash laws" require that dogs in public be on a leash that is less than six feet long.

E arly one fine spring morning, Tyler (a large Golden Retriever), Zoe (a large red Doberman) and I (a woman of a certain age) headed out for a walk. Our destination was the lake in the neighborhood. First, though, we visited the local coffee shop so I could get a cup of tea to drink as we walked.

I tied Tyler and Zoe, who were very sweet and obedient dogs, to the base of a metal table that was in a cordoned-off area for the restaurant next door. When the restaurant was closed, I often tied them to a table. As usual, I turned to look at them before going in and said, "Be good. I'll be right out."

It was a Saturday morning, and very few people were about or in the coffee shop. After getting my tea, I went over to the condiment station to doctor it with some sweetness. My back was to the door. While stirring in the sugar, I had slipped into a bit of absentmindedness. All of a sudden, a man's voice boomed from behind me, bringing me out of my reverie. "Someone own those dogs out there?" he called out.

Leaving my tea, I sprang to the door. Outside, mayhem reigned. Tyler, Zoe and the table were gone. Tables and chairs were knocked over. The black straps that cordoned off the area along with their metal stands were on the ground. I ran to the middle of the street. Tyler, the table, and Zoe — in that order — were running away as if the devil himself was chasing them. The metal table bounced, making a loud noise, which caused Tyler to run faster.

I ran after them, yelling, "Tyler, stop! Stop, Tyler, stop!" I could see that Tyler was the instigator since he was in the lead. He looked back at me, then at the table, and then back to me. His eyes said, "Mom, I can't. There's a table chasing me!" He kept running.

Zoe looked back at me, and her eyes said, "Mom, he's gone crazy; I don't know what to do." She was definitely at his mercy, and Tyler was at the mercy (in his mind) of the table.

I continued to run after them and yell at Tyler to stop. He'd look back at me, wanting to obey, but then he'd look at the table that kept chasing him and continue running. He'd swerve toward a parked car, causing the table to swing out, and I'd pray, "Please don't hit a car." Thankfully, he'd correct his course to the middle of the road and somehow avoid hitting any cars with the table.

I was not in shape to be running full tilt, and I had no idea how long the "table chase" was going to last. It appeared as if the threesome was headed toward our home, but there were six or so blocks still to go with a couple of parking lots, woods, and busier streets along the way. And poor Zoe, she had no choice but to run. I think she had her senses about her and would have stopped if she could, but as Tyler was in the lead, she was an unwilling accomplice. When I called out, she'd turn her head to look back at me, and with her eyes would say, "He's gone mad. Help me."

A few blocks into the run, with me huffing and puffing, it occurred to me: I could be mad and frustrated, or I could laugh. I chose to laugh, which made the running even more aerobic. But the absurdity of a woman of a certain age running after a dog who thinks he's being chased by a bouncing table was too much.

Soon, I was winded and could feel my heart beating fast. Then another thought came, "Oh, my God! I'm going to die of a heart attack chasing these dumb dogs and a table. What a stupid way to die. I hope my family will get a good laugh out of it."

The dogs crossed a grassy median that sent the table bouncing and swinging even more. The trio was headed to a parking lot with several cars in it. Tyler came close to a new red truck, and I thought, "I'm going to be buying a bumper today." Luckily, he veered away from it just in time.

Out of the corner of my eye, I noticed an employee standing in front of a Michael's craft store. He looked at the dogs, looked at me, and then did a double take. Then he took off after the dogs, running diagonally to them, and stopping them just as they were about to cross a busy road and careen into another parking lot filled with more cars.

I slowed down to catch my breath as I saw he had the dogs under control. Then a new thought sprang to mind: How the heck was I going to get the metal table back to the restaurant while controlling two large dogs? Should I leave the table? Tie the dogs to something stationary at the coffee shop and come back for the table? Could I even carry it after running so fast? Or should I take Zoe and Tyler home and bring my car for the table?

By the time I walked up to David (my hero) and the dogs, he had untangled them. The table was up on one of his shoulders. I thanked him while he passed Zoe and Tyler's leashes to me and marched off to the restaurant like it was an everyday occurrence to rescue a damsel in distress from renegade dogs and a fiercesome table. He was a godsend.

By the time Tyler, Zoe, and I got back to the coffee shop, David had just finished reestablishing order to the outside dining area. It looked as if nothing had ever happened. I can't remember ever being so grateful for a stranger's help, and I profusely thanked my Good Samaritan.

But it didn't seem enough. I wanted to show him my gratitude with more than just words; I wanted to give him something that was heartfelt. Cooking is something I do from the heart, and my apple pie is a favorite among friends and family.

So, I went home and made David an apple pie. It was still hot when I took it to the store just before he got off work. Months later, I was in Michael's and saw David. I repeated my thanks for his help, which he kindly brushed off. However, he thanked me for the apple pie, saying it was the best he had ever eaten.

By the way, from that point on, Tyler and Zoe were always tied to a stationary object, such as a lamppost, when we went to the coffee shop.

~Ann Denise Karson

Bedtime with The Moose

*Fun fact: Dogs make great heating pads because
their normal body temperature is higher than that of
humans — around 101 degrees Fahrenheit.*

Walter Liddy aka "The Big Guy" aka "The Moose" is a four-year-old Mastiff–Presa Canaria mix. He is a big boy, solidly built, but under the mistaken impression that he is a member of the teacup variety. Walter was found wandering alone on the streets of New Bedford, starving, frightened and covered in mange. Like most rescues, this dog flourished with love and kindness, shedding both his fear and his patchy skin to become a solid member of our family. Technically, "The Big Guy" belongs to Brigid, our oldest daughter, who adopted him from a local rescue, but he's a frequent flyer here at home base. He is our pet by proxy.

Walter Liddy is like many spoiled family pets. He begs for food (and usually gets it), makes himself comfortable on the furniture at the expense of one or more of his humans and is generally overindulged at every turn, but it is his bedtime ritual that makes this gentle giant unique.

Brigid had briefly described his new behavior to me. "Walter likes to sleep under the covers," she explained. Big deal, I thought, but I didn't fully comprehend Walter's ritual until I experienced it myself one night last winter. Walter woke me from a sound sleep around 2:00 a.m. by standing on my side of the bed and looking at me intently through the darkness. My husband was asleep next to me. Walter let out a grunt, waited and grunted again. He was obviously trying to tell me something.

"Do you want to go out?" I asked with a bit of annoyance, wondering why he wasn't asking his "mother." Walter didn't budge. Nope, that wasn't it. Then I recalled Brigid's words earlier. I lifted the blankets, and Walter immediately hopped up and dove under layers of bedding: sheets, blankets, and comforter — the works.

He slid his humongous carcass down to the foot of the bed, made a half-turn, plopped down, stretched out and promptly fell asleep. It was like having a third person in bed with us. I couldn't believe it. "How can he breathe?" I wondered, as I tried to get comfortable again with no luck.

After that, it was a done deal. Night after night, this crazy dog roamed from room to room, bed to bed, squeezing in with a different family member every night. The routine was always the same: Walter Liddy didn't want to sleep *on* the bed with his people; he wanted to sleep *under* the covers, DEEP under the covers. And once situated, he would remain there until morning, immovable as an oak tree.

One night, I heard The Moose get off the couch and walk to the girls' room. I heard a loud thud in the dark as he attempted to use his huge cranium like a battering ram, but someone had inadvertently shut the door, preventing him from entering. I got out of bed and quietly opened the door for Walter to go in. As I stood there in the dark hallway, I knew exactly what this determined canine was doing. He stood next to the bed. He grunted and then waited, expecting the occupant to lift the covers and invite him to crawl in. That night, it happened to be his auntie Barbara, our youngest daughter. When Barbara didn't respond, Walter gave another deep grunt, as if asking, "What's the hold-up?" Now half-awake, Barbara groaned and said, "Oh, you gotta be kidding me." There was a pause and then, "Walter, come on, get up. Uppee, Walter, uppee!" His collar jingled as he jumped up, and Barbara sighed, "Now go to sleep." I heard the rustle of bedding, a deep satisfied canine groan, and then silence.

I peeked into the darkened room and saw he was completely gone, all one-hundred-plus pounds of him. Walter was nothing more than a slight bump in the bed linens. He had ignored all the extra mattress space available on the bed and was stretched out flat against Barbara, stuck to her like a pilot fish to a shark. She had gone back to sleep as if this was the most normal thing in the world, and for some reason that struck my funny bone. I began to laugh so hard I was crying. The thought that this dog had trained his family to do his bidding, in the middle of the night, with a grunt or two, was hysterical. I was just catching my breath when I heard his tail go THUMP, THUMP, THUMP under the blankets. From his cocoon, The Big Guy was responding to my laughter. He was happy and content with the world, his wagging tail said. It was a small but profound thing, and it touched my heart. I whispered a silent prayer to heaven that every animal could know such love and security. If I live to be a hundred I'll never forget this silly, affectionate boy and the quirky, crazy habits that make him so precious.

~Liz Lombard

Hungry Like a Wolf

*Fun fact: Australian Shepherds, unlike Australian
Cattle Dogs, aren't actually Australian; the breed was
developed in the United States.*

My husband Michael has the equivalent of a preschool education when it comes to food preparation. He knows the basics, like how to spread Nutella on rye. His food pairings are imaginative and desperate. He shouldn't be in the kitchen in the same way a color-blind person shouldn't be an art director of a fashion magazine.

Michael does know his way around a refrigerator filled with leftovers though. The key to his survival has always been his prowess at warming up said leftovers in the microwave.

This brings me to the most sacred day of leftovers: Yom Kippur, the holiest day of the year for Jewish people. Many non-Jewish people know it as the annual Jewish observance of fasting. The fast begins at sundown on the night known as Kol Nidre and continues to sunset the next day. There is always an extravagant feast on Kol Nidre before sunset to hold everyone over for twenty-four hours of starvation.

I love all the Jewish holidays because my mother-in-law does the cooking. The agreement we have is that I set the table and she provides the food. This has served us well through the years, and was negotiated on a table napkin one year after an especially challenging cooking experience. As part of the deal, I even get to keep the leftovers.

Notwithstanding the Jewish holiday contract, I am still entrusted with the care and feeding of the entire family and that includes taking care of our Australian Shepherd, Slugger Free Spirit Red Sox Koenig, who does not participate in the Yom Kippur fast.

Slugger is a purebred Aussie, a stunning red merle with a soft coat in shades of white, tan and reddish brown. Unfortunately, as Slugger has aged, he has developed a throat condition. He often gags as if something is caught there. So one September, around the time of Yom Kippur, I tried changing his food from dry pellets to wet food. I hoped it would be less harsh on his throat. So it wouldn't be wasted, I spooned his uneaten moist food into a plastic container and put it in the refrigerator.

As she does every year, that Kol Nidre my mother-in-law brought a complete holiday dinner to my house. We rushed through eating so we could get to temple in time for the evening service. We stuffed chopped liver, brisket, and noodle pudding into plastic containers to be eaten the next day when we would break the fast on Yom Kippur.

That year, as he does each year, Michael fasted the entire day. His ritual is to break the fast at exactly 5:00 p.m., even if the sun has not set. He is fond of saying "It's always sundown somewhere in the world."

While Michael struggled through the last half-hour of his fast, I took Slugger for a walk. When I returned home twenty minutes later, I saw that Michael had pulled a container of leftovers out of the refrigerator. The top was removed from the container and placed next to a box of crackers on the center island in the kitchen. Dry, beige crumbs littered a blue disposable plate. A dirty knife rested on the black granite countertop.

How nice, I thought. Michael has helped himself to some chopped liver.

"How are you doing?" I asked.

No response. He pointed to a mouth full of food.

Michael had moved on from the appetizer portion of the evening to a warmed plate of beef brisket and kugel, which are egg noodles baked in soft cheese and sugar. He was watching a movie with a TV tray in our family room.

I picked up the plastic container to put it back into the refrigerator, but something didn't look right. I took a closer look at the contents. I showed it to Slugger, who raised his nose into the air. Sniff, sniff, and sniff. He licked his chops.

I sniffed the contents, too. I imagined what Slugger must be thinking, "Why is Michael eating my food?"

"Yeah, that's what I'm wondering, too," I said aloud. "But thanks for sharing. You're a good dog."

I wasn't sure what to do next. Should I tell Michael that he had just broken his holiday fast with dog food? Or should I call all the family members on my contact list and tell them the story? After a twenty-four-hour fast, some entertainment is needed.

"What do you think, Slugger?" I said. "Call the relatives? Post the story on Facebook?"

Slugger cocked his head to the side.

"That's what I thought. You're such a bad dog."

I looked at Michael happily enjoying the rest of his dinner. I decided that if the dog food was good enough for Slugger, then it was good enough for my husband. I spooned the rest into Slugger's bowl, grabbed my cell phone and called anyone who would answer the phone. Like food, this was a story best served fresh.

~Tina Koenig

Top Dog

Fun fact: July is National Doghouse Repair Month.

"Come on, boy. That's right, go inside," I said to my new puppy after buying him a doghouse. My eight-week-old puppy, Strider, was apparently afraid of his doghouse. I didn't understand it. Most of the dogs we had growing up didn't have doghouses; they slept outside or sometimes inside the house, but what dog wouldn't want its very own house? Every day I would come home from work, collect my bag of treats, and go to the back yard to train little Strider to go inside his doghouse. I offered him treats, but he would just look at me like I was out of my mind. I put the treats inside his doghouse, but he just turned his head away from me.

After weeks of not getting anywhere, I decided I would crawl into the doghouse myself, along with the treats, to show him that it was safe. He ended up running away while I struggled to get out. I persevered in spite of that unfortunate setback. "Come on, boy, it's dinnertime," I said sweetly, placing his dog dish inside the doghouse. Strider sat down about six feet away, nose in the air, and gave me the most pitiful look he could muster. I sat down on the swing and decided I would wait. This was going to work for sure.

Two hours later, Strider still lay six feet away from the doghouse, looking at his food. I, too, sat there, staring at his food. "I give up!" I said sternly as I threw up my hands and walked over to his doghouse. I picked up his dish, set it just in front of the house, and stood up to look at Strider. He barked at me and stayed where he was. I said to Strider, "Who is training who here?" I gave in and put the dish closer to him and a little farther away from his house. To be fair, he met me halfway.

The next day, I started over. First, I tried his treats to no avail, so I set them on top of his doghouse and went inside to get his dinner. As I came to the door, I saw him jump up on the roof and stick his head in the treat bag! I was a little miffed, but I had to admit it was a pretty cute thing to see. I put on my stern face and swung open the door, yelling, "Bad dog! Get off of there right now!" He jumped down, still gripping the bag with his teeth, and I proceeded to chase him around the yard to win back the bag of treats. Eventually, I got the bag away from him and figured that was enough training for one day.

Before going to bed, I decided to check on him. I took a quick look out the window like I did every night. I had to do a double take because he was asleep, quite comfortably I might add, on top of his doghouse! I couldn't help but laugh. I'd never known a dog afraid of a doghouse, let alone one that slept on top of one! I was so tickled that I couldn't help but gaze out the window at him for a few more minutes before going off to bed.

Months passed, and I finally managed to get Strider to retrieve his treat from inside the doghouse. He wouldn't eat it inside, but he would quickly run in, grab it, and run right out. It was frustrating, but entertaining to watch. A few more months went by. One day, I put his dog dish inside the doghouse, and as I was heading back inside, I turned around and saw that Strider had gone inside the doghouse and was eating his food in there. "Yay, Strider, good boy!"

That night, I looked out the window, sure that I had finally gotten him comfortable enough to sleep in his doghouse. I pulled away the curtain and there lay Strider — on top of his house. I went to bed in a huff. Almost a year, and poor little Strider would only go in his house to get food or treats.

Finally, I decided enough was enough, and I left Strider to whatever sleeping arrangements he chose. For another year, Strider chose to sleep on top of the doghouse, but he was growing into a pretty big dog, and he found it harder and harder to balance himself on the roof. Even so, I stopped trying to get him in his house and started focusing on other, more useful commands.

One day, we got another dog. Lady didn't mind the doghouse at all. Her first time in the yard, she went right in. Strider barked at Lady, lying inside his house. I called them over to have dinner. Lady ran out of the doghouse, and Strider ran right in. He was finally lying in his house, and he wasn't coming out any time soon!

~Christina Eichstedt

A Tail-Raising Tale

*Fun fact: Many commercial products are now
available that do a better job of "deskunking" dogs
than the traditional tomato-juice bath.*

My heart melted when I met him. Scooping up the
light-as-a-feather puppy, I held him nose-to-nose.
The tiniest pink tongue flicked out and graced the tip
of my nose with a moist kiss.

Convinced this teeny brown pup was part Chihuahua, I named
him Pancho and slipped him into my coat pocket. But he morphed — in
size and attitude. He was fearless, and his reckless abandon often
landed him smack-dab in the middle of trouble.

Overnight camping trips particularly brought out Pancho's wild
side. He would rocket out of the car with excitement when we arrived
at our campsite. One time, he leaped out the open window the moment
we arrived. I lost him in the nearby meadow, but occasionally I'd see
him hopping up and down like a jackrabbit. As I set up camp, and then
fished, my eyes scanned the valley for signs of my wayward friend. It
was growing late — too late. I bit my lip. Time to go into tracking mode.

Halfway across the meadow stood a gnarled climbing tree, so
up I went. Perched out on a limb, I gently rocked my body back and
forth to allow my eyes to catch movement in the twilight. What kind
of trouble was Pancho in this time?

A-ha! There he was, leap-frogging near some boulders. I licked
two fingers and whistled his call. His head swiveled toward me — but

only for a second. His nose went straight up in the air. He rotated his body and then dashed into the thicket, hot on the trail of a great sniff.

Scraping both hands, I bumped down the tree. "Get back here!" I yelled.

He didn't.

I charged into the deepening shadows of pines and aspens, but I couldn't see well enough in the twilight to realize something was amiss.

Then it hit me. I sniffed again, and realized exactly where Pancho must be. And there he was, legs planted far apart, glaring at a small black-and-white animal.

"Pancho," I whispered. "That's not a cat. Come."

He didn't.

The skunk, on the other hand, did move. His beady black eyes stared straight at the dog, ignoring me completely. He arched his back and hissed, tiny sharp teeth showing white against his black face.

I took one step back and also hissed. "Pancho, back away now."

He didn't.

The dance began.

The skunk was kind of adorable, stamping his clawed feet. But when he started hopping backward, all cuteness melted away. I took three steps back.

He raised his gorgeous, plumed black-and-white tail. Swallowing, I slithered behind an ancient aspen tree, several more feet away.

My canine cocked his head and held his ground.

Suicidal fool.

"Come. Now," I squeaked in horror.

The skunk wobbled forward, and my dog's growl shifted to frantic barking.

Oh, this was not good.

The skunk whipped his rear around and sprayed. Pancho shook his soaked body, whining pitifully while the skunk serenely waddled away — in triumph.

Pancho eyed me cowering behind my tree and made a beeline to me.

I panicked. I didn't want to touch him, so I grabbed a low hanging branch and swung my feet off the ground, dangling just out of his reach.

Fortunately, Pancho dashed to a thick patch of grass, flopped over, and rolled on the ground. I lowered myself and slipped back to camp. There, I grabbed some defensive tools. The last thing I wanted was for him to spread his stink on the sleeping bags.

When Pancho slunk into camp, tail firmly between his legs, I was ready—lasso and stick in hand. With my head turned to the side, I prodded him to a bush far away from camp and tied him there.

Now, all I wanted to see was red—red tomato juice, tomato sauce, tomatoes.

I scrambled back to my family's freshly made sandwiches and, in a blur of motion, lettuce and pickles flew over my shoulders. Gleefully, I held up slices of tomatoes. "There you are, you red beauties."

Glancing at my stunned family, I asked, "Do we have catsup?"

The speechless group held their noses and backed away. Apparently, I hadn't fully escaped the skunking after all.

I growled. "Well, do we?"

Finally, my sister rustled in a bag and, with her arm ramrod straight, bravely handed me a bottle. I locked eyes with her, and she froze. "Make me a garbage-bag apron. Dump the stuff out of two plastic grocery bags—no, make that four—and tie them on my hands. Tie my hair back, too. Now."

Bless her. She also pinched a clothespin on my nose.

I turned, ready for battle.

After Pancho and I both had several tomato and mud baths, we returned from the river, dripping. Pancho smelled less horrendous. Still, he would spend the night whining, tied far away from camp.

Just as we drifted off to sleep, someone mumbled, "How are we going to get him home tomorrow?"

Windows wide open—that's how. We drove away from the serene valley with our heads poking out the windows and Pancho blissfully asleep at my feet.

~Sandy Wright

Reprinted by permission of www.offthemark.com

Every Farm Needs a Dog

Fun fact: Up to fifteen percent of dogs may experience some form of separation anxiety.

Our dog had died the previous year, shortly before we had left to go to Mississippi for a year on a mission for our church. When we returned home, it didn't feel quite right to have a farm without a dog, but my husband wasn't eager to start over with another one.

Then one weekend, when he was at our son's dairy farm, our son said, "Dad you need a dog. Every farm needs a dog."

My husband looked at the four dogs there and commented, "The only dog I would want would be one like old Comanche there. He just lies around and stays out of trouble."

They both laughed and went on with their work.

Comanche, a German Shepherd mix, was a brother of our dog that had died. He was about five years old and well past the puppy stage.

When my husband returned home, he repeated the conversation to me. We laughed and soon got busy on our mini-farm, forgetting all about it.

A few weeks later, our son and two of his children were heading south and "just happened" to be coming our way.

Our son called and said, "We have a surprise for you. Something you really need on the farm."

For the next hour, we wondered what we "really needed on the farm." We should have guessed, but we were so surprised when our son and his children walked in with Comanche in tow!

Comanche was not an overly friendly dog; in fact, he had always barked at us when we went to visit our son and would not let us get too close. We were not sure that we really wanted this dog, but here he was. And how do you say "no" to two grandchildren who are excited to give you one of their prize dogs?

At first, my husband was concerned that the dog might run back to our son's farm if we left him alone too much. So, for the first time in over forty-five years, we had a dog *in* the house. We let him sleep by our bed the first night, and that turned into the second night, and the third night. He wasn't really any problem. When he was in the house, he would find a good spot and lie down. Soon, he was following my husband everywhere he went, even if he just went into the next room. I could see that my husband was getting very attached to this dog, and before I realized it, we officially had an indoor dog!

However, the first Sunday we had a dilemma.

"Where do we put Comanche while we are at church?" I asked.

"We can't leave him outside," my husband said. "He is not all that familiar with things. And he still might head for his previous home if no one is here for several hours."

We decided to leave him in the basement.

At least, we thought he was in the basement. When we returned home, we found a mess. There were lamps turned over, flower pots emptied on the floor, and curtains moved in every room, even upstairs. As we walked into the kitchen, I noticed my honey-bear jar was on the floor. It usually sat on top of the microwave.

"What happened to that?" I asked, looking around the floor to see other things in disarray. Reaching down to pick it up, I caught movement from the corner of my eye.

I glanced up and was totally stunned! My mouth flew open, but I was speechless. There on top of the refrigerator lay Comanche. His tail wagged in greeting. All I could do was point.

"Oh, my goodness!" my daughter exclaimed.

Suddenly coming to my senses, I hurried for my camera — this scene could never be duplicated. But when I moved, everything changed.

Comanche carefully slid around and jumped on to the sink and then to the floor. He hurried over to my husband, who was always good for an ear rub. He seemed so happy to see us.

We discovered that he had opened the basement door and checked out every window. It was as though he had a panic attack when he could not find us anywhere in the house and could not see us outside, so he found a tight place where he felt secure.

As time went by, we discovered that he knew how to open the back door and the garage door, so he could come in whenever he wanted unless we locked the doors. Fortunately, he also figured out that we always came back once we left, and he did not have another anxiety attack. And we never found him on top of the refrigerator again!

~Shirley M. Oakes

7

Buried Treasure

Not-so-fun fact: The side effects of chocolate consumption in dogs can range anywhere from a little bellyache to death. In general, the smaller the dog and the darker the chocolate, the more dangerous this snack is for your pet.

Droopy was our first rescue dog. He was a Basset Hound with front legs shaped like bananas. His badly formed legs didn't slow him down and he loved to run laps around the house and play with our other Basset, Buster. Droopy liked to snuggle, and slept in bed with us every night. Apparently, Droopy also had a sweet tooth.

One evening after we had Droopy for a few years, my husband Brent and I were eating dinner at the kitchen table, and we heard Droopy chewing on something in the living room. When I went to check it out, I found him chewing on a mini Tootsie Roll. After I took it away from him, Brent and I went back to eating dinner. A few minutes later, we again heard Droopy chewing on something. I found him chewing on another Tootsie Roll and took it away. This went on multiple times: Droopy appearing with a Tootsie Roll, me taking it away.

Finally, Brent and I looked at each other and wondered where he was getting the candy. Just then, Droopy came walking through the dog door. A-ha! I walked outside, and Droopy quickly followed. Then I saw him retrieve a Tootsie Roll from the yard. When I went to follow him, he led me to Tootsie Rolls that he had buried all over the yard. It seems Droopy had found a bag of candy and had the willpower to bury them all over to save them for later. Each time I took a candy away, Droopy had another one waiting for him.

I spent the rest of the night outside with a flashlight, searching for Tootsie Rolls buried in the yard.

~Kimberly Crawford

8

The Tomato Thief

*Not-so-fun fact: The ripe tomato fruit is generally okay
for dogs to eat in moderation, but the tomato plant,
which contains tomatine and solanine, is highly
toxic to dogs.*

I was about to give up trying to grow tomatoes. I had dreamed of delectable tomato sandwiches, bruschetta and more. I planted and fertilized three beautiful plants of the Better Boy variety. But there was nothing delectable about my mostly fruitless plants. I saw flowers… and then nothing!

By season's end, I had what my husband described as three of the "area's most expensive tomato sandwiches" and not much more.

So what was happening to my sweet, beautiful fruit? I'd always been good at growing plants. In fact, I still maintain a now twenty-two-year-old aloe plant.

What I didn't know is that I was competing with another gardener.

Our five-year-old Pug had been rescued from a North Carolina puppy mill. She was abused and frightened of everything. We adopted her after two previous placements — one foster, one adoptive — proved she needed more.

We knew the moment she made it through our door that she would spend the rest of her days with us, and an unlimited supply of hugs, love and protection. My husband, son and I took special care to speak softly and not drop any pots or pans. It took months, but finally Dora untucked her tail and displayed its signature curl. That was a teary, joyful day for us.

Dora had over a half-acre of fenced-in yard as well as our home in which to find peace and security. She also had three defenders whose mission was to make sure that no one would ever hurt her again and that her days of abuse would become a distant memory.

We watched her blossom, but maybe a little too much! We had a lot to learn about her breed, including the fact that Pugs have no food filters. She was ready to eat at all times of the day and night. At ten pounds overweight, she was now struggling in a different way.

We researched and realized she could maintain her lust for food with a healthier option: carrots! She lost all the weight and looked like a brand-new, healthy dog. But our Dora is still always on the hunt to find food, and the mischievous nature of her breed has her wanting to find things her humans know nothing about.

So, let's get back to the tomatoes.

Feeling a little deflated about what looked like a sad end to my annual attempt at tomatoes, I left my husband in charge and went to spend a long weekend with a dear friend, who has the ultimate green thumb. I bemoaned my garden, and she tried to assure me I was doing the right things.

Back home, my husband made a discovery. He was finding half-eaten tomatoes all over the yard. We have woodland creatures, so maybe they were the culprits.

Then again... maybe not.

Something flashed in his peripheral vision, and he looked to see where Dora was. He walked toward the flash and stopped dead in his tracks.

Our beautiful, innocent Pug had dashed behind the box garden so she wouldn't be seen and then hopped into the box. My husband could only watch and laugh as she went after one of the few remaining tomatoes.

He most certainly had a dilemma. He didn't want this Pug that we had nursed into happiness and security to get in trouble, but he didn't want his wife to continue thinking she was the worst gardener ever.

He had to be sure it wasn't a fluke, so the next time he was out, he was armed with the camera on his phone. It didn't take long to get the evidence proving our sweet Dora had an alternate career as a tomato thief!

I don't think I've ever laughed so hard or been so relieved to solve a mystery.

Dora, who maintained a face of innocence through it all, suffered no major consequence.

My husband did.

The very next year, he had to help me fence in the box so we could keep the criminal away from Mommy's tomatoes!

The result: I have a bumper crop, Dora stands no chance of tomato poisoning, and my husband can no longer claim he is forced to eat the most expensive tomato sandwiches ever!

~Carol Andrews

The Price of Protection

*Fun fact: Dogs have only about one-sixth the number
of taste buds that humans have. Often, they prefer
strong-smelling foods since they enjoy their food more
with their sense of smell than taste.*

We don't have a home security system. We have a dog — a good-tempered pooch who sheds a lot, eats a lot, sleeps a lot, and loves us in that uncomplicated way animals have. Whenever he gets into mischief, my husband reminds me, "One day, he will save your life."

I'm not so sure. He seems more concerned with his stomach than our security. If he's done any guard-dogging, it hasn't been in my presence.

One evening, my husband and I were running the kids to various activities. I arrived home first with our older daughter. It was dark, and when we pulled into our driveway, we saw the interior door was open. My daughter panicked.

"We've been robbed!"

More likely, the last kid out was running late and forgot to shut the door. Still, I needed to exercise caution. I opened the car door, and my daughter grabbed my arm.

"Mom! Don't go!"

We have a dog, I told her. He's either in the house or not. If he's not, I'll come back.

She looked at me as if she might never see me again. She nodded her head, and then locked me out of the car.

I approached the house, calling my dog. Nothing. I opened the storm door and called again. Still nothing. I poked my head inside and saw a flash of tail scurrying behind the television.

Phew.

Then, I saw the problem.

We have a split-level home, which means I can see into my kitchen from the front door. And in the kitchen, all over the floor, was garbage. Apparently, my nine-year-old "puppy" was taking advantage of our absence to nibble the trash. Now, guilt-ridden but not terribly sorry, he was hiding.

Never mind if there was an axe-wielding burglar in the upstairs bathroom.

I called his name, trying to hide my annoyance. The dog wasn't fooled and remained hidden. I looked at the car. My frightened teen peered back at me. I looked at the tail behind the television. Unbelievable. It was a dog's shining moment — the moment my husband had alluded to for years — and our dog was cowering in the corner.

I entered the house, walked to the fridge and opened the cheese drawer. My dog knows the cheese drawer. Sure enough, he bounded over the trash-strewn floor and sat like a prize show dog. My champion.

Holding the cheese in my hand, I inspected the house. Every room he entered with me, he got a bit of cheese. My feelings were conflicted. On one hand, I was bribing my dog to protect me. On the other, I did feel safer entering those dark rooms with him at my side.

Once I confirmed the house was safe, I got my daughter and swept up the garbage in silence. My dog watched me expectantly.

Was he in trouble? Was he a hero? Was he thinking, "Eat trash, get cheese?"

My husband returned. While the dog circled his legs, I explained what happened. He frowned at his trash-eating pooch, but couldn't resist patting the dog's head.

Granted, it only took cheese to get him to come with me. And cheese is cheaper than a home security system. Let's just hope his loyalty doesn't hinge on who's holding the cheddar.

~Nicole L.V. Mullis

Backyard Buddies

*Fun fact: All dogs have pink tongues, except for
the Chow Chow and Shar-Pei, which have black or
purplish tongues. Many dogs have black spots on their
tongues, though.*

Lacey, our female Yorkie, saw me opening the front door to check the mailbox and took that opportunity to slip out into the yard. She was usually very good about staying in the house, but she had an incentive to escape that day — our neighbor, Sarah, was in the front yard watching her son ride his new bike up and down the sidewalk while she fed her toddler.

Lacey was a mousey little dog who did not come into her own until she had a litter of puppies. She was a great mother and truly enjoyed taking care of her brood. She had three litters with our male, George Mutt, before we had her spayed. She had adored being a mama, but during her last pregnancy she had come down with milk fever and we decided it best not to breed her again. Her mother instincts still lingered, though. Every time she heard a puppy cry — even on television — she would search for it so she could "mother" that baby. Her maternal instinct went beyond puppies, too. She would mother all young things, from kittens to human babies. When she heard any distress call, Mama Lacey was there to comfort and quiet the little ones' fears.

That day, Sarah's baby, Kim, was teething and fussing as her mom attempted to feed her. When I opened the front door, Lacey heard the baby cry and was gone like a shot to help. Before I could stop her, Lacey had run next door to where Sarah and Kim were on a blanket on the ground. Lacey immediately stood on her hind feet and started licking Kim's face. The child was startled at first and drew back. But I said, "It's okay, she won't hurt you. Those are just puppy kisses." Kim relaxed, stopped fussing, and began to pet Lacey. Sarah was relieved — she said it was the first time that day Kim had settled down. When it was time to go, I literally had to pull Lacey away from Kim's grasp to take her home.

After that incident, when both our dogs and Sarah and her kids were each in our fenced-in back yards, Lacey would always run to the fence, wag her tail and excitedly greet Kim, who always responded with a smile and an outstretched hand. If she could reach Lacey to pet her, Kim would. Sarah and I thought this bond between dog and baby was delightful. We were glad the two had found each other.

Spring had sprung, and Sarah and her husband built a play fort in the back yard for the kids to play in while they planted flowers in the flowerbeds. I noticed that when I was cooking in my kitchen and the kids were playing next door, Lacey would cry to go out. I'd let Lacey out in the back yard while I was finishing supper and I would hear the squeals of laughter from Kim next door when she caught a glimpse of Lacey. When the kids were playing, it got harder and harder to get Lacey to come back in the house.

One afternoon, Lacey did not come back at all when I called, and it was eerily quiet in the neighbor's back yard. Wondering if something was amiss, I dried my hands and went into the yard to see what was happening. As I cleared the corner of the house and looked in the direction of our neighbors' house, I witnessed what was going on just about the time Sarah looked up from her flowerbed to check on her suddenly silent toddler.

There, both clinging to the chain-link fence that separated them, were Lacey and Kim. They had each pulled up to the eye level of the other and were intent on joyfully touching tongues through the links of the fence. Sarah and I simultaneously started laughing and went to separate our "kids."

~Janice R. Edwards

Pet Rock

*Fun fact: Mother dogs are called dams. Father dogs
are called sires.*

We grew up on a farm in Colorado, situated at the base of the Rocky Mountains, surrounded by cats, goats, pigs, cows, and horses. My sister and I loved the outdoors, and our dog Kelly was our constant companion. Her fat belly and long ears almost dragged on the ground as her little legs labored to keep up with us. The only thing that took precedence over tagging after us was chasing rabbits. When she picked up a rabbit's scent, she'd follow it, yipping, with her nose to the ground. Sometimes she'd be gone for hours. One time, she actually came back carrying a bedraggled baby bunny.

"Kelly, no!" Alarmed, I took the baby bunny away from her. Not knowing what else to do with it, I took it home and placed it in a cage. I would try to raise it and release it back to the wild.

In the spring, my sister and I often ignored Kelly for a while when there was a new litter of kittens, a nest of baby bunnies, or a new baby calf. One day, as we stopped to inspect a litter of kittens, we noticed that the gray striped one was missing. The mother cat had been known to move previous litters, so we searched all the places where she had hidden them before. We came up empty. I decided to search in one last place — a rarely used shed. Peering into the gloom, I heard a crying kitten, and who did I find there but Kelly, lying next to the kitten. She looked up at me and thumped her tail, smiling, as if to say, "See? I'm taking care of her."

I gently scooped up the kitten and carried it back to its mother. A few days later, the same kitten went missing. Again, my sister and I found Kelly nestled in the shed with it. This earned her a stern scolding as we carried the kitten back to its mother.

All summer long, we battled — Kelly stealing a kitten, my sister and I hunting her down and taking the kitten away. It didn't matter how much we scolded her, Kelly continued to steal the kitten, bathing it and trying to nurse it. For the next three springs, Kelly, my sister and I fought that same battle with a new kitten every year. Then one year, we stumbled across a goose nest. Canada Geese migrated through every year, but this was the first time we'd actually found one of their nests.

"No, Kelly, no!" we told her as we shoved her away from the nest. A few days later, I saw her coming from behind the house, carrying something in her mouth.

"What does she have now?"

She had robbed the goose nest! I looked at her in exasperation, but didn't try to take it away. I doubted that the mother goose would want her egg back.

Kelly carried her goose egg around with her all summer. She would stop and gently lay it down to follow my sister and me when we went horseback riding, swimming, or fishing. But upon returning to the house, she would go straight to check on her goose egg, gently pick it up, and carry it to a new resting spot. She totally ignored the kittens.

Then one day, as I was going around the back of the house, I spotted Kelly standing with her legs splayed, head hanging down with the saddest look on her face.

"Kelly, what?" I started to say, but then the smell hit me. Gagging, I whirled and hurried away. When I came around the other side of the house, I stopped, gulping in fresh air. Yikes! I didn't know which smelled worse — rotten egg or skunk! They were both foul. When I could breathe again, I found my sister and informed her that Kelly had dropped her goose egg. We both tried to console Kelly when she finally joined us. I don't know if dogs can actually cry, but it sure did look like a few tears actually slid out of her eyes, although maybe it was just a reaction to the noxious smell. After all, she'd been standing right over the egg when it broke!

For a while, it seemed that Kelly had given up on having her own baby. She now ignored tiny kittens, baby rabbits, and eggs of any kind. But that was soon to change. My dad drove us up into the mountains every Saturday during summer vacation, and we spent the day exploring. I was a rock hound, fascinated by all the different quartz crystals and mica flakes I found.

One day, I rounded a boulder and came upon Kelly digging and worrying at a rather sizeable moss-covered rock. "What did you find, Kelly?" I asked as I knelt to help her move the rock, expecting to see something interesting underneath it. Finding nothing, I left her to her rock and continued with my own hunt for mica. When my search brought me past her again, she was still pawing at the rock, trying to get it into a position where she could pick it up. I watched as she tried several times, her neck muscles bulging with the effort. "You silly dog, you'll never be able to pick that up," I told her as I hunted around for a smaller rock. "Here, try this one." I handed her a rock slightly larger than my fist that fit in her mouth nicely. Wagging a thank-you, Kelly picked up the rock and followed me back to the car.

When we arrived home, Kelly tried to carry her rock everywhere she went. Deciding that was too cumbersome, she settled for just bringing it out when we were around the house. She had finally found the perfect pet! It would not die, break, or be taken away.

When the Pet Rock craze hit the shelves a few years later, I laughed to myself. After all, my dog Kelly, a pudgy Dachshund with overly long ears and chestnut brown eyes, was the proud owner of the Original Pet Rock.

~Karen Cooper

Riley

Chapter
2

My Very Good, Very Bad Dog

My Miraculous Dog

Fun fact: According to legend, dogs and other animals are given the miraculous ability to talk at midnight on Christmas Eve.

12

The Rainbow Bridge

*Fun fact: Cocker Spaniels were given their name
because they were good at helping people hunt the
woodcock, which the Spaniel flushed out of low bushes.*

Ten years ago, my father was seventy-one, but still not retired. He had always taken great pride in his work and defined himself by it, so, to his mind, retirement equaled uselessness and loss of identity. My mom was growing increasingly resentful at being left alone so much during what were supposed to be their golden years. I suggested to her many times that she get a dog for company around the house, but she always said, "We don't want the carpets to get ruined."

I tried to convince my parents that a little carpet damage would be a small price to pay for the loyal companionship of a dog, but they still refused. Their last dog was my childhood pet, which had died twenty years earlier, so I figured they were overdue for another one. My plan was to find a puppy so cute they couldn't possibly resist it. Of course, every puppy is adorable, but the one I found was off the charts — a Cocker Spaniel smaller than my hand, with long, silky ears and big, brown, soulful eyes.

The only problem was that it would pee when I leaned over it or picked it up. As I wiped off my hand, the breeder said, "Oh, that's just submissive urination. He's recognizing your dominance. It's kind of a compliment!"

It didn't feel like a compliment. It felt like pee.

He added, "It's a puppy thing. It'll stop when she's older." I took his word for it, figuring a little wee-wee could be tolerated for such a bombardment of cuteness. Armed with this secret weapon, I returned to my parents' house. My mother fell easily, but my dad remained stony. While my mother cuddled and spoke baby talk to the puppy, he leaned in and whispered to me, "I'll get you for this."

In his younger years, my dad was a semi-professional boxer and a reserve policeman in Belfast, Northern Ireland. He was as tough as his upbringing, but he had a soft side, too. I often joked with him that he was "rock candy with a gooey center" — tough on the outside but mushy on the inside.

In time, as I had hoped, the dog did her magic and won him over, too. They named her Molly, and she became my dad's constant companion. I think she was even instrumental in helping him finally retire. It was still hard for him to sit around the house, but having Molly to play with made it much easier. My mom was happier than ever, too.

A few months after I gave them Molly, Dad told me, "That dog is the greatest gift you've ever given us."

I joked, "But, Dad, you said you were going to get me for this, remember?"

He smiled slightly and said, "Shut up."

Molly filled their days with laughter and slept at the foot of their bed every night. They walked her several times a day, getting exercise they otherwise wouldn't have had, and meeting neighbors they might never have met.

Five years ago, my father was diagnosed with light forms of Parkinson's and dementia. He became very depressed. He even stopped singing, the one thing that had given him the most joy in life. We all felt helpless. He had always been the life of the party, the one his friends called on to sing a song or tell a joke, and so the change was painful to watch. I visited him as often as I could, but work and family obligations often kept me away. I was always glad to know Molly was with him when I couldn't be.

Last year, on the day after Thanksgiving, Dad fell and fractured his hip. He spent three agonizing weeks in the hospital. Since my wife, my mother or I were always at his bedside, we took turns going home to tend to Molly. She always greeted me enthusiastically and then looked out the window to see if my dad was with me. I would tell her he would be home soon. One day, I entered the house so quietly she didn't hear me come in. I found her sleeping on his pillow.

My father never came home. He developed aspiration pneumonia in the hospital and died of respiratory failure a few days before Christmas. We fought hard to save him because there was still a lot of him left to save, despite his brain conditions. The day before he broke his hip, we had had Thanksgiving dinner and he was very much his old self, so it was devastating to lose him.

When I took my mother home, Molly greeted us as enthusiastically as ever, and then looked out the window again for my dad. My mother sat on the couch and cried. Molly looked over from the window, then ran and jumped onto my mother's lap, lowered her head and actually seemed to cry with her. She knew something was very wrong.

It was a dark house for several days when tragedy struck again. Molly, who was only ten years old and had always been perfectly healthy, died suddenly of a brain aneurysm on Christmas Day, four days after my father's death. My mother was inconsolable.

Some say everything happens for a reason, but for the life of me, I couldn't figure out why my father had to suffer so much during the last three weeks of his life, and why their dog had to die a few days later and leave my mother completely alone. It just seemed cruel and senseless.

A few weeks later, I was talking with a good family friend; Kathleen asked if I had ever heard of the "Rainbow Bridge." I hadn't. She said, "It's a place between earth and heaven where animals wait for the person they were closest to. The Bridge is in a beautiful place with fields for dogs to play in and everything they could desire. Sometimes, the animal dies before its owner, and sometimes they die because they know their owner has passed away and they want to find him or her again. Your dad may have been confused and in need of a guide. The dog is there to lead its master over the Rainbow Bridge and into heaven."

I was very cynical at the time because of so many unanswered prayers in the hospital, but I hoped that this was true. When I doubt the existence of the rainbow bridge, or heaven itself, I remind myself that a healthy dog somehow knew my father was not coming home and died a few days after he did. I remind myself that my dad had a brain condition, and Molly died of one, as if by some empathetic response, and as if she knew dying was the only way to be with him again. It seems to me life can be meaningless or it can be filled with magic and great mysteries. I choose a mystery.

My four-year-old daughter asked where my father and Molly went. I didn't want to explain death to her so early, so I told her they both went to Ireland. I imagine the land around the Rainbow Bridge is a lot like Ireland, so it's a white lie.

Someday, when I'm old and it's my time to go, I hope the dogs I've loved on this earth will guide me across the Rainbow Bridge, too. And I hope my father and Molly will be waiting for me on the other side, happy and healed. I'll hold him tight, then kneel down and tussle Molly's hair like I always did. She'll look at me with those big brown eyes and her doggy smile again. My father will put his arm around me and say, "Isn't this something, son? It's all true! And Molly is still the greatest gift you ever gave me."

~Mark Rickerby

13

Listening to Our Hearts

*Fun fact: Most experts agree that dogs dream. They
may also grunt or jerk while sleeping because they
relax their muscles when they're asleep,
just like people.*

Daisy was stuck on her back, her legs rigid in the air, her big brown eyes filled with fear. She was a black Labrador mix, only six-and-a-half years old, and always happy and cheerful. She had trotted into the back yard and we found her five minutes later, unable to move. All she could do was move her head a little.

The veterinarians confirmed that Daisy was paralyzed from a sudden stroke and suggested that we give her the weekend to heal. If she wasn't walking by Monday, we were told to think about her quality of life. We had a large dog cot and placed Daisy on it, keeping a soft pillow beneath her head. We put puppy pads on the bottom half of the cot, as she had no control over going to the bathroom. We hand-fed and watered Daisy — she couldn't lift her neck to do so for herself. We bathed her daily and flipped her to lie on the opposite side every hour or two to prevent bedsores, including during the night.

Monday came and went, but we opted to wait. We didn't want to give up on Daisy so soon. After extensive online research, we found that many dogs had suffered this type of stroke and had a nearly full recovery, although it often took at least six weeks for the improvement to become evident. We were definitely waiting. Daisy still wagged her tail as she lay on her cot. Her eyes were still vibrant. Mentally and emotionally, she was the same happy Daisy she had always been — she just couldn't move.

We provided Daisy with daily range-of-motion therapy and massage. We carried all fifty-three pounds of her on her cot up and down the stairs to be with us wherever we were in the house. She was just as much a part of our life as she had always been, despite being paralyzed.

Three weeks went by, and there was little improvement. Then she developed a bad urinary tract infection. Her urine filled with blood, and we worried that she was shutting down internally. Thankfully, after testing and medication, Daisy's infection healed. The nights remained sleepless, however.

After five weeks of around-the-clock care, Daisy began to run in her sleep. She still had no feeling or motion in three legs, but we thought the sleep running (most likely dreaming about running) was helpful for her muscles to regain the memory of movement. Instead of waking her up, we let her dream, hoping that the movement produced in her dreams would one day translate into reality.

Around the five-week mark, we bought a large rug for Daisy. We called it the therapy rug. In addition to daily range-of-motion therapy and massage, we thought that providing her with a large area rug would give her a location with traction — a place to pull herself around if and when she was ready.

We laid out the therapy rug and carried Daisy from her cot onto the carpet. Daisy wagged her tail in appreciation, and within a day of the rug's arrival, she began trying to pull herself forward. We still had no idea if she would regain feeling or strength in her three legs, but we held onto hope.

At exactly six weeks from the date she became paralyzed, Daisy attempted to walk. We had a fresh snowfall — good packing snow — and we decided to carve a narrow passageway in the snow. Its sides would support Daisy's body as she stood. Daisy stood on all four legs for the first time in six weeks with the help of our self-made snow bumper walls. This was a huge victory, and we knew at this point — although we still had a long road ahead of us — there was no turning back.

From six weeks on, Daisy began to use the bathroom outside. We bought multiple area rugs, and she could pull herself to her food and water bowls anytime she wanted to. The transformation was miraculous. We had a set of wheels made to support her back end as she re-learned how to walk. However, Daisy was determined to walk on her own. We never pushed her to try; we only encouraged her when she did. We knew this wasn't something that could be rushed. We did our part with the ongoing care and therapy, and we took it one moment at a time.

Before we hit the seven-week mark, Daisy took off — running! It was far from graceful, but she was running and doing it totally on her own. In the days leading up to this, she had been merely pulling herself a few steps or standing for a few seconds before falling over. Now she was running!

Although the situation had looked hopeless when Daisy first became paralyzed, we listened to our gut — and our gut said to do our own research. Daisy was fully alert, mentally and emotionally, even just after becoming paralyzed. She had the will to live. And so, after researching and listening to our hearts, we moved forward, helping Daisy regain mobility and strength.

Now the snow has melted. Summer is here, and Daisy trots in the back yard. Her tail is always wagging. She searches through her pile of favorite toys and brings one to us every time she goes outside. Her spirit is contagious. Her attitude of gratitude is mesmerizing. Her journey exemplifies what hope can bring about. Patience, dedication and faith carried us through the journey as Daisy went from paralyzed to mobile. Now, when we see Daisy's eyes dancing with happiness, her tail wagging with excitement, when we see her trotting around the house or the back yard on her own four legs, we are reminded that amazing things can occur if we simply follow our hearts and cling tightly to the belief that everything will be all right.

~Stacey Ritz

14

A Really Good Dog

*Fun fact: Most dogs that are used in TV and movies
have been rescued from an animal shelter.*

W hile some friendships grow over time, others happen fast. The first time you meet, it's like you've always been friends. That's how it was with my friend Cathy, who I met when I volunteered for a canine rescue group.

Cathy had her own tribe — two dogs — as did I, plus two cats. She also had a long-term foster, Gus, who had some behavioral problems she was working on. I had a large yard, so she often loaded up all her dogs to come over and play with all of mine.

One day, Cathy called sounding fairly panicked and asking if I could take Gus, who had bitten a repairman. It didn't seem to be a bad bite, but the repairman apparently didn't like dogs and pretty much wanted him shot on the spot. The police were called, and tickets were written.

Cathy had to appear before a judge within twenty-four hours, at which time Gus had to be removed from the village or be put down. The rescue had rules about dogs that bit, so it couldn't help. My house was pretty full of dogs already, and I had kids about, so I wasn't eager to take him. Things weren't looking good for Gus.

Cathy was also trying to reach another friend, Mary, who was especially fond of Gus, but she had been having some health problems lately, suddenly passing out for no reason anyone could discern, so we weren't sure she would be up for it. Plus, she was at her limit for allowable dogs and had a neighbor that would have liked to ban dogs altogether. She was always watching Mary's dogs and counting them. As it turned out, Mary was delighted to take Gus, feeling that since he looked so much like her own dogs, the neighbor wouldn't know the difference!

Not long after, Cathy called to tell me that not only was Gus doing well with Mary, but he suddenly seemed to develop a sense for when Mary was going to have a "spell." He would nudge her persistently until she sat down. Mary was able to have him designated as a service dog, and therefore he was not included in the maximum number of dogs she was permitted to have. He was also able to go to work with her as an official service animal, further relieving her angst over possibly having to quit her job because of her condition.

As an added benefit, Gus got to accompany Mary's husband to visit the neighbor, wearing his service vest, to explain there would now be three dogs at their house.

We were delighted, thinking it couldn't get any better, when Cathy called me again. She had received a call in the middle of the night. Seeing it was Mary's number on the caller ID, she feared the worst. But as it turned out, it was Mary, not her husband, on the phone. Gus had woken her up, something he had never done. When he wouldn't settle, she thought maybe he needed to go out. When she got up, he jumped in her bed. For all his problems, Gus had never gotten on the furniture.

It was then she noticed that her husband's breathing didn't seem right. She called the paramedics, and in the dead of that Midwestern winter night, they arrived in record time and rushed him to the hospital. Time was truly of the essence. With no previously known cardiac problems, he was in heart failure. They arrived in the emergency room with very little time to spare, saving Jim's life.

Cathy and I have talked many times about how it seems that foster dogs seem to be on a journey. It's as if they have a destination known only to them and will do what they have to in order to complete that journey.

In this case, I guess Gus had to be a bad dog in order to fulfill his destiny to be a really good dog.

~Beki Muchow

15

Making a Family

Fun fact: The Bichon Frise actually has a double coat,
with a soft, thick coat underneath its cottony-looking
outside coat.

"**P**lease?" "Please?" "Please?" Three sets of eyes looked up at Dad. During dinner, Mom announced that one of her English students at the college was a dog breeder and was offering the runt of her latest litter of Bichon Frise puppies at a special price.

"We'll take care of him," I promised.

"Please, Daddy, please!" my sister begged.

"I always grew up with dogs," Mom added.

For years, Dad had avoided getting a dog. Whenever the topic came up, Dad put on his grumpiest face and uttered stock phrases: "Dogs are a pain. They're a big responsibility. I don't want to be bothered." But he never refused outright. He'd hidden "Nos" behind "Somedays" and "Maybes."

This was our "Someday."

Dad barely made it through dinner before he caved. A few weeks later, Mom brought home a little ball of fluff named Chip. Dad watched from afar, muttering, "Don't think for one second I'm going to feed, walk, or brush him."

We were almost too in love to hear.

For me, at age thirteen, Chip offered a solid foundation, a way out of all the trouble I could get into as a teenager. While many of my friends were flirting in online chat rooms, sniffing permanent markers, sneaking their parents' alcohol, or meeting for trysts in the woods, I was outside playing with our new puppy.

Instead of being a self-absorbed teenager, I had someone else to look out for: Chip. Before long, I had him waiting at crosswalks until it was safe, and responding to "shake," "sit," and "stand up." I kept him out of the trash, filled his water bowl, groomed his coat and brushed his teeth. I had promised my parents that if we got a dog I'd be responsible, and I was. Chip taught me about actions and consequences. I learned that when we take care of what is important to us, we reap the benefits. For me, this meant a loyal companion, someone to greet me at the door when I returned from babysitting, someone to keep my lap warm on cold winter nights, and someone to kiss my face when I was sad. And this lesson stayed with me as I grew.

Chip brought out my responsible side and he helped my younger sister with her self-confidence. We'd had a dog once before — years earlier, and only for a few weeks. My mom had been allergic to his dense fur, and my sister, then only a small child, had been terrified of the Samoyed. She approached Chip with caution. As if Chip could sense her feelings, he remained extra gentle with her. He would crawl gently onto her lap and curl up with a contented sigh. She grew confident with him and was eventually able to walk him on her own. She even taught him his most unusual trick — "Look" — a command that caused him to run to the nearest sewer drain, push a pebble into it with his nose, and watch it plummet into the water below. This new confidence stayed with her as she grew, and she took on leadership roles in sports and at school.

But Chip's magic didn't stop with us kids. Mom had always been happiest when she had someone to just sit and listen — and our busy family didn't sit still for that. Bichons are particularly adept at listening and discerning the nuances of language, so Chip would sit with mom, his head cocking from side to side as he tried to make out the meaning of her words. Before long, she had him discerning the difference between all his toys: "Christmas-bear," "cat-bear," "flat bone," "squeaky toy," and more.

Perhaps the most amazing transformation was Dad's. From the start, Dad was adamant: "He's your dog, not mine. No table scraps. No sitting on the furniture." It was hardly a month before Chip's adorable personality won him over. Dad was the first to feed Chip table scraps, and the first to allow him to sit on the couch. Chip even allowed Dad's under-utilized (but amazing) creative side to blossom. Before long, Dad was making chew toys and obstacles for Chip to play with. In the deep winter snow, it was Dad who shoveled a path in the back yard from the patio door to Chip's favorite tree. Chip had won over the heart of the sternest member of our family and softened him.

Chip brought us together as a family. It was a time when my friends were becoming more isolated from their parents and a time when teenagers thought it wasn't "cool" to associate with younger siblings. After dinner, children would escape to their bedrooms, parents fled to their newspapers, and no one interacted. But Chip united us. After dinner, we all followed Chip into the family room. We'd teach him new tricks or reinforce his old ones. We'd recount stories of the cute things he'd done that day. We'd help Dad create a new chew toy with ropes from the garage or collaborate on an obstacle course of buckets, blankets, and toys. The important thing is that we'd do this together as a family.

When Chip passed away at seventeen, Dad suffered the most. "I never thought a pet could mean so much to me," he admitted. He told us this together — grown-up kids coming home again from college and jobs as Chip brought us together one final time. And it was Dad who called from the road not too long afterward — letting us know he'd found a puppy on a pet-finder website and was on his way home with it.

People who are not dog lovers sometimes complain about those who treat their pets too much like humans. What they don't understand is that it isn't that dog lovers are abandoning humanity for their pets; rather, their pets are what elicit in them the best aspects of their humanity. In my family's case, Chip strengthened our responsibility, confidence, companionship, love, creativity, and togetherness. It isn't that we aspired to make Chip human; it's that he succeeded in doing that for us.

~Val Muller

16

The Birthday Miracle

Fun fact: A study by the ASPCA found that pet owners become just as attached to pets they've received as gifts as to pets they've chosen themselves.

His pleading blue eyes always got to me, and Devon knew it. I sat in my favorite tattered armchair watching TV, a blanket tucked around me against February's winter chill. Devon stood next to the chair in his stocking feet.

Devon had played the man of the house since his father left the year before, but tonight I was not looking into the eyes of a man. Tonight, he was a twelve-year-old boy who wanted a puppy for his birthday, and his birthday was tomorrow.

"They say every boy should have a dog of his own, don't you agree?" His brow wrinkled into such a serious expression that I wanted to giggle. He had obviously put a lot of thought into how to talk me into getting him a puppy for his birthday.

The old chair groaned in protest as I leaned forward to match his gaze. "I kind of figured you were going to say that."

"So? What do you think?" He bounced up and down in anticipation.

I sighed, knowing what my answer would have to be. It seemed to be the answer to every wish since his father left us. "I would love to get you a puppy, but puppies are expensive. They need food and shots and a license. We just can't afford all that right now, honey." I lowered my head so he wouldn't see my tears.

He stood there for a moment. Then he knelt down and placed

his small hand on my knee. "That's okay, Mom. I understand," he whispered. "But some day, when things get better, can we get a puppy?"

"Absolutely, Dev. I promise." I forced myself to smile. I hated disappointing my sweet son on his birthday.

"Well then," he announced with a brave grin, "when we get a puppy, I am going to name him Rusty."

"Rusty? That's a fine name." I breathed a sigh of relief as he crawled onto my lap for a hug.

The next morning, I awoke to the grim reality that I could not afford a birthday gift for Devon, let alone a party. The house was quiet as I slipped into my shoes and gathered our recyclable bottles and cans. In Oregon, they were worth five cents each. I thought of the video-game system Devon would be receiving from his father and the look on his face when he saw nothing from me.

Standing at the foot of Devon's bed, I cried "Happy Birthday!" as soon as he opened his eyes. "Come on, we have some recycling to turn in. Let's get you a birthday donut."

We drove to the nearby convenience store, and I crossed my fingers while the cashier counted our bottles and cans. There was just enough. Devon and I took our time choosing the two most scrumptious-looking donuts, one covered in sprinkles and one dripping with chocolate.

Devon grabbed the bag and fished out his treat. He took a huge bite before pushing his way through the glass front door. On the front sidewalk, he froze in his tracks so fast that I almost ran into him.

A puppy caught his eye. A young woman was parked just outside the door. The morning air was barely above freezing, but she sat with her car window down and bundled in a big jacket. Her face was wet with tears. A fluffy puppy was curled up in her lap with his nose resting on the driver's door. He had a copper coat and warm brown eyes.

Devon rushed over to the car and stood stroking the puppy's fur and laughing as the puppy licked his face. Then I turned to the woman: "What's wrong?"

The woman sniffled and wiped her face before answering. "I got this puppy from a lady giving them away in front of Ray's Market a couple weeks ago. My husband is a truck driver, and he is gone from home a lot. I thought maybe the puppy would be fun company for the kids and me, and my husband would get a kick out of him."

She stopped to blow her nose and then continued. "Instead, he was furious! He demanded that I load him into the car right now and take him to the animal shelter." She paused as tears started to form again. "But I just can't."

Devon giggled as he fed the rest of his donut to the puppy and was thanked with a wet puppy lick across the face. The woman ran her fingers through the puppy's thick fur.

"He sure likes you," she told Devon. "Any chance you guys could take him?"

"Really?" Devon gasped and turned to me. I stepped back from the car. Could we?

"Listen," she begged. "I know it's a lot to ask, but he already has his license and shots. He is even potty-trained. He eats cheap, generic dog food, and he loves kids." I reached forward and touched the soft fur.

"He sure is cute," I mumbled.

"Please take him," she begged. "He is such a friendly and well-behaved dog. He stays outside during the day and is content while I am at work. The kids named him, but you can change it if you like. They call him Rusty."

"Rusty?" Devon whispered.

Moments later, Devon buried his face in the soft fur while the puppy dozed on his shoulder during the short ride home. Devon's birthday wish was granted, as well as my prayer to give him the perfect gift. His name was Rusty. How could I say no to that?

~Tea R. Peronto

17

Blind Faith

*Not-so-fun fact: Progressive retinal atrophy (PRA), an
inherited disorder, causes degeneration of the retina
and eventual blindness. It's found in more than
eighty-six dog breeds.*

We are the proud owners of a snowy-white, twenty-three-pound Poodle mix named Curley. He's an adorable rescue dog. He's affectionate, playful, loyal, gentle, and happy. He loves absolutely everyone and is always by our sides. Did I say always? Yes, always. Turns out, Curley doesn't like to be left alone — ever — probably as a result of being abandoned.

We discovered this early on when we would leave for a little bit. In our absence, he'd chew through doors, windows, window blinds, curtains, doorknobs, anything. Sometimes, he'd get out, dig a hole through the fence, and trot down the sidewalk searching for us. I considered adopting a companion for him, but he does not like other dogs, only people. We tried doggy kindergarten to get him socialized, but he flunked out twice.

It took me several months to piece together the puzzle that is Curley, so buoyantly happy in the presence of others, but hysterical and distraught on his own. It was my mission to help him heal. In retrospect, I should have known we were adopting a high-maintenance case. The shelter volunteer had whispered to me as we were putting Curley in the car, "Oh, yeah, I'm supposed to tell you that he's been returned — twice. He might be a little bit, like, destructive."

I read *The Dog Whisperer* and consulted blogs. I tried all sorts of security devices like toys, treats, blankets, and stuffed animals. Nothing worked. If we were going out to dinner, we had to first "Curley-proof" the house. Lock and block the windows and doors! Leave the TV on for some background noise. We'd hope for the best, but it was anyone's guess what we'd come home to, and the thought of him being so worried broke our hearts. I can't begin to list the doors, screens, windows, curtains, blinds and fences we ordered and reordered, but there was never any part of us that didn't want Curley in our lives. His smile, his soulful eyes, and his willingness to be by our sides are all the qualities that melt our hearts.

Over time, Curley improved — not because of any toy, or treat, or doggy kindergarten, but because everything consistently stayed the same. He could finally trust that he was home and loved forever. His outbursts subsided, and sometimes we'd walk in the door and find him resting peacefully on the couch. It was a beautiful sight. Then came our next challenge.

One evening, as it was getting dark, my daughter and I were walking back from the park with Curley, and he sat down on the sidewalk, refusing to go any farther. This was highly unusual since he loved his walks. He wouldn't budge. We finally had to carry him home. Once we were back in the house, he acted fine, but he refused to go outside that night before bedtime. We started seeing his behavior change whenever he was in dim light or darkness. He was tentative and would creep slowly along the ground. I took him to our vet, who referred us to an animal ophthalmologist.

The "doggy eye doctor" (as we liked to call her) ran several tests. She set up an obstacle course for Curley. With the lights on, he was okay. With the lights off, he failed. She had him track cotton balls, dropping them to see if he would track them as they soundlessly hit the ground, and he failed again miserably. She looked deep inside his eyes with her various instruments and then completed her diagnosis. "Your dog is going blind," she told me bluntly. "He has progressive retinal atrophy, or PRA. There is no cure. He has maybe six months to a year left of sight, and then he will be completely blind."

"But he's only five years old," I said. "Isn't he too young for something like this?" The doctor explained that PRA happens at any age, and we would have to move forward from here. "Don't move the furniture around. Keep encouraging him, and he'll be fine," she assured me. My heart broke. It just seemed so unfair. Curley had finally settled into a new life with a family that he could trust and he was so happy. Now this? I was devastated. "I'm sorry," I told her. "This is so upsetting. He's a very special dog, and I just don't want to see him struggle through one more thing."

The doctor broke out of her "clinical doctor mode" and actually got real. She looked at me with compassion and said, "Shawn, he does not know he is going blind. Even if he has less sight day after day, he will accept and adjust to his circumstances with your encouragement and support. Keep doing what you've been doing. Trust me. It will be okay."

Curley has been blind for several years now, and not once has he ever responded to this challenge with any of the behaviors he presented upon adoption. He finds his way around the house with ease. He still "looks" out the car window with the breeze blowing in his hair, blissful and free. He follows me everywhere by tapping his little wet nose across the backs of my legs. As predicted, he adjusted.

I find it all so ironic. Once Curley had true, unfaltering, trusting, never-let-you-down love in his life, he went completely blind without even a whimper. I can't help but wonder whether, had he been given the same sense of security as a puppy, he might have handled being alone now and then. I mean, could you survive being returned twice? It probably sounds a bit sappy, but Curley is my inspiration.

I experience an important truth when I think about his story: Love makes all the difference. He didn't have love as a baby. He had no reason to believe that he'd be okay, but now he does and he moves forward in faith—blind faith—with a kind of enthusiasm and hope that reminds me every day that I should trust love, too.

Curley can see that.

~Shawn Lutz

18

Back to My Roots

Fun fact: Due to overpopulation, many governments charge more for a license if the dog hasn't been spayed or neutered.

I had always had a passion for animals and I had co-founded an organization to help animals in need. Helping animals through rescue and adoption, and helping their new families through a multitude of programs such as affordable spay-and-neuter options, made me feel alive. I also loved to write in my free time.

Those were my two passions, but I had taken a new job, thinking the additional money would provide a lifetime of security and freedom. All of my effort and energy went into this new office job that I didn't love, while my rescue organization stagnated and I found I had no time to write.

One bitterly cold winter day, I was heading back to my car between appointments when I saw her. The dog was shivering in the below-zero temperature, and my heart sank. I bent down to pet her and found icicles hanging from her matted fur. Her nails curled into her paw pads, making it difficult to walk. She allowed me to pet her and even spun in circles with excitement. I placed her under my coat to warm her up and I walked from house to house asking if anyone had seen her before.

No one knew anything about her. I left my information at each house just in case, and I took her home. When I took her to the vet, I learned that she had not been spayed or micro-chipped. She was covered in so many fleas that her apricot hair looked gray, and her stomach was full of parasites and worms. The poor thing was severely underweight and dehydrated. Instead of working into the wee hours of the night for my job, I went to buy dog food and spent the evening giving her a bath.

I assumed I would foster the dog myself and place her for adoption with my rescue organization just as soon as she was healthy enough to be spayed and fully vetted. I didn't have time for a dog in my life. I was too busy with my job, and I was never home. But as each day passed, I couldn't wait to get home and see the little dog that had wandered into my busy life. We named her Lady, and after a few veterinary visits and a nice haircut, it was determined that she was a Poodle mix. Lady got along well with my cats. She sat on my lap as I worked from home in the evenings, and she snuggled with me when I finally crawled into bed, exhausted.

Lady fit right in, but I reminded myself I did not have time for a dog. I was pursuing financial security, and that meant sticking to my plan, even though I was so unhappy at work.

Each day, Lady grew healthier and stronger, and our bond grew. She loved to go on walks and really loved running with me, which surprised me for a small dog. Rescuing Lady reminded me of my true calling—helping animals—and my other passion for other things, too—running and writing. She reminded me to slow down and actually live life.

A few months after I adopted Lady, I was sexually assaulted at work. Lady helped me find the strength to leave the job and she was there to comfort me through my endless nightmares. It took five years before I was strong enough to seek help in the form of therapy. Once a person full of words, I hadn't been able to find my own voice since the trauma occurred. But Lady didn't force me to talk. She did the best thing anyone could have done for me during that difficult time—she stayed by my side and was there for me. When I suffered from debilitating panic attacks, she would sense an attack and jump into my lap, licking my face and forcing me to come back to the present moment instead of allowing the replay of past events to hold me hostage in my mind.

It may have looked as if I saved Lady, but Lady really saved me. I went back to my animal-welfare organization and got it back on track, adding more volunteers and life-saving programs. We officially became a 501(c)(3) organization. I also resumed writing.

Today, our non-profit organization has saved more than 11,000 lives, and I write for a living. Because one furry life found her way to me when I needed her most, I have found the courage and strength to live the life of my dreams.

~Stacey Ritz

One for the Road

*Fun fact: Ancient Greek and Roman physicians
thought dogs' saliva had healing properties and could
even be an antidote to poisoning.*

I had just changed into my running clothes and was leaving my office, off for a run even though it was well over 100 degrees. I couldn't explain it, but I felt the need to run despite the record heat and my colleague's admonition not to go.

A quarter-mile into my jog, I saw spots. I admitted defeat and turned around. As I approached my car, in what had been an empty parking lot, I saw an animal circling it.

"Is that a dog?" I asked of no one.

It was a dog, an unintimidating one at that. "Hello," I said. When I reached for the door handle, the dog disappeared underneath the car into the shade. I grabbed my bottle, desperate for water, took a long swig, and then lowered to my knees to look for the dog. When I stood up, I found it sitting in the driver's seat, panting.

I reached across him, started the car, and turned the air conditioning on high. I poured water from my bottle into the cap and offered it to him in the driver's seat. He drained it in a few desperate gulps. I refilled it several times before he had his fill.

"Who do you belong to?" I asked. He wore no collar. "Stay here. I'm going to look for your owner."

He turned his face toward the vents, relishing the cold air, his moustache blowing.

There was no one in sight. I walked in each direction, toward the river's edge and back. I stood there, looking at the dog staring back at me through the window. He waited patiently as if he'd been in my car dozens of times. I didn't know what to do. Leaving him in that heat was out of the question. He would die.

"Move over," I said. The dog moved obediently to the passenger seat. Before I was out of the lot, he had climbed onto my lap. "You stink," I said. He looked up at me, panting, and then licked my sweaty face. "Ugh! No licking!" He turned his gaze out the window, and I wrapped a protective arm around him for safety. His black fur was warm to the touch and caked with dirt. His unusually long nails dug into my thighs.

"Let's go figure out what to do with you."

I was never a dog person, which I often confessed without a trace of shame. "How could you not like dogs?" people asked me. "Easily," I'd answer. "They smell, they're loud, and they're messy, to name a few reasons." With this attitude, my soon-to-be husband had already resigned himself to the fact that we would never have a dog.

And now one was in my car, on my lap no less! I pulled into my driveway and shrugged as my fiancé saw the dog, his eyes wide at this sudden development.

"Don't worry," I said, as I lifted the dog out of the car. "I'm calling animal control." I set him down in the yard and filled a bowl with cold water. I sat in the shade beside him as he lay on the ground panting heavily. He was lethargic. Upon closer inspection, he appeared quite old, with a Fu Manchu-style moustache, white whiskers and dirty teeth. He didn't look up when there was a noise, so I assumed he was partially deaf.

We sat together waiting for animal control. The dog didn't move except to lick my salty face, a foreign sensation that I was already starting to like. I petted him, assuring him that everything would be okay. When animal control arrived, I filled in the representative on how I found the dog. "Also, I think he's old and possibly deaf," I added.

She performed some sensory tests, snapping her fingers near his ears and shining a light in his eyes. "He's not old or deaf," she concluded. "He has heat stroke."

Soon after, the dog was loaded into a crate and into the van. I felt a strange mixture of relief and sadness. "What happens now?" I asked.

"His owner has ten days to claim him. After that, he'll be available for adoption."

"I'll look for signs in the area and check the papers and websites. If he has an owner, I want to help find them."

"Based on his condition and where you found him, my guess is he was abandoned. He's been a stray for a while now."

Suddenly, looking at that sweet dog panting in his crate, I realized that this was no chance encounter. I was meant to go running and find him. My heart spoke before my brain could interfere: "If he isn't claimed, I'll adopt him."

Ten days later, I brought Cooper home. He expressed such gratitude to have found his forever home. But it was I who was grateful, for the opportunity to experience such an unexpected bond with an animal.

Learning Cooper's personality and quirks was entertaining. I had no choice but to acquiesce to the licking. He's a kisser! Although not always welcome, he usually has good timing. He's kissed many of my tears away over the years and brought me comfort. Also, he loves the car. A proper mom now, I learned how to secure him in the back seat, but that never stopped him from placing his front paws on the center console and staring attentively out the windshield. He stands guard. No matter how long the drive, he stays on duty the entire time, even if he is exhausted after a day at the beach.

And that is a fortunate thing. I may have saved his life by letting him into my car that hot summer day, but he returned the favor by saving our lives in that same car years later.

We'd spent the day at a picnic an hour north and were headed home late at night. We were both exhausted, struggling to stay awake. "Take a nap, Coop. Mommy's fine," I told him. But he wouldn't nap, nor was I fine.

I fell asleep and veered onto the shoulder. Cooper head-butted me, startling me awake right before we surely would have crashed. I gained control of the vehicle, fully alert from the adrenaline surge, and pulled Cooper's face against mine. "Thank you, baby," I said, kissing him. "Good dog. Thank you for saving us." Terrified, yet relieved, tears fell from my eyes. As always, Cooper promptly licked them away.

"It had to happen this way," my husband has often said. "She'd have never gone to a shelter and picked a dog." That hot day, when that angel of a dog appeared from nowhere, truly was a miraculous day for me.

~Jessica A. Walsh

The Fear Factor

Fun fact: The American Society for the Prevention of Cruelty to Animals (ASPCA) is 150 years old, having been founded in 1866 by Henry Bergh.

For my dog's first birthday, I entered him in a K-9 fun run sponsored by our local Society for the Prevention of Cruelty to Animals (SPCA). I'm not much of a runner, but the run was only a 3K, so I thought it would be fun for both of us.

We practiced in the weeks leading up to the run. On our practice runs, he was always raring to go and usually dragged me along behind him. I worked on his leash manners so that he wouldn't trip me on the big day. I felt we were ready for anything.

The fun run was downtown amidst the big buildings, so the noise of barking dogs all around us was amplified to a deafening pitch at the start of the race. My dog bolted when the starting tone went off. He had trouble running in the right direction with all the confusion around us. Soon the runners began to thin out, and my dog was running straight and fast. We were passing people and making great time. I was dreaming of a gold-medal finish.

At the halfway point in the course, we turned right, then right again at the next block, and then headed back on the parallel street. When we were six blocks from the finish, my dog screeched to a stop and dropped to the ground like a sack of potatoes. I almost dislocated my shoulder from the sudden stop as I was jerked backward by the leash.

He was lying flat on his belly with his head down in the middle of the intersection. At first I thought something bad had happened to him. He was shaking and whimpering. I did a quick check and couldn't see anything wrong. I tried to get him up, but he refused. The police officer doing traffic control at the intersection was impatiently motioning for me to move along so he could release the cars.

But I couldn't get my seventy-five-pound dog to get up. The harder I tried to pry him off the pavement, the more he fought me. I tried to drag him over to the curb, but he was dead weight. The officer was yelling at me. Cars were honking. I pulled and pulled. My dog wouldn't move.

Finally, I got my arm under him and lifted him up in a fireman's carry, throwing him over my shoulder. As I staggered to the curb, people at the nearby bus stop were taking my dog's side. "Poor dog is tired." "You were running him too hard." "He needs a ride back." And laughter. Lots of laughter. I was fuming. My dog would run all day long at the dog park if I let him. He wasn't the least bit tired. He was scared.

When I adopted him, he and his two siblings had been rescued from death inside a tightly tied black trash bag that someone had dumped on the side of the road. An alert garbage man noticed the bag was moving and used a metal rake to tear open the bag to look inside. My dog and his siblings were only puppies at the time. The rake damaged the nerves in my dog's back so he limped a little, but he could run as fast as lightning.

Another half-block of carrying my getting-heavier-with-every-step dog brought the answer. A garbage truck was idling at the curb. The sound of it must have hit my dog's sensitive doggie ears when we turned the second corner. He cried louder and clawed at my back as we drew closer to it. I held on tighter and tried to comfort him. I don't know where I found the strength, but I ran as fast as I could to get my sweet baby dog away from that scary garbage truck.

I ran with him on my shoulder until I felt him relax, and then I set him down. He wagged his tail in gratitude for me saving him from the garbage truck. We stood there until I could breathe normally again, and then we ran like maniacs to the finish line. We didn't win any medals, but I won his trust forever.

~Kathryn Lehan

21

Chicken Soup for the Soul

A Marine's Mission

*Fun fact: The Boston Terrier, an American breed, is a
cross between a white English Terrier and an
English Bulldog.*

M y husband John heard about an older Boston Terrier
at the Williamson County Animal Shelter and he was
determined to rescue him. The dog had been named
"Hard Luck Harley" because he had lost his original
owner to the war in Iraq and his second owner to a fatal car crash.
John asked no more questions because, being a retired Marine, he
believed that you take care of your own. Little did he know that
Harley would change his life.

Harley was eleven years old and was in the vehicle during the
accident that killed his most recent owner. He and another dog survived. Harley had been injured and had bitten one of the rescuers as
they were trying to remove him from the vehicle. As a result, Harley
had spent the last two weeks in quarantine. When they brought him
out to meet John, he waddled over and then lay at John's feet. John
had never seen such a large Boston Terrier. Harley was a whopping
thirty-eight pounds, fifty percent above normal.

John did not see an obese senior dog with a mysterious bump on
his backside. He saw a dog that needed a new home to live out his final
years. John knew there were medical issues but he didn't care. On the
way home, he took Harley to the vet, Dr. McBride, and was advised
that Harley had a perennial hernia, which meant that his intestines

were extruding into his pelvic area. Dr. McBride advised John to feed Harley soft foods and make sure that he had daily bowel movements. He also said that Harley wouldn't live long.

Once John and Harley were home, John began to investigate exactly where Harley had been. He knew the date that Harley had arrived at the animal control facility, so he researched accidents with fatalities on that date. There was only one: Rose Marie Gill. Then John learned that Harley had originally belonged to Rose's son, Steven Patrick Gill, a United States Marine who had been killed in action on July 21, 2005. John was shocked. Fate had placed a Marine's dog in his care.

The more John looked, the more information he found. There was a post office in Round Rock named for Steven Gill. He searched for people who had placed messages on Steven's memorial page and found Karen Cupples, who was Rose's best friend. She filled in many of the blanks about Harley. Eventually, John even met Steven's father Bill, who answered more questions.

John got very little sleep in those early days with Harley, who was having nightmares. He would whimper until John curled up on the floor next to him. Of course, that meant that Harley ended up sleeping in our bed.

Harley was seen all over Burnet County and went everywhere John went. Harley had a Facebook page where he gained many friends and helped spread the word that senior dogs need to be rescued, too. As a result, people started opening their hearts to the frosty-faced senior dogs that found themselves in rescues, animal shelters and city pounds. Harley touched many lives and was an inspiration. His friends loved to read about his adventures on Facebook and all of the witty remarks "Harley" made.

Sadly, on February 12th, Harley went on his last patrol. John was lost without his sidekick. Harley's Facebook friends were also shocked. John decided to memorialize Harley with a tattoo. He visited American Gypsy Tattoo in Marble Falls, Texas, and met the owner, Dave Justice, also a Marine. Dave picked a picture of Harley from his Facebook page and then designed a tattoo of Harley that was so lifelike it took John's breath away. American Gypsy made a video of the tattoo and the moving story of a man and his dog. The video can be found on YouTube by searching for "Sarge Harley."

As John grieved, he didn't know that he was going to rescue another Boston Terrier and also create a non-profit organization to keep rescuing dogs. The Sarge Harley Memorial Fund was born, and already it has met with great success on Facebook. An auction was held to kick off the organization, and $700 was raised in just a week to help pay medical bills for a Boston Terrier named Tulu that had begun having seizures and was in need of testing and medication. Money has been donated toward the purchase of a wheelchair for a little pug, medical treatment for a little Boston Terrier in Dallas with a severe skin problem, and even a little dog in California that needed emergency surgery to remove an eye.

A new Boston Terrier rescue named Recon has joined our family now. John was floored to discover that Recon was born on July 21st, the anniversary of Steven's death. To make it an even bigger coincidence, Steven Gill was a Recon Marine. Recon may not be Harley, but he is working his magic and making himself at home in John's heart.

~Cindy Lou Ruffino

Azure

My Very Good, Very Bad Dog

My Therapeutic Dog

Fun fact: Many therapy animals are dogs, but there are also therapy cats, rabbits, horses, pigs, birds, and other animals.

22

Watchful Devotion

Fun fact: It's believed that the Icelandic Sheepdog was brought to Iceland in the late 9th or early 10th century by Viking settlers.

My finger slipped. The word escaped me: "Oops." My dog, Kai, hurtled across the room, barely cleared the screen of my laptop, and landed squarely on my chest. I laughed even as I scrambled to shift my laptop to a side table — an awkward task with twenty-five pounds of Icelandic Sheepdog on top of me — then wrapped my arms around him, ruffling the long, silky fur that had never really lost its puppy softness. "I'm fine, bud. I made a typo. Okay? A typo. I'm fine. I promise."

He was not immediately convinced, but I made my breathing slow and calm as I petted him, and after a minute or so he seemed to conclude that all was indeed well here. He hopped up over my shoulder and onto the back of my chair, where he sprawled like a cat resting lazily on a branch, draping down to rest his nose and one front paw by my ear.

If he could talk, I thought, he would probably mutter, "I only left for a minute."

I understood. It was different when he first came to live with me. I was different: washed out of grad school, and so anxiety-ridden that I doubted I would ever again make it out of my room at my parents' house for long enough to have anything resembling a normal life. I was having panic attacks daily. Virtually anything could set them off — even, on bad days, something as small as a typo.

But when Kai came to my home, this began to change.

I will always remember that first day. He was a nine-and-a-half-week-old ball of black-and-white fur with ears that didn't quite stand up yet, all kisses and tail wags, completely unbothered by the fact that he had been plucked away from his siblings and his familiar yard and playpen. I sat on the floor of my room playing with him, tossing a stuffed toy that he happily chased. He would pounce on it, then snatch it up and prance around the room with his head held high and proud, as if he had just found the world's greatest treasure.

I laughed at his delight, but then the dark got in, as it always did. This moment was good, but it couldn't last. I knew something would go horribly wrong. My breathing changed, and Kai spun to look at me, toy forgotten. Head on one side, he trotted over to where I sat, climbed up on my lap, and put his nose a few inches from mine as he studied my face, his dark brown eyes curious.

I made myself smile at him. "It's nothing, bud. It's okay. I'm okay." I didn't entirely believe it, but it was close enough to be true. The nightmare that had invaded my thoughts had disappeared quickly in the face of Kai's support.

It happened again the next day. I sat on the floor, head in my hands, and hyperventilated. I couldn't stop.

Even as the panic attack started, I worried about Kai. He was a very young dog in a new place, very sensitive to the moods of those around him, and here I was hunched over on the floor, screaming at my imagination. He was a confident little boy, but this might be too much. I might scare him, make him wary of me. I knew it and hated it, but I couldn't stop.

With no hesitation, as if it were a job he'd been preparing to do since he was born, he marched across the room and climbed into my lap again. He was very quiet, but the set of his ears and his tail suggested no stress on his part. He leaned his small weight against me, letting me feel his steady heartbeat and unhurried breathing, and stayed there calmly while I hugged him and sobbed. Slowly, my own breath settled until it was under control again.

Over the next weeks and months, Kai got older and more obser-vant. If I panicked, he was there to sit with me until I wasn't panicking anymore, but his self-appointed duties did not stop there. If I started pacing with too much urgency, he would put himself in my way and jump up on me, interrupting my steps. If I started talking to myself — a thing I did so much I didn't always realize I was doing it — he would climb in my lap, whining and wanting to kiss my face, as soon as he heard stress in my voice. If I gesticulated too wildly as my thoughts tripped over themselves, waving my hands as I tried to get out what I couldn't express in words, he would paw at my arms frantically until I stopped. These were not responses that I or anyone else trained him to give; they were his own, and apparently instinctive.

Whatever was actually going on in his head, the result was that whenever I began to work myself into a panic attack, he interrupted me. Soon, he was catching subtler signs, warning me at hints of agita-tion that only he could see. With his patient help, I gradually learned to catch myself when I was in trouble, early enough that most of the time I could pull myself out of it.

Kai is three years old now. Most of the time, he doesn't have to play the role of mental-health monitor anymore. I still have dark days, but I've learned I can get through them. Real panic attacks are rare beasts now instead daily occurrences, and it's largely thanks to my dog and his watchful devotion.

I'm back in school, something I never thought would be possible when I left. Kai curls up near me when I do my homework, ready to jump up and stick his nose in my face if I so much as say, "Oops." I don't mind. He knows, and I know, that sometimes little problems lead to bigger ones.

These days, when he does this, I smile back and tell him it's okay. And I believe it.

~Cris Kenney

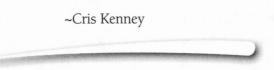

23

Resting at Her Feet

Fun fact: Most dogs can't see enough detail or color to enjoy watching TV.

It wasn't that he didn't like her. It was more that Benny just didn't care about her one way or the other. The only reason he paid her any attention at all was because his best buddy did, and that was only for a few minutes at dinnertime. Only then would Benny acknowledge her presence, and then, only until his food was served.

Surprisingly, she didn't mind getting the canine cold shoulder, because she knew a sacred bond existed between a boy and his puppy — even if this one-year-old dog wasn't quite a puppy anymore, and this sixty-nine-year-old man wasn't quite a boy anymore.

Unfortunately, one night, Benny's best friend became ill, and people that neither of them knew came to help. They took his buddy away, and Benny never saw him again. In the days and weeks that followed, he searched for him, and several times he thought he'd found him. After all, his scent was everywhere — on his chair in the kitchen, on his coat hanging by the stairs, and even in his shoes — still waiting for him out on the breezeway. Benny became excited when he heard a car pull in the driveway or voices in the street, but in the end, it wasn't him.

For weeks, he moped and refused to eat, but then one day he realized something that previously had meant little to him: She was still there. That night, when they were alone, Benny slowly came over and sat at her feet. She gently began to stroke his shiny golden hair, and then something totally unexpected happened: She hugged him.

From that moment forward, their relationship changed, and for each of them, the healing began.

They would become inseparable companions who enjoyed taking long neighborhood walks, stopping to talk with everyone they met along the way. Whether watching *Animal Planet* on TV or doing nothing at all, they did it together — a team of two — her confidant and his new best friend. The proof of this relationship was revealed in the greeting cards she routinely sent to friends and family acknowledging holidays and special events. Depending on one's relationship with her, the card was signed: "Love, Doris & Benny," "Nana & Benny," or "Mom & Benny." And those of us receiving these cards understood the importance of the closing salutation. We knew their story was one of recovery and rebirth, of two needy souls who found each other, and of the enduring friendship that resulted. It was a good story, too, but like all stories, it had to end eventually.

If Benny had one fault that clearly surpassed all others, it was that he wasn't immortal. As he approached his thirteenth year, his body began to reveal evidence of the passage of time. Their long walks gave way to shorter excursions — a consequence of his new hip difficulties. Other issues developed, and by early December she wondered whether he'd make it through New Year's.

And then, she received a devastating diagnosis of her own.

They both survived the holidays, and for the next few months, the three of us spent practically every day together as she suffered the procedures that took her strength and, eventually, her hair. And Benny continued to be her most faithful friend and supporter. It was as if he knew that she still needed him, and in truth, she did. Although rising from his rug and walking required increasingly more effort, he struggled to greet her every time I brought her home from her daily treatments. His puppy-heart still overflowed with unconditional love. His old body was still ready to snuggle. When her exhaustion forced her into her chair, I would sit nearby in the rocker, but Benny knew just where she needed him to be… resting at her feet.

Benny continued to provide his love and support throughout the duration of her treatments, and when they were finally over, he died.

Sadly, her healthy reprieve didn't last. For a second time, she fought the good fight, but this time, when she knew the battle was lost, she gracefully accepted the inevitable and had but one request — that the ashes of her beloved Benny be interred with her.

On a sunny November morning, we lay Mom to rest with Dad. And just as she'd asked, Benny was there, too. As always, he was just where she needed him to be... resting at her feet.

~Stephen Rusiniak

Reprinted by permission of Bruce Robinson

24

My Slobbery, Comforting Shadow

Fun fact: Studies have shown that the stress-reducing effects of petting a dog occur after just five to twenty-four minutes — much more quickly than taking a stress-reducing medication.

"Welcome home, honey," my mom said, ushering me inside the front door of my childhood home. My dad followed close behind with my suitcases. As soon as we stepped through the door, we were greeted by a wriggling, eighty-two-pound bundle of brown-furred energy: our family dog, a Boxer named Murray. I hadn't seen him in five months, not since I had been home for Christmas. He yelped and barked with joy, leaping up to kiss my face, then ran around the living room — his own version of welcoming me home.

"It's good to be back," I said, petting Murray's head. He slobbered all over my hand, but I didn't mind.

"I'm going to make you a sandwich," my mom said, heading into the kitchen. "I can tell you haven't been eating enough."

I didn't argue — I hadn't really been eating or sleeping much the past month and a half, not since my engagement had quite suddenly but irrevocably unraveled. At the time, I had been living halfway across the country from my family, finishing up my third and final year of graduate school. My brother flew out to be with me for the shell-shocked initial week of the break-up, and he was a godsend: hugging me as I cried, walking with me to class, sitting patiently with me at the kitchen table, and gently plying me with a few more bites of food, a few more sips of water.

But then my brother had to return home for work. I told my family — and myself — that I could make it through the final five weeks of the semester on my own. I was strong. I could take care of myself.

I managed to keep it together on the outside — I finished up my teaching obligations for the semester, turned in my thesis, and completed all my course requirements to graduate — but inside, I was an emotional wreck. I had trouble sleeping. I lost an unhealthy amount of weight because I simply wasn't hungry. For the first time in my life, I suffered from anxiety, a near-constant pressure in my chest that sometimes made it hard to breathe.

Finally, the semester ended, and I boarded a flight home to California. I arrived home shaken, unsure who I was, scared to be on my own facing a wide-open future. Only months before, I had everything mapped out. I thought I would spend the summer planning a wedding to my best friend. I thought the two of us would get jobs at a university together. I thought I was done looking for my life partner. But now, all of that was gone. I was back at square one.

"This is exciting!" my friends said. "You've got a fresh start." But I did not feel excited. I felt lost.

My family only talked about my ex-fiancé in negative terms. "We could always see he wasn't right for you," they said. "You're better off without him. You dodged a bullet." I knew their comments were meant to make me feel better, and I was grateful for their unflagging support of my choices. But, despite everything, the truth was that I missed my ex deeply. And I felt confused and guilty for missing him.

Out of everyone, it seemed that Murray, our family dog, was the one who best sensed my bewildered, raw grief. He looked up at me with his large, concerned eyes, and I felt understood. He didn't prod me forward when I wasn't ready to move yet. He didn't judge me for my inconsistent emotions. He loved and accepted me, just as I was.

Murray is not normally a cuddler. He's been known to leap off a queen-sized bed if someone else dares to invade his personal space by lying down beside him. Yet, as May melted into June, and June gave way to July, Murray was my shadow. He followed me around the house. He snored under the desk as I wrote on my laptop. Every night — as if sensing that nights were the toughest time for me — he curled up at the foot of my bed and kept me company as I tried to sleep.

As July faded into August, I began to sleep more. And eat more. And laugh. And smile. The hollowness and fear inside me slowly began to dissipate, like fog in sunlight. Excitement and energy began to grow anew in my core. I was healing. I was becoming myself again, passionate about life, unafraid to try new things. When I came home from my new yoga class or volunteer work at the food pantry, Murray would greet me with his sloppy dog kisses. Always, he made me feel safe and loved for exactly who I was.

In September, I moved out of my parents' house and on to the next chapter of my life, which is still being written. Murray stayed behind — he is, after all, our family dog, and my parents' house is his home. I get to see him whenever I visit. He is still not a cuddler, but whenever I return to sleep in my childhood bed for a night or two, I hear his doggy footsteps padding upstairs. His big head will nudge my bedroom door open. And he'll curl up at the foot of my bed for a little while, as if to remind me that no matter what happens, he's there and he understands.

~Dallas Woodburn

Best Friends

*Fun fact: About ten percent of people may be allergic
to dogs. Allergic people should choose breeds that don't
shed and produce less dander, the source of
most allergens.*

When my neighbor Ellen retired recently, one of the first things she did was to get her dog, Lucy. She had always wanted a dog, she told me, and now she had the time to care for one.

"I had a dog very briefly when I was a little girl," she said, "but it turns out that my brother was allergic to it, and we had to give it away."

She paused, gave a rueful little laugh, and then said, "I've never forgiven him."

It was clear, though, that she was finding her time with Lucy well worth the wait. Lucy is a charming mix, with the velvet ears and sleek coat of a Labrador Retriever, the elegant posture and black-and-white markings of a Boston Terrier, and the endearing curved tail of a Spitz breed. The shelter from which Ellen adopted Lucy told her that Lucy had likely lived most of her life on the streets in the South. Lucy's affection for Ellen is palpable, almost as if she can't believe her good fortune in finding such a loving home. And Ellen's delight in everything about Lucy is a joy to behold.

Seeing them so happy together, day after day, I couldn't help but think of Kenny, my younger son, who has also wanted a dog his whole life, but couldn't because of my husband's allergies. One of Kenny's first three words was "dog." His favorite toy as a baby was a Labrador Retriever stuffed animal. (It went everywhere with him for years—I don't think there is a photo of him as a toddler that doesn't include it.) He long considered Jenny, my sister's chocolate Lab, his favorite cousin. He would talk about visiting her with the same enthusiasm that most kids his age reserved for a trip to Disneyland.

He would ask for a dog for every Christmas and birthday, and my husband, Dan, and I would always gently turn him down. We'd explain that even if my husband could find a way to manage his allergies, Kenny would still have to wait until he was old enough to walk his puppy around the neighborhood by himself. When he was little, it seemed like the perfect solution. We didn't need to break his precious heart by telling him "no"—we just had to encourage him to have patience.

Before we knew it we had a persistent eleven-year-old who insisted that we make good on our promise. Kenny was well prepared to combat the allergy argument, providing us with a long list of hypoallergenic breeds. He also sent me a long text with all of his reasons for wanting a canine companion, ending the message with the simple words: "A dog would make me happy."

I received his message on a dreary morning after I saw Kenny off to school. As a fifth-grader on the cusp of entering middle school and adolescence, Kenny was chafing at any and all attempts to restrain his independence. It was a constant source of conflict between us.

I thought about all the arguments we had had in the past month. He was increasingly moody and full of pre-teen angst. I thought about my own childhood, and how hard the middle school years were. By the time I reached high school, I knew a bit about myself, but the awkwardness of early adolescence had been almost unbearable.

"A dog would make me happy." The last line of his text haunted me for days while I pondered what to do. I was not sure that I wanted to add more tasks to my to-do list. But how could I deny Kenny the one thing that he had always wanted? Would he, like Ellen, have to wait until he was retired to have the dog of his dreams?

Dan and I discussed the pros and cons endlessly. In addition to

Dan's allergies and all the work involved in taking care of a dog in New York City, we worried about the expense and the fact that we would likely own the dog for a decade or so after Kenny left for college. Just as I was becoming convinced that after all those years of stalling, we would have to tell Kenny "no" after all, I experienced an incident that completely changed my mind.

One morning, I spotted Ellen and Lucy walking toward our apartment building about a half-block ahead of me. They leaned into each other as they strolled along. Every now and then, Lucy gently caressed Ellen's leg with her Spitz tail. A bit of a breeze ruffled Lucy's fur and she reacted with joy, leaping and jumping around. Even from the distance, I could see Ellen's broad smile and hear her chuckle as she reached down to give Lucy a pat on the head. I knew then and there that I wanted that always-there, easygoing companionship for my son.

Kenny, of course, was ecstatic. Yes, he would agree to take total responsibility for the dog, to feed it, walk it, train it, bathe it, and clean up after it. Yes, he would agree to our house rules for the dog: It wouldn't be allowed on furniture or in the master bedroom; it would sleep in Kenny's room; it would have to be trained to listen, not jump up, etc. Yes, he'd prove he was responsible by walking the neighbor's dog every morning before school and every night before bed for a week. Yes, he'd read a book about dog training. Yes, he'd talk with an experienced dog owner to help him consider everything involved in owning a dog. Yes, yes, yes — whatever we wanted — yes.

Dan did some online research about hypoallergenic breeds. He decided we should get a Goldendoodle and set about finding one. Within a few weeks, we had a new member of the family, whom Kenny named Jenkins.

The change in Kenny was dramatic. Everyone, from his teachers to the doormen in our apartment building, remarked that since we got Jenkins, Kenny seemed to stand taller, smile brighter and, yes, be happier. He worked hard to train Jenkins, patiently cleaning up when the puppy had an accident, and setting limits regarding what is okay to chew (dog toys) and what isn't (Mom's favorite high heels).

Toward the end of our first summer with Jenkins, I happened to catch a glimpse of Kenny and his dog walking side-by-side on their way home from the park. Jenkins loped along on still-too-big-for-him puppy paws, feathery tail straight up and wagging happily. Kenny beamed with pride as a passerby complimented him on his adorable, well-behaved buddy. Boy and dog exhibited exactly the kind of relationship that I had hoped they would have: loyal, faithful, best friends.

~Victoria Otto Franzese

26

Saved by the Dog

*Fun fact: Small dogs like Chihuahuas, Maltese and
Shih Tzus are often referred to as "toy dogs."*

I'd always been an intense neat freak. When people wanted to enter my room, I would force them to wash their hands and put on hand sanitizer. Oh, and my famous book problem: I had started my own little library and I love books, but I wasn't very good about sharing them. If my brother asked to borrow a book, I'd have him wash his hands four times and put on my favorite lotion. Also, I prohibited food around my books because I didn't want crumbs stuck between book pages.

When my friends came over, I wouldn't let them in my room because I didn't know what they had touched before coming over. Eventually, I prohibited everyone from entering my room. I took many showers and constantly washed my hands.

I wouldn't play with my brother because he was "dirty." My mom said my obsession with cleanliness was abnormal. My dad just shook his head and said it would pass. But it didn't pass. I was caught in my own little world, terrified of the myriad bacteria around me.

Then, after two years of this, along came Teeny, a Chihuahua–Shih Tzu mix with a lovely coat of black, velvety fur, as well as white paws and a white nose. She was playful, energetic and adorable. On the one hand, I was extremely happy, but on the other, I was horrified and disgusted. A dog was a bacteria machine, always slobbering and shedding. Whenever Teeny started licking me, I'd panic and get mad.

She was covering me with bacteria! I loved petting her, but I taught her not to kiss me, even though she found that confusing as no one else prohibited it.

We brought Teeny along with us to my aunt's house for her first Thanksgiving. She jumped all over my aunt's family with kisses and joy. I was jealous of the affection that Teeny was giving my cousins, and jealous of her playfulness around them. Teeny jumped and played with my cousins more in one evening than she ever had with me. That evening was a long one, and I remember every little bit of it.

After that Thanksgiving dinner, I decided to retrain Teeny. I tried everything. I sat down on my knees and begged her to come to me. I held treats on my lap hoping she would sit there. I even imitated my cousin's voice calling for her. At first, Teeny hesitated, but slowly she started paying more attention to me, and the feeling of acceptance was beyond amazing. Little by little, Teeny started becoming more comfortable with me. I realized she had been scared of me.

I stopped thinking of Teeny as a "bacteria machine" and realized that she was a true treasure. It took a while, but my obsession with cleanliness disappeared.

I hadn't realized how mean and rude I must have been to my mom, dad and brother. I felt so guilty. What kind of daughter was I? How could a big sister be so mean? What kind of friend wouldn't let her friends into her room? What did my parents think of me? I wondered how I could show them I no longer cared about bacteria and dirt.

I decided to act as I did with my dog. Little by little, I grew more and more open-minded with my family. I no longer complained when they entered my room. I made no more remarks about washing hands or using hand sanitizer. My mother no longer commented on my "mental illness," and my brother and I built a great brother-sister relationship. My father, in his corner, even smiled at the progress I made.

Teeny taught me a valuable lesson about acceptance. By reaching out to her, I overcame my obsession and learned how to reach out to everyone who matters in my life.

~Laura Yoon

27

Little White Dog

*Fun fact: Dogs have forty-two teeth: two pairs of
canine teeth, six pairs of incisors, and the rest
are molars.*

"Should we even be thinking about getting a dog right now?" I asked my eager fiancé as we drove to the shelter that hot July morning. "The wedding's nearly five months away, and we still have so much to do for that and the house. I still have to move, and you'll be alone with the dog most of that time. Then we're headed to Hawaii, and we'll have to find someone to dog-sit. It would be easier if we waited until after Christmas, or even spring."

Stephen hadn't grown up with dogs as I had, and I had a feeling he didn't really understand the amount of work they could be.

"That's exactly why we should get a dog," he countered. "I'll be alone until you move, so I'll be lonely. Dogs relieve stress, so it will actually help with all the things we have to do. It'll help us relax, you know? I've already looked at the shelter online and made a list of dogs that would be good."

A half-hour later, I closed the door of the small-dog room, muffling the high-pitched cacophony our presence had set off. I crossed to the desk, staffed by a volunteer. "Could we meet that little white dog, please?" I asked. "The one in the bottom corner by the door."

She looked at me blankly, trying to pull the dog's information from memory. I persisted. "It looks like she only has one eye."

That one eye had locked on mine as Stephen left the room, passing a message: "I am your dog. I don't like this noise any more than he does. Let's get this show on the road."

"Oh, oh, Chippewa," she said. "Yes, I'll get someone to bring her out to you."

We sat at a picnic table in the dusty driveway of the shelter, watching our little white dog walk out to us. The shelter said she was a Beagle-Lab mix. Her ears and tail turned out to be biscuit-colored now that I saw them in the light.

The shelter worker handed me the lead, and Stephen patted the bench. The little white dog knew what that meant. She hopped up and sat between us, drinking in the attention. Not only was her left eye atrophied, but her teeth were mostly nubs.

Now that she was in the fresh air with us, the little white dog was cheerful and energetic. She raced to the end of the driveway and back, Stephen trotting beside her to keep up.

"She's probably at least ten," I said. "She has one eye and bad teeth. What are those bumps on her face and head?"

Stephen leaned down and patted her gently. "Buckshot, I think." He looked disgusted. "Someone shot her in the face. That's probably what happened to her eye."

Our own eyes met. "It doesn't matter," one of us said. "This is our dog."

It's a cliché to say that the dog rescued us, but it's true. We renamed her "Hildy," short for Hildegard, a name Stephen had chosen for a dog years before. We bought her everything an old dog could want. We took her to the vet, who ran a panel of tests and sent us home with pills for her thyroid disorder and a heart condition and told us she probably didn't hear well. He also said her tiny nubs of teeth were weakened by poor nutrition and ground down by attempts to gnaw on hard things like rocks and cans to fill her hungry tummy. They also could have been ground down if she had been kept in a cage by a puppy-mill operator.

We took her back later that year for minor surgery to remove the buckshot that was drifting close to her good eye.

Meanwhile, our newlywed dreams fell apart. Our wedding was beautiful, but afterward we were alone in a small town in the Midwest, seven hundred miles away from family and friends and our East Coast homes. We were young, we were miserable, and we blamed each other.

But Hildy united us. She loved both of us, and we both loved her. We were stuck together and forced to make our marriage work because neither of us was willing to leave her. Hildy was our constant, our friend even when we were not friends to each other.

At last, three years after we adopted Hildy, we were able to move, not home to the East Coast, but at least to a city that was more our speed, and into jobs that were a better fit. We rented a small house that Hildy loved because she could sit in one place and see most of it. There weren't any stairs to challenge her arthritis. She loved going for short walks four times a day around the block, and people in the neighborhood came to recognize her and us. Despite her new diagnosis of Cushing's disease, it was a happy year for all of us. Stephen and I found our way back to the relationship we had had before, the one we were now so glad we hadn't given up on.

In June, a year after our move, Hildy's health declined sharply. Her vet suspected bone cancer. Despite her illness, she was cheerful until the last walk she took into the emergency vet clinic early on a Sunday morning, when it was time to let her go. The night before, we lay on the floor beside her bed, petting her and trying to tell her what she meant to us.

"You saved us," I whispered. "You saved our marriage. Thank you so much. Thank you for loving us when we couldn't love each other. We love you, little white dog."

After Hildy died, I started writing again, something I had given up on in those dark, mostly miserable years when I felt my life had gone horribly wrong in every way except for the little white dog at my feet. I felt Hildy would want me to.

My first novel was published four years after Hildy's death, two weeks after the birth of our first child.

The dedication reads, "In memory of Hildy, who saved my life in the wilderness."

~Courtney McKinney-Whitaker

28

The Gift of a Caring Companion

Fun fact: Studies have shown that the unconditional love of a dog can help people feel less depressed.

Back in high school, I had a hard time fitting in and felt really lonely. It was getting harder and harder to hold back my tears every day when I came home from school. I didn't know if the tears were of relief that the day was done, or of sadness that I had to get up and go back to a place full of bullies and people who didn't like me.

One day, I came home in tears and ran upstairs to my bedroom. I couldn't stop crying. I sat on my floor and started ripping pages from my diary. I can't believe I liked him, I thought. I had liked this boy for a long time and had actually been feeling pretty happy lately, but that day he had said he could never like someone like me. I was crushed.

I finished ripping the pages out of my diary and continued sobbing when I felt something brush against my leg. I looked up and saw Myla staring at me with a tilted head and a wagging tail. I scrunched up my face and began crying hysterically. Myla's tail stopped. She backed away a little bit and tilted her head to the other side. Her eyes grew wide. Then she started whimpering.

I curled my legs up to my stomach and hugged them with my arms. Myla nudged her head between my legs, put her paws up on my chest and sniffed my face. She had never done this before! She was a pretty placid dog who usually sat on the couch and unenthusiastically watched the cars go by. I knew she cared about me but I was shocked when she put her paws on me, sniffed my face, and licked my tears away. It was as if she was replacing a caring parent at that moment.

I patted her head, and her tail started wagging again. I laughed at her funny little tail trying to wag as fast as it could. She then started chasing it, and as I watched her, I forgot what I was so sad about. I took a moment to catch my breath and lifted myself up off the floor. Myla followed me to the bathroom where I washed my tear-stained face. I flicked some water at her, and she sneezed. Her tail never stopped wagging.

Myla followed me around the house until late into the evening. Every time I would sniff or make a sound, she would cock her head and look at me like a worried mother, as if to confirm that I was okay.

That night, as I crawled into bed, exhausted from the day's events, I realized how thankful I was for Myla. I had gotten her for Christmas the year before just as I had entered high school. I went through many emotional ups and downs throughout high school — as most people do — and came home to my favourite little pooch who would follow me up to my room and insist on comforting me the only way she knew how: with doggy kisses and tail wags.

Myla comforted me with her puppy compassion until someone else needed her. Two years after I started university, my mom told me her friend was lonely after being widowed. It broke my heart. I knew that Myla would be a perfect addition to her household, with her easygoing nature and huggable coat of fur.

It was really hard to give Myla away, but I will never forget the look on that lady's face when I gave her a new companion. Her big smile and happy tears made me feel like I did the right thing.

After caring for me for so long, it was time for Myla to care for a widow who just needed someone to talk to and feed. I think I gave the best gift one could ever give. From an emotional high-school life to a widow's bedside, Myla served her purpose as a caring and friendly presence in times of need. My darling Myla proved to me that dogs make not only the best pets, but also some of the best friends, teachers, and caregivers we'll ever know.

~Sarah Wun

29

Promising Monroe

Fun fact: According to a recent APPA survey, six percent of dogs and twenty-seven percent of cats in the U.S. were adopted as strays.

Headstrong. Defiant. Smart. Quick. Mischievous. That's what I thought when I first met Monroe, a little wiry Terrier mix I found abandoned in a cornfield. The first time I saw her, I was driving down a country road that divided two such fields, and she was trotting in and out of passing cars, dirty and scared.

I was immediately drawn to this little being. Despite the fear she clearly felt, she had an air of confidence and feistiness that fascinated me. She refused help. She would run, and she was fast. She would be gone in seconds at one false move.

"She could be a reflection of me," I thought.

Having recently experienced a disastrous end to an engagement, I, too, had become quick to discount new and wonderful possibilities out of fear. Headstrong, I would not accept help from anyone, especially if they made a misstep. Monroe and I both had to learn to trust again after being abandoned.

It took me over a week to bring this quirky girl to safety. I tried trapping her, baiting her, chasing her, sitting quietly with her on the side of the road talking softly, and making myself small and nonthreatening. As I talked to her, I promised I would never harm her. I wanted to help her, and if she'd just trust me, I would never let her down. It was important to do this with little movement and breathing. She was always careful not to get too close.

She had made a makeshift home under a cluster of trees at the top of a hill. Wild kudzu cushioned the shaded floor under the branches, and every day that I rode out to check on her, she would be waiting majestically atop her throne of kudzu.

I would toss her bologna, her favorite food, piece by piece, trying to get her to inch closer to me. One day, I managed to get her within a foot of me with this wonderful, magical bologna, and with a swift movement of my left arm, I had her. She flipped and flailed like a fish out of water, yelping and growling. Worried that I was hurting her, I thought, "I can fix a broken leg, but I cannot let go. She'll never come to me again." I wrapped her in a towel and gently shoved her into the safety of a pet carrier. She never once bit me.

She got a little sick in the car, so we went immediately to the emergency veterinary clinic to have her checked out. She bit a vet tech and trembled in extreme fear. It was quickly observed that this little pup had very little socialization and was going to need a long time to recover from her months out in the cornfield scavenging for food and avoiding the coyotes. The vet told me to be prepared for her to become deeply bonded to me from that point forward.

Every little sound upset her; any movement frightened her. She lived in that pet carrier for a month before she felt comfortable enough to come out on her own. After that, we would curl up in bed and watch TV to help her acclimate to noises. We would walk through the neighborhood at midnight to avoid contact with others. She had extreme separation anxiety, and my doorframes, windowsills, furniture and even my walls became victim to her nervous chewing habit over many months.

We took it one day at a time. She gradually learned to go outside during daytime, warming up to other people little by little. She always loved a car ride, so we would ride around, giving her a little more freedom.

As she recovered, and I watched her grow into a more confident and trusting dog, I grew, too. We rehabilitated each other. If she could learn to trust people, so could I. Monroe and I became quite a pair, overcoming our fears and our distrust of the human race together.

Our daily conquests were documented online for friends and followers to see, complete with funny photos and descriptions of the progress Monroe was making. And as the two of us grew, so did our audience. Monroe was an inspiration and entertainment to many. While she wasn't ready to meet everyone personally, her followers became engaged in her life and mine, cheering us on each day.

I knew there was something very special about this little Terrier full of potential from the first day I met her. And I upheld the promise I made to her sitting alongside the country road.

The inspiration she brought to me and others evolved into a small non-profit organization to help other animals like her. She even went on television to publicize the non-profit named in her honor. Recently, we opened up our home to a new rescue — a little male dog, Monty. Together, we live each day helping others, confident that we have each other. I will never regret promising Monroe my devotion and dedication. This little twelve-pound mess brought me back to life.

~Jennifer R. Land

30

Right

*Fun fact: "Sight hounds" have superior eyesight and
speed, quickly spotting their prey and catching it.
"Scent hounds" track animals better through their
sense of smell.*

"Hi, I'm Jessica, and I have an anxiety disorder." I did
all the right things for it. At least, I did all the right
things eventually, when it all came crashing down
and the panic attacks took over my life. It got so bad
that it was all I could do to make it to the end of the day, when I'd
hand the care of my kids over to my husband so I could go curl up in
a ball on my bed, sure that going outside would kill me.

I did all the right things: I saw my doctor. I got medication. And
I saw a therapist.

It's complicated, of course. My therapist and I talked about my
marriage, my hang-ups and, of course, my childhood.

But then came the question from my therapist: "Why don't you
get a dog?"

A dog. A calm, loyal, protective animal that would be there when
I was scared. That would stay present and warm and near when the
adrenalin coursed unwelcome through my veins. When the waves of
fear made my heart pound and my stomach clench and sweat drip
down my face. A dog.

"I can't get a dog," I said. "I live in an apartment."

My therapist looked amused. "Do you think people in apartments never have dogs? What do you think they do in New York?"

She was right. I couldn't pretend she wasn't.

And I loved dogs. I always had. I'd grown up with them. There was Sofie, the shy rescue puppy we named after her love of curling up secure on the sofa. There was Charlie, the big, bounding Dalmatian–German Shepherd mix who could stand on his hind legs and put his front paws on my shoulders. There was Sarah, the sight hound who looked sleepy but could bound up and catch an opossum on the back fence faster than I could blink.

But I'd grown up in a house, and so for some reason, I had it in my head that people who lived in apartments—like the one I lived in now—couldn't have dogs.

Nevertheless, I came home and, with a hint of hope in my voice, mentioned the idea to my husband: "What if we get a dog?"

He wasn't hard to convince. He'd grown up with dogs, too. So, we brought home Callie, a fluffy, medium-sized black mutt. Gorgeous. Her fur was so long I could sink my fingers into it and so soft that it rivaled the fur of a cat. Callie was so affectionate that she'd wiggle herself under my hand for just one more scratch every time I stopped petting her.

And she made me feel safer.

"What do you think people in New York do?" my therapist had asked.

And now, as a person who had a dog—and who lived in an apartment—I had my answer: They take their dogs for walks.

They take their dogs for walks outside. Away from the safety of their homes.

It was the exact opposite of everything my anxiety disorder screamed at me to do. My anxiety disorder said: Stay inside, stay safe, and hide yourself away.

But the fluffy black mutt who looked at me with adoring eyes said: "I love you and I trust you're going to walk me to some fresh green grass where I can pee."

It sounds silly, but it was simple, really. Callie became both my reason for going outside and also my protection when I did.

With Callie on a leash, I began to fight my fears. I started going on walks again. Just around the block at first, but that counted. I was outside with my dog at my side; I was reclaiming my place in the world. My neighborhood streets became mine again.

Mine... and Callie's.

My therapist was right.

~Jessica Snell

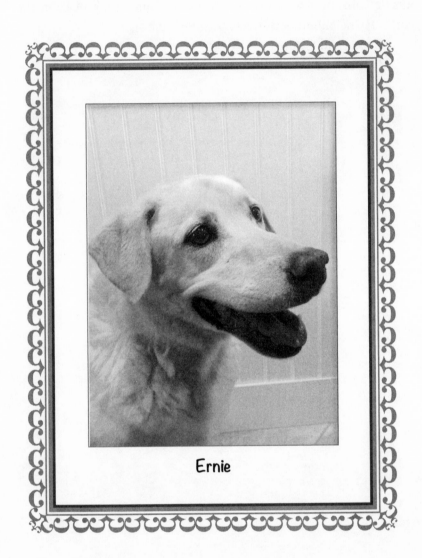

Ernie

My Very Good, Very Bad Dog

My Naughty but Nice Dog

*Not-so-fun fact: Excessive barking is one of the most widespread
behavioral problems in dogs.*

31

The Busboy

*Fun fact: Most experts say that "guilty look" our dogs
give isn't really guilt but rather the fear of
being punished.*

As my sister and I washed the dishes after our holiday meal, we heard a loud tinkling noise in the dining room. It sounded like glass, though not a breaking noise. I sent my sister in to check it out and bring in another stack of dishes to wash.

"Oh, my God!" I heard her gasp. I hurried into the room to find my sweet, one-year-old, seventy-five-pound Alaskan Malamute–German Shepherd mix standing in the middle of the dining table licking the meal's remnants off my fine china. His tail curled up into the crystal chandelier, and as he licked with gusto, his tail automatically moved inside the chandelier, causing the tinkling noise.

"Sitka!" I hollered. He stopped licking and turned his head to look at me. I swear I saw him smirk, a look I had seen on his face every time I found him doing something he knew he shouldn't. He was one of the sweetest dogs I'd ever known, but he was clearly still a teenager and often challenged behavior norms. I never knew what to expect from him. I'd already taken him to puppy training where I was pretty sure they had only passed him so that I wouldn't bring him back.

"Get off the table!" I said in a loud, stern voice. Instead, he crouched into a play position. A doggie grin spread across his jokester face, and his huge tongue dangled out of his mouth. He began rapidly moving his giant paws from side to side — his game challenging me to play. I envisioned my fine china and crystal glasses flying and shattering into millions of pieces. I had to act quickly. I didn't want to reward him for bad behavior, but I knew I had to do something to save the china and crystal. I changed my demeanor and tone.

"Sitka, sweetie, lie down nicely," I cooed, taking slow, easy steps toward him. His big brown eyes softened as he watched me. When I reached him, I began to gently pet him and continued speaking in soft, soothing tones. "Oh, you're helping me clean the dishes. What a thoughtful doggie." He mellowed and began lowering his large white-and-black body onto the table, right on top of the dishes, eventually lying sideways and offering up his stomach for a tummy rub. As he spread out his legs, he began pushing the crystal and china to the table's edge. I grabbed them before they fell and handed them to my sister. "Yes, that's right, you lie down, yes, anywhere you like," I cooed affectionately.

My sister stood in mild shock, her eyes asking me what to do. I whispered, "Very slowly, gather up the dishes. I'll keep him preoccupied." Jordana began removing dishes, first those behind him, but as soon as she reached for the dishes in front of him, he playfully laid his paw over her hand, preventing her from removing them. He began thumping his tail in a hard wag, attempting to play with her and causing the remaining china and crystal to rattle and jump in place. I reached over and laid my hand over his tail while still rubbing his stomach, gazing into those sweet chocolate eyes full of adolescent love and whimsy. It worked. Within a few minutes, Jordana was able to remove all the dishes, except those under his body.

"Now what?" she asked.

I rolled Sitka over to scratch and massage the sides of his stomach and chest. "Grab 'em quick!" I said, as the window of opportunity to remove the dishes was brief and fleeting. She grabbed them, and finally the only thing remaining on the table was my silly dog.

I stood back, hands on my hips. "Bad, bad dog!" I admonished him. "Get off the table! Now!" He stood up and looked at me with understandable confusion, turning his head from side to side. "I said now!" Sitka lowered his head, the silly grin gone, his tongue firmly inside of his mouth. He jumped off the table and started to slink away in shame and dejection. He didn't get far before I grabbed him by the collar and led him out to the back yard where he stayed all evening.

I was prepared to leave him outside all night but my husband said he probably learned his lesson, as we hardly ever banished him to the yard. When I went outside to bring him back into the house, he got up slowly, hanging his head low. He wouldn't look at me. Like a child who knew he had done something bad, he focused on the ground.

"You know you were a bad dog, right?" I asked him. No answer. He wouldn't even look up. I kneeled down in front of him and gently took his face into my hands, massaging the sides with my fingers and forcing him to look up. He stared at me with all the sincerity of a child truly sorry for being caught with his hands in the proverbial cookie jar. "Are you going to be a good doggie now?" I asked in as sweet a voice as I could muster. He bumped his big black nose against mine, giving me a little lick, which I took for an apology.

I stood up. "Okay, you can come inside," I said in a cheery tone. "No more standing on the dining table. Got it?" He cocked his head to the side. "All right, come inside," I said, waving him toward the back door. "Time for bed!" He got it and raced me to the door — winning, of course.

~Jeffree Wyn Itrich

32

Power Struggle

*Fun fact: A study by the Mayo Clinic Sleep Disorders
Center revealed that fifty-three percent of pet owners
in the study said their pet disturbed their nightly rest.*

I felt my husband, Loren, flip back the covers and climb out of
bed. A dim light from the hallway disappeared when the bathroom door clicked shut.

Seconds later, I felt the mattress beside me sink down. I
snuggled closer and draped my arm over his quilt-covered body, then
drifted deeper into sleep. My eyes fluttered open moments later when
I heard the elevated pitch of Loren's voice.

"What are you doing? Get down."

The reluctant lump beside me rolled over and plopped to the
floor with a thump. The nails of my four-legged companion, Charlie,
clicked across the linoleum as he left the bedroom.

Our eighteen-month-old Basset-Lab mix was engaged in a bit of
a power struggle with Loren. Charlie considered no territory off-limits.

The next morning at breakfast, Loren said, "I don't know what
made him think he could sleep in our bed, and on my side. You notice
he didn't get in on your side?" I drew a deep breath while I considered
my response.

Loren spread jam on his toast. "I just don't get it. We've had him
over a year, and he's never done that before."

"It's not really his fault," I confessed. "When you went to Oregon
for your fire-department training, he slept in bed with me all week."

Charlie stood next to the table between us, his ears perked. With a scowl, my husband stared into those brown Basset eyes. "Hmm…" Charlie wagged his tail. He looked at Loren and then at me while he waited to hear his fate.

Loren shook his head. "Well, no more, or he'll have to stay outside. No more getting on the bed, no begging for dinner scraps at the table, and I don't want him on the couch either."

Charlie gave Loren a defiant glare. He lifted his nose in the air as he lumbered into the living room and leaped onto the couch.

Before he could plop down in his usual corner and rest his head on the arm, Loren waved his hand in the air. "Oh, no, you don't. You get down. You're spoiled, that's what you are."

Charlie lowered his head, skulked across the room, and flopped down on the rug in front of the fireplace.

Loren grabbed his lunchbox off the kitchen counter. "Sometimes, I think we work just so he can lounge around here all day enjoying the comforts we provide."

I laughed, giving him a kiss on his way out the door to work. "Don't be so put out. You love him, too, and you know it."

Loren shrugged. "Well, let's try to keep him off the furniture."

By that evening, Loren had relented and let Charlie reclaim his spot on the sofa. "I guess I was a little harsh this morning, but I don't want him on the bed."

Over the next few years, the two developed a silent understanding between them, acknowledged only by a certain lingering eye-to-eye contact. As long as Charlie stayed off the bed, he continued to edge his way further into Loren's heart. My husband may have protested his spoiled ways, but one evening I noticed him sharing his dish of ice cream. Charlie wiggled and wagged his tail while he licked the last few bites from Loren's spoon. Still, my husband insisted it was a bad habit to allow dogs to beg at the table. However, as Charlie gained ground, even that restriction became obsolete. Toward the end of our dinners, Loren would hand leftover morsels from his plate under the table where an eager unseen someone waited for the tasty scraps.

The longer we had him, the more Charlie advanced from pet

status to family member. Still standing firm, Loren maintained that our bed was a Charlie-free zone. On occasion, our beloved and persistent hound would sneak into our room for a quick snooze. But as soon as Loren discovered him, he escorted Charlie from the room with a gentle scolding. And so the back-and-forth battle continued.

That is, until I underwent unexpected major surgery and had to stay in bed for several weeks. Loren did everything he could to make me comfortable. One afternoon, with a sheepish grin on his face, he brought Charlie into the bedroom and hoisted him up next to me on the blankets. "I guess there's no reason he can't be on the bed during the day. But he's not going to sleep with us at night."

Of course, that final restriction didn't last a month. From then on, Charlie jumped up on the bed anytime he wanted, rested his head on the pillows, and sprawled out in king-sized comfort. Finally, he declared victory in the battle for the bed.

~Kathleen Kohler

Reprinted by permission of Bruce Robinson

33

A Second Too Long

Not-so-fun fact: Never leave your dog alone in a hot
car. He can quickly become overheated and even die.

"Let's go, Maximus," I said, snapping a leash onto his red collar. My parents had called to offer a Sunday meal, and I jumped at the invitation. Plus, I was taking my new pup to play with his grandpa and grandma for the afternoon. I would get great eats, and they would get time with their grandbaby. Max's stubby tail, or to be honest, his whole butt, wiggled back and forth in anticipation of going "bye-bye." Car rides were one of his most favorite things—even if he had no clue where he was going. A trip to the vet even elicited this response… at least until we pulled into the parking lot.

I gathered up all the necessary items I needed to take along: Max's toys, his food, and two videos I needed to return to the store on our way, and piled all of it into the car. I buckled Max into the passenger seat for safety reasons, and he sat obediently within the confines of the belt, still vibrating with anticipation.

The day had turned cold and blustery, and snowflakes had begun to fall on my windshield. After running the car for a bit, I turned the heater up full blast to warm up the car, and we were on our way. Max immediately tried to bounce around on the front seat, anxious to see where we were headed.

"Sit!" I commanded, and he dutifully sat back down, looking at me with his big panting smile. He had not taken too many car rides since I adopted him two months prior, but he already knew most rides ended up at my parents' house, so he tried his best to be patient. He knew Grandma and Grandpa had the best treats. We were both on this trip for one thing: food.

The snow had just begun to stick so I maneuvered my car gingerly down the street. Due to the weather and because I was in a hurry, I pulled up outside the store along the curb instead of parking in a space. It would only take me a second to run inside and drop off the movies, and then we'd be on our way to a home-cooked meal.

"Stay here, Max," I said, giving him a brief pat on the head. "I'll be right back, buddy!"

I left the car running, heat blasting, and jogged into the store. I heard Max bark a few times in dismay as I left him behind, but I would only be gone a few seconds.

I took two steps inside the door and handed the movies to the cashier. Turning on my heel, I headed right back outside. The snow was falling in earnest now, and I wondered if I should still continue on to my parents' home. But they were looking forward to getting together, and Max and I were looking forward to the meal, so I decided to keep going. Dad could always drive us home if it got too bad.

I could see Max's whole body wiggling with excitement and his tongue hanging out of his smiling wide jaw as I approached. His exuberance made it seem like I'd been gone for weeks. It made me smile to have someone adore me so much and miss me so deeply when I'd only been gone a few seconds. Adopting him had been the best thing I'd ever done.

"Hey, buddy," I said from outside the car in the voice everyone uses when speaking to their pets. "Yes! Who's a good dog?! Let's get going!"

I reached for the handle, watching Max bounce with pure joy inside the car. Just as I put my hand on the handle, Max's bouncing paw found the door-lock switch.

I heard the locks engage, and it felt like one of those slow-motion moments in the movies.

"Nooooo!" I screamed.

Several passersby glanced in my direction as I pulled unsuccessfully at the locked car door. I tried every door, but the electronic locks had engaged every entrance.

My loving but slightly-too-exuberant dog had just locked me out of my still-idling car.

My mood instantly changed to one of shock and despair. I heard my car's engine droning on as visions of gallons of gas going up in unnecessary fumes filled my mind.

Max, however, didn't understand the dilemma and panted gleefully at me from the now really warm interior.

I could almost hear him say, "C'mon, Mom! Let's go! What's the hold-up?"

I debated walking home to get the spare key, but it was over two miles away. Plus, the snowy, cold weather put a damper on walking that far. I didn't want to leave my car or my pooch, and the car would probably be out of gas by the time I was able to retrieve a key. I tried to get Max to step on the same button to unlock the door, to no avail.

"Come on, buddy! Step right there... no... there... no... argh!"

Max quite enjoyed this new game, panting and barking at my weird commands, and fogging up his side of the window. I rubbed my hands over my increasingly cold arms and tried to think of another solution.

As each second passed, I saw dollar signs drifting out of the exhaust. Finally, I gave up and went back into the video store. The only solution was to call Dad before my car ran out of gas. After briefly describing what had happened to the cashier and ignoring her smirk, I asked if I could use her phone to call my dad, who also seemed quite amused at my situation.

"He did what?" he asked. I could hear the smile in his voice.

After explaining it again, he promised to come straight away with the spare key.

I hung up the phone, thanked the clerk and went back out to check on Max. I watched as he fogged up the windows of the car, sitting dutifully on the passenger seat and looking at me shivering in the cold like I'd lost my mind. I tried to reassure him that everything was okay, but it was really myself I was comforting. I went back inside to wait.

When my dad finally arrived, he didn't say a word, but just grinned and handed me the spare key. I followed him back to their house and endured hours of endless amusement about how the dog had locked me out of my own car.

After this incident, I now make certain that Dad always has the spare key, and when I bought a new car, my top priority was the feature that wouldn't allow the doors to lock while the car was running.

Now Max rarely gets left alone in the car, even if it is only going to be "just a second."

~Sue A. Fairchild

Heidi's Gift

*Fun fact: Miniature Schnauzers are known as "ratters"
because they were developed by German farmers in
the late 19th century to keep the rat population
under control.*

Both teens retired to their rooms. My husband Freddy let our Miniature Schnauzer Heidi out for her final yard inspection before bedding down in her crate. Though she was not a large dog, she would do whatever was necessary to guard her family. Checking out the yard before bedtime was one of her many self-imposed duties. I looked in on the kids while Freddy called Heidi back into the house.

Instead of going to her crate, Heidi rushed past me into my daughter's room. As she darted by, I tried to grab what looked like dried grass hanging from her beard. In one flying leap, she landed on Teri's bed among open books and homework.

I went to tell my son goodnight. I'd be back for Heidi when she'd had a few scratches behind her ears.

As I chatted with John about his day, the quiet evening was disrupted by Teri's shrieking. Her screams were so loud I thought a burglar was in the house. As John and I ran down the hall, we met my husband headed in the same direction.

There was no burglar, but the shrieks continued. Puzzled, we stepped into the room.

Heidi sat in front of Teri on the pink bedspread, tail wagging, ears up, and paws together. She looked like a little general standing at attention. Teri was bouncing up and down flailing her arms about while she continued to scream.

She was able to get out a few words to give us a clue as to the cause of her terror. She pointed to Heidi. "Look. Look. Look." We hurried over to the bed.

Heidi seemed so proud as she sat behind her offering to Teri: a mouse. Somewhat crippled but still alive, the mouse wriggled as Heidi stood guard.

Schnauzers are mousers. They earn their keep catching—and usually killing—mice for their owners. Teri had been chosen from the four people in our home to receive the spoils of her backyard reconnaissance. Perhaps in Heidi's mind, a live mouse was better than a dead one.

My husband stepped forward. He took the treasure outside and didn't bother us with the details. Meanwhile, my son and I were laughing so hard that my daughter's terror turned into indignation.

We laughed even harder at her version of the story. When Heidi jumped on her bed, Teri reached over to pull a piece of dried grass out of her beard. When she discovered she was pulling a live mouse's tail, the screams began. Hoping to appease her mistress, Heidi laid the mouse as close to Teri as possible.

Later, as the house returned to normal, I remembered trying to grab what I thought was dried grass in Heidi's beard. Had I succeeded, I would have denied Heidi the chance to bestow her gift on Teri and we would have been deprived of a great family memory.

~Carole A. Bell

His Just Desserts

Fun fact: Humans have five million scent receptors in their noses, but dogs have more than 200 million scent receptors in their noses and the roofs of their mouths.

It was dog-treat baking day — time to create those homemade treats that my pups love so much. Somehow, they always know when I'm about to start cooking. Two seconds after I pull out the cookie sheets and grab the bone-shaped cookie cutter, the dogs appear. I suddenly become the most popular person in my house.

Sadie, our Lab-Shepherd mix, and Coco and Pixel, the Maltese pups, waste no time dashing into the kitchen. They jockey for position, extending their moist noses, anxious to see what I'm doing. I usually have quite a bit of help with my baking project.

This day was no different from any other. With pups underfoot, I assembled the ingredients. I mixed and measured flour and cheese, adding in some bits of bacon as I stirred and kneaded the concoction. Beautiful smells filled the air, tantalizing their senses. The puppies gathered under my feet, bouncing into my legs and demanding my attention. They whimpered and whined, begging for some small scrap to come their way as I loaded the cookie sheets with rows of tiny treats. A modest pile of cheese and bacon pieces was left on the kitchen counter. Feeling generous, I knocked the mound to the floor. Three wet tongues scurried along, slurping up the tiny scraps. Keeping them occupied allowed me to pop the treats into the oven without their help.

I mused that baking time must be sheer agony for the dogs.

Delicious smells wafted from the oven. The puppies never stray too far from the kitchen during the baking process, so, as usual, they lay down and stared at the oven door. When the oven timer went off, it was almost like someone had rung the doorbell. (We all know what a frenzy that drives our dogs into!)

Buzz… buzz… buzz. The howling and barking began. In dog speak, the buzzing must mean "hot treats are done — you can eat them now." I quickly scooped out both cookie sheets, turning off the pesky timer in the process. Foolishly, I thought the absence of noise would make the dogs calm down. No way. As soon as I put both of the cookie sheets on the stovetop to cool, another chorus of howls greeted me. I'm pretty sure they were saying they wanted their treats — right now. How was I going to explain that none of the delectable goodies was intended for immediate consumption? I didn't even try. I just made a general announcement to the universe that the treats needed to cool. I also added that any puppies in the kitchen needed to vacate the area. For the next fifteen minutes, three dogs sat very still on the kitchen floor, gazing up at the stovetop. They looked as though they expected the treats to come to life and jump into their mouths. Occasionally, they'd look forlornly at one another, whimpering and barking quietly.

I never suspected that they were hatching a plan — that can be the only explanation for what happened next. I can still see it happening as though in slow motion. I grabbed the cookie trays, one in each hand, moving them to the kitchen counter. I was silly enough to think that I'd be able to load up their treat jar with the freshly baked goodies.

That's when it happened.

Simultaneously, three dogs sprang to their feet, charging toward me. Three dogs under two unsuspecting feet doesn't end well. I tripped, twisting and turning in several directions at once. Meanwhile, the dog treats were slipping and sliding precariously on the baking sheets.

Down I went along with both cookie sheets. The puppy treats scattered like dry leaves in a hurricane. They slid in several directions across the slick tile floor. Sadie dashed off in one direction, scooping up treats as fast as she could. Coco scampered off in another direction, munching and chomping on the warm goodies along the way.

And there sat Pixel. At his feet was a perfectly formed dog treat. Untouched. I was eye-to-eye with him at this point, after my not-so-graceful landing on my rear end. He stared at me, just waiting. With a whole floor covered in dog treats, he wouldn't eat a bite.

Finally, I reached over and picked up the treat, snapping it into two pieces. I placed one piece back on the floor at his feet. The other piece went into his open mouth. Pixel looked at me as if he was smiling before he wolfed it down. You see, that's the only way Pixel will eat his treats. One piece must be placed gingerly into his mouth with the other piece placed at his feet. Even when the whole floor is covered in his favorite thing to eat.

You tell me — is he spoiled, or what?

~Debby Johnson

36

Independence Day

*Fun fact: 17th century Swiss monks in the Hospice
of Saint Bernard bred St. Bernard dogs to search
for lost travelers crossing mountain passes between
Switzerland and Italy.*

My first dog was a St. Bernard named Sir Lancelot. From a fluffy puppy we carried in our arms, he grew to be a powerhouse weighing nearly 200 pounds. Lancelot was not only large, he lived large, trotting across the lawn with an old tire clamped in his jaws or turning a discarded mahogany tabletop into a teething ring.

Our dog was not a star pupil in obedience class. Lancelot pulled on the leash so hard he yanked my mom and sister off their feet. Only my father and I walked him. Sometimes, I wrapped his leash around my arm, the chain digging into my flesh with bruising force, to hold him back when Lancelot growled at strangers who shared my sidewalk.

Lancelot may have frightened strangers, but he was still a little puppy at heart. We made the mistake of leaving him home alone in the yard his first Fourth of July while we went to see the fireworks show at the high school. We came home to an empty yard.

Lancelot had hurled himself against the gate until it broke open, then disappeared into the night. Dad drove slowly around the neighborhood. Mom and I walked up and down our street calling his name. None of us spotted any sign of our missing St. Bernard.

Late that evening, the phone rang. "Mrs. Lendroth, is your doggie home?" asked the mother of my best friend, Denise Woo.

Her parents had returned home from a night out to find something unexpected on their shadowed porch. A deep, long growl rumbled from the darkness when they opened their front gate. The Woos quickly slammed it shut again. Whatever creature barred them from their home was large, very large.

Mr. Woo called the police from a neighbor's house. The officers angled their patrol car to throw light up the walkway and onto the porch. When Mrs. Woo saw what stood there, she called us.

Somehow, our terrified St. Bernard, running to escape the booming fusillade overhead, had found Denise's house a half-mile away, remembered from the two or three times we had walked there months ago in cooler weather. Her porch spelled safety, Denise's parents, intruders.

Dad quickly drove to the Woos' house. When he approached the gate, Lancelot growled deep and low, warning him and everyone else to stay back from the porch he had claimed. The policeman warned Dad, too. "That dog's scared; you'd better not go near him."

Dad simply opened the gate and yelled, "Lancelot, you damn fool, it's me!"

At those magic words, our dangerously frightened St. Bernard bounded to Dad, panting happily and wriggling like a puppy. Clipped to his leash, he was eager to greet the Woos, the police and anyone else he met — a happy-go-lucky dog whose person had finally arrived to take him home.

~Susan Lendroth

37

Midnight Thief

Not-so-fun fact: According to the Association for Pet Obesity Prevention, 52.7% of dogs in the United States are overweight or obese.

I love to visit my son and his family in Fountain Inn, South Carolina. Not only do I get to enjoy the weather there versus winters at our home in northern Illinois, but I get to see their three adorable dogs: Mason, a yellow Labrador Retriever; Max, an overweight Basset Hound mix; and Jake, a cute, caramel-colored Dachshund.

The dogs love treats and perform to get them. Jake "speaks" in a special way, Mason balances a bone on his nose, and Max rolls over and plays dead.

The dogs are obsessed with food, of course, but they are fed a healthy diet, with a minimum of "people" food. When we sit in the dining room to eat, three little heads poke around the door and move closer and closer to the table, hoping against hope for an accident.

One day, my daughter-in-law, Tammy, had made a beautiful and delicious cake for dessert. After dinner, we loaded the dishwasher, covered the leftover cake, and went to bed.

The next morning, Tammy shrieked and yelled at Mason, who being a Lab, was the only one of the three tall enough to reach the kitchen counter. I stepped into the kitchen to see what the fuss was about. "What's wrong?" I asked.

"Look!" She held out the empty cake plate. "Naughty dog!" She stared at Mason.

"What happened?" I had wanted another piece of that cake.

"Mason ate all the leftover dessert." She grabbed the dog, saying "No, no," and putting him out in the back yard.

After dinner the following night, we wrapped the leftover apple crisp and slipped it into the refrigerator — out of sight and smell, and temptation. I rolled the potato chip bag tightly closed, clipped it, and put it on the counter.

The next day, the bag of chips lay flat and empty.

Mason got another scolding and was put outside in the yard again. When it came time for doggie treats, Mason didn't get one bite. The next night after dinner, we cleaned the kitchen and wiped the counter clean.

Early the next morning, my son went to the bakery for pastries and jelly-filled donuts to surprise my daughter-in-law before she got out of bed. He tapped on my door. "Breakfast, Mom."

The strawberry-filled pastries were heavenly. The dogs hovered around the table, drooling, with their noses twitching.

Later that evening, we closed and taped the boxes of pastries and donuts, stuck them in a plastic sack, and pushed them to the back of the counter.

That night, I read my novel until midnight. When I closed the book, I heard a noise like someone drumming his fingernails on something. Then, a soft tap sounded on my bedroom door.

I slipped on my robe, shuffled across the room, and opened the door. My daughter-in-law stood there with her index finger across her lips and motioned for me to follow her. I quietly followed her down the hall in my slippers. When we stuck our heads through the kitchen doorway, we caught the snack thief eating pastries and gobbling down donuts.

Max, who could barely walk because of his weight problem, had jumped onto an upholstered chair and climbed from there onto the counter.

Tammy brought in Mason and gave him a special treat for all the scolding he had undergone in Max's stead. Mason was happy to accept a treat as an apology.

Max had a good thing going for him for a while. If we hadn't seen that overweight dog on the counter, we would never have believed it.

~Marie Elizabeth Bast

38

Yoga Spirit

*Fun fact: Classes in "doga" — yoga with dogs — are
growing in popularity nationwide.*

I was holding her bowl of food over her head. She danced around
me, her twenty-two-pound body wiggling in excitement. "Say
a prayer," I commanded Spirit. Obediently, she barked out a
prayer.

My daughter and I adopted Spirit, an energetic six-year-old white-
and-chestnut Jack Russell–Terrier mix, from the local shelter when she
was just four weeks old. We later wished that we had brought home her
sister and her mama, too, but at the time we still had our Australian
Shepherd, Sydney, who taught Spirit how to be a wonderful addition
to our family before she passed on four years ago.

Spirit's morning medley of hard-boiled egg, fresh carrots, black-
eyed peas, corn, green beans, and cucumbers is quite the nourishing
meal, but I was not ready for breakfast myself yet. First, I wanted to
do yoga on the fuchsia mat in the other room. Before placing the lid
back on the cucumbers, I grabbed a couple of slices. I had not slept
well the night before, and my tired eyes were puffy. The cucumber
slices might help reduce the swelling.

Taking my hair clip out and my glasses off, I lay back on the mat
in the corpse pose with a cucumber slice on each eye. The cooling
sensation was instantly soothing. Stretching my backbone on the floor,
shoulders pressed down, arms out, palms up, I straightened my legs,
relaxed my toes, and concentrated on calming my breath and quieting

my mind.

I heard nails clicking on the tile floor, as Spirit came in from the kitchen to do yoga with me. Every day when I am on my yoga mat, she joins me and does some of the same stretch poses that I do, sometimes even simultaneously. Though she doesn't hold the poses as long as I do, she keeps me quite amused.

The living room is carpeted, and I heard Spirit's paw steps transition from tile to carpet. Lying on the mat with eyes closed, I flowed into a state of yoga stretch and relaxation.

I could sense Spirit standing close, hovering — a typical move she performs when she initially finds me on my mat. In one breath, her nose was at my face, a little sniff, a tender sensation on my cheek, and in a swift action, the cucumber slice upon my eye was snatched.

Opening my eyes, I caught Spirit nonchalantly chomping away as if I had handed her the cucumber. She finished the delectable cucumber and looked at me, as if waiting for something. In a sitting position now, I couldn't hold it in anymore and burst out in laughter. Spirit continued to stand beside me, eyeing the other cucumber slice I held in my hand.

"Geez, Spirit!" I chuckled. "You might as well have the other one, too." I lay back down on the mat, placed the cucumber slice upon my eye, and in a sudden burst, Spirit moved in for the prize. No sniffing this time, just a delicate snatch and a wagging tail.

Upon finishing the cucumber slice, Spirit stretched out on her stomach and into the cobra pose. I followed suit and, together, we continued our yoga practice.

~Elizabeth Anne Kennedy

39

The Not-So-Long Down

*Fun fact: The "long down," during which a dog must
remain in a down position for an extended period
of time, teaches self-control and helps establish the
human as the leader.*

I am seated at the round kitchen table with my mixed-breed puppy Sneeks lying near my feet. You might not know it to look at me, but I'm actually doing homework.

You see, shortly after Sneeks joined our household, we signed her up for obedience class. Well, I suppose you could say that both Sneeks and I have been enrolled in the class. Since I have a tendency to be a soft touch, the training is helpful in establishing who gets to be the alpha dog. At least, that's the theory.

In reality, the training hasn't been a scintillating success in this regard, through no fault of the instructor. Beneath Sneeks's shorthaired black-and-white coat beats the heart of a rebel, a born leader. A cross between a Border Collie and some kind of Terrier, she has been endowed with a combination of smarts and stubbornness, and is insistent about getting her way about certain things. The fact that she is saucy and impertinent in the process makes it hard not to laugh at her antics.

Today's homework, with Sneeks a reluctant participant, is an exercise known as the "long down." The objective is to teach the dog to lie obediently at one's feet. Equipment needed: collar and leash. Method: get the dog to lie on the floor, then place your foot on the leash to restrain her in place until you release her.

Sounds simple, right?

Each time I have tried this exercise before today, Sneeks has put up a fuss, struggling mightily for several minutes before sulkily complying. Today, though, she settles right down, and I allow myself a few seconds of smug self-congratulation before immersing myself in an earnest study of the newspaper.

Moments later, I hear a noise that sounds suspiciously like the clicking of dog nails on a vinyl floor. I dismiss this because I can still feel the leash under my foot.

The sound persists, so I lift my head and survey the kitchen.

Sneeks is standing in the far corner of the room, defiantly staring me down. Dangling from her collar are six inches of lime-green nylon fabric leash. I look down. The remainder of the leash is under the table, including a section still — somewhat uselessly — pinned under my foot. It's clear what she was doing while I thought she was demonstrating a newfound flair for obedience.

With a sigh, I begin to acknowledge that Sneeks may never master the "long down." On the bright side, I have an excuse for our next obedience class.

The dog really did eat my homework.

~Lisa Timpf

40

Pumpkin Pie

*Fun fact: A dog's pregnancy is relatively short, usually
between fifty-eight and sixty-five days. Thus, many
of puppies' organs, including the brain, aren't fully
developed at birth.*

Wiping my hands on a towel, I looked out the kitchen window and laughed. Nine Golden Retriever puppies chased their sixty-pound mother across our fenced-in back yard, trying to nurse as they ran. The five-week-old pups had been on dry dog food for a week but still enjoyed frequent milk breaks. As a first-time mother, Chelsea was still unsure how to handle her large brood.

I stepped out the back door, and the harried mama skidded to a stop beside me on the patio. "What's the matter, girl? Are they pestering you to death?" I scratched her behind the ears. "I bet their teeth are sharp, too, aren't they?"

Chelsea knocked away a persistent pup with her back foot and looked at me with imploring eyes.

"Sorry. I can't bring them in. Not with eight people coming for Thanksgiving dinner." I turned to go back into the house, and Chelsea tried to nose her way through the door. "No, you can't come in either. I'm too busy, and you don't behave well inside."

A few hours later, with the pies baked and the smell of succulent turkey filling the kitchen, I glanced out the window again. This time, Chelsea was running backwards, the pumpkin-colored pups in hot pursuit.

I looked at my watch. Two hours until dinner. Maybe it wouldn't hurt to bring Chelsea in and give her a little break. I opened the back door and whistled. She streaked into the house before her tormentors could catch up. After settling her onto the laundry-room floor, I went to straighten up the bathrooms. I returned to the kitchen in time to see the pitiful, overworked mother with her paws on the counter, licking up the last of our pumpkin pie.

"Chelsea!" I grabbed her collar and shoved her outside, all sympathy for her plight gone.

Back in the kitchen, I searched the pantry, hoping I had another can of pumpkin. Green beans and English peas lined the shelves, but no pumpkin. Now what? My family doesn't think it's Thanksgiving without pumpkin pie. I jumped in the car and sped to the closest convenience store, expecting to find pumpkin sold out. Luckily, there was one can left.

As I mixed ingredients, I fumed over having to bake another pie with so many other things left to do. I should have known better than to bring Chelsea in. Slipping the new pie beside the roasting turkey, however, I remembered past holidays and what it felt like to have kids hanging onto my leg while I cooked and cleaned. Maybe I could identify a little with my beleaguered dog. But wait until everyone found out they almost missed out on pumpkin pie because of her!

I had just taken the pie out of the oven when our dinner guests walked through the door.

"Poor Chelsea," my mom, the inveterate dog lover, said. "Those babies are chasing her all over the yard. Couldn't you let her come in for a little while?"

I shook my head. "Not on your life, Mom. She's already had her Thanksgiving dinner."

~Tracy Crump

41

Understanding the Dog

*Fun fact: Your shoes pick up plenty of interesting scents
while you're out and about, and dogs love to chew on
them and sniff them to learn where you've been.*

Bo an Alaska Husky
Was a boy of two
And even though he had his toys
It was shoes he liked to chew

He'd chew upon the leather
Then tuck them neatly away
As if it never happened
Fearing what I'd have to say

So one day while shopping
A pair of sneakers I did buy
Thinking this should cure the problem
They were only five ninety-five

The next day before leaving
I placed them on the floor
Goodbye, my little Bo
As I locked the old front door

Upon returning home that night
The sneakers I did see
Without a scratch upon them
Near my chewed heels by Gucci

I've had it, Bo, I said,
Placing the leash around his neck
A new home is where you belong
While racing for the vet

I told the vet what happened
How Bo needed a new home
The vet looked sympathetic
Letting out a little groan

Bo chews upon your shoes
For the scent, it keeps him warm
The brand-new shoes you left him
Were shoes you had not worn

It's your scent that keeps him happy
It's your scent that I speak of
It's your scent that he will search for
For it's you that Bo loves

But I will take this dog from you
And find him a happy home
Although he will need time, you see
For he'll miss you when alone

I suddenly felt panicked
As I grabbed upon the leash
He's my dog, dear doctor
And it's him I wish to keep

After getting home that night
With Bo at my side
I put on those new sneakers
And ran with him in pride

The next day while leaving
I patted Bo's head
Leaving out the now worn sneakers
Following what the doctor said

Upon arriving home that night
The sneakers they were torn
But tears ran from my eyes,
For the laces he had adorned

Wrapped around his tiny paw
And held up to his nose
Was a lace he had been sniffing
As though it were a rose

Bo now is eight years old
And still to this day
He drags around those sneakers
Whenever I'm away

~Sylvia Macchia

Hank

My Very Good, Very Bad Dog

My Heroic Dog

Fun fact: An eleven-year-old Golden Retriever named Bear was the first search-and-rescue dog to arrive after the World Trade Center attack on September 11, 2001.

42

Dolly, the Wonder Dog

*Fun fact: Dogs for Diabetics trains dogs to recognize
chemical changes in humans' blood sugar and alert
them to the possible onset of hypoglycemia (low
blood sugar).*

On a quick jaunt to Yuma, Arizona, we ended up at a motel due to a strong storm. The young couple that found refuge in the room below ours had a young Shih Tzu, a toy Pomeranian, and six of the cutest puppies you ever saw. The young wife came out of her room holding a little ball of dark brown and black fluff with the biggest eyes you ever saw. As we looked into one another's eyes, I knew I had to have her!

My husband reminded me sternly that we already had one dog, a spoiled Poodle named Ruby. But Ruby was definitely *his* dog... and there was something about this little girl that caused me to know beyond a shadow of a doubt that she was meant to be mine. My husband argued against owning her all afternoon, and I gave in. Finally, he asked me if I *really* wanted that little pup, and I said, "Oh, honey, I already have her named!"

The dilemma was that she was not quite three weeks old, and we lived some 250 miles away. I finally convinced the couple, who were getting ready for the husband's deployment to Afghanistan, that I could bottle-feed her and wean her onto solids myself.

We settled on a price and Dolly came home with us.

Feeding her, weaning her, and housebreaking her were the easy parts of our early life with her. Dolly loved me so much that she loved everything of mine — my shoes, my purses, and even my clothes! I used to shudder every time we walked into our home after being gone for more than a couple of hours.... I never knew what she would find and love (and chew) beyond repair!

Dolly is tiny, weighing only about six pounds, but she is a real powerhouse and knows how to get her own way. I know I should feed her only high-quality dog food, but when she looks up at me with her huge brown eyes, I can't help but sneak her a tasty morsel or two.

She, like Ruby, has complete run of the house, including sleeping in our bed with us at night. Our bed is extraordinarily high, forcing me to use a little stool to climb onto it, but Dolly jumps and claws her way up until she is lying below my cheek with her head on my pillow.

My husband and grown children liked Dolly all right, but they believed she was "good for nothing but love" — a phrase I disagreed with every time I heard it. I would tell them that someday she would do something so amazing that "You'll all be glad I brought this little girl home"! That fantastic act finally happened during the deep of night some weeks ago....

We live in the country on a mountainside in northern Arizona. As a result, we keep our "girlies" in the house, letting them out only on a leash, or into their fenced and covered dog run. Coyotes, hawks, eagles, javelinas, snakes, mountain lions... we've had them all near our home, and these two little dogs would be a good "snack" for any of them.

Our "doggie door" is in our bedroom on the first floor, and we keep it closed after dark. The girls let us know if we need to let them out in the middle of the night. On this night in particular, Dolly indicated (I thought) that she needed to go out. I got up and opened the doggie door, but she wouldn't go out. So I went back to bed and fell asleep quickly.

I felt her running up and down my torso as I slept and chose to ignore her, thinking since she didn't need to go out, she'd give up sooner or later and settle down to sleep.

Suddenly, she jumped right on my face with all fours! As I swung my arm to move her off my face, I noticed that the pillow next to me was sopping wet. Thinking she had urinated in our bed, something she had never done, I got up to check the damage.

It was then that I noticed my husband's arm on that sopping wet pillow, cold, clammy, and drenched with sweat. I lifted his forearm, trying to wake him, but it dropped limply back onto the pillow as I let go.

In a panic, I jumped down off the bed and ran around to his side. I could smell his breath as I leaned over him... a sweet, almost sickening aroma. Having been a first-aid instructor for several years, my training kicked in immediately, and I recognized that my husband was in a diabetic coma. I tested his blood sugar, and it was dangerously low.

Having no juice in the house in which to add sugar nor any glucose tablets, I shoved candy into his mouth, stirring him into a somewhat conscious state, and then continued giving him sugar and monitoring his glucose level. It took nearly an hour for his level to come up to a number we could live with, and Dolly stayed right at his head as if she were also monitoring him.

When morning came and my husband was truly stable, we both realized that if Dolly hadn't forced me to wake up, my husband might very well have died in those hours.

She is no longer a "good for nothing but love" dog in our eyes, our children's eyes, or in the eyes of anyone else who has heard about the heroic way she saved the "dad" she loves so much!

~Bette Haywood Matero

Amazing Onyx

Fun fact: Many dogs love water, but not all breeds can swim. Bulldogs, for instance, don't swim well. Pool owners should make sure their fences are dog-proof.

She was the prettiest Lab puppy we had ever seen, and the whole family immediately fell in love with her. We named her Onyx because of her thick, shiny black coat. She spent her first vacation with us when she was only ten weeks old and had her first bath and swim in the St. Lawrence River. We had no clue that this amazing little ball of fur would end up being our hero.

As she got older, Onyx learned to fish. Standing perfectly still while waiting patiently in the clear, shallow water, she'd carefully watch a smallmouth bass dart around her feet until she dunked her head underwater and, amazingly, caught one in her mouth without leaving a tooth mark. We taught her the concept of "catch and release."

Onyx was also a wonderful hunting dog, never afraid to show up her larger, more mature counterparts. She would not hesitate to crash through the ice on a tributary of the Chesapeake Bay in order to retrieve waterfowl. She braved the defensive posture of a hissing, wounded goose to bring it back to her master. She loved being by her master's side, whether in a duck blind or riding in the front seat of the pickup truck.

Onyx smiled. It was a real people-like smile, but it intimidated those who didn't know her. Strangers misunderstood the showing of her teeth until they saw the upturn of her lips. If she was happy and content, Onyx smiled.

When she wasn't hunting, Onyx enjoyed all our family activities. On hot summer days, when the humidity was oppressive, Onyx enjoyed floating on the river with us in her own inner tube. Resting her front legs and paws over the edge of the rubber tube, her eyes would droop shut as she floated until she'd had enough of the warm sun on her black coat. Occasionally, Onyx floated with us while standing on a huge tractor tire tube that had been inflated just for her. Amazingly maintaining a four-point stance on the top of the tube, she smiled while showing off her perfect balance.

One hot day, our eighteen-year-old daughter, Margie, announced she was going to swim across the bay. No one in the family was free to go with her. The unwritten rule, regardless of swimming ability, was to have a buddy in the water with you, especially when swimming the width of the bay. Margie never argued about that rule even though she had been an accomplished member of a swim team for many years.

Her father said, "Take Onyx with you."

Having heard her name, Onyx roused from a nap, ready for action.

"Go with Margie," he said to the dog.

Margie beckoned to the dog with a hand signal. Onyx trotted to the water next to her.

They entered the chilly river together and swam side by side across the bay. I watched from the deck as they reached the sandbar on the far shore.

Margie stood and smoothed her wet hair back from her face. They rested a few minutes before diving into the water for the return trip.

I felt uneasy for some reason and continued to watch the pair swim side by side. Then I heard Margie struggle, calling out, "I have a cramp!"

Onyx began swimming circles around her, sensing her distress. Margie was trying to massage the cramp, but began struggling in the water. I ran to the dock, got into the boat and started untying the ropes wrapped around the dock cleats.

Onyx knew Margie was in trouble. She came up behind and to the side of Margie, poking her head underneath the girl's right arm.

Margie desperately grabbed onto Onyx's collar. Onyx began digging deep, slicing through the water with her webbed paws, swimming with every ounce of strength to bring both of them back to the dock.

Watching the drama, I realized I didn't need to take out the boat. I simply waited until the pair approached me. Calling out encouragement to both my daughter and my dog, as they got closer I extended an oar to Margie. She grabbed it and held onto it with one arm while the other gripped our heroic dog's collar. Onyx had brought our girl to the safety of the shore where her father and I could help her get out of the water.

Onyx jumped up onto the dock and shook vigorously several times. After Margie was wrapped in a large towel, she lowered herself to the grassy front lawn to rest. Onyx eagerly ran to her, covering her face with sloppy dog kisses. Wrapping our arms around both of them, we praised our amazing dog and gently tousled Margie's wet hair. Everyone was grateful for their safe return to shore.

Later in the afternoon, Onyx got an extra treat. She didn't quite understand all the fuss; she just wanted to jump off the dock again and swim around in the bay.

During subsequent family gatherings at the summerhouse, we'd reminisce and lift our glasses to our amazing Onyx and the day she became a hero.

~Nancy Emmick Panko

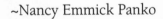

Because of Kasey

*Fun fact: Shelby was named the 45th Skippy Dog Hero
of the Year for saving a family from carbon monoxide
poisoning by waking them up and getting them
safely outside.*

"Hey, I like your car!" Karen said, as the new hybrid pulled smoothly into the driveway.

She walked up to its front door, smiling, as her husband, Paul, rolled down the window. "I know! Thanks. It is so quiet and smooth, I love it," he said, and then pulled into the garage.

After they shut all of the garage doors, they walked inside where Kasey, their six-year-old Golden Retriever, greeted them with a smile.

"Kasey hasn't even memorized the sound of the motor yet, with it being so quiet." Paul grinned as he set down his things from work and gave Kasey a good scratch behind the ears.

Kasey had come into their lives as a six-week-old puppy, adopted from a neighbor who was moving and had an unwanted litter. Their daughter, Julie, adopted one of the puppies and gave it to her boyfriend, Chris. Chris and Julie taught Kasey good manners, took her on duck-hunting trips, and taught her to retrieve. But college rolled around, and they had to leave. Kasey would have to go to Chris's parents' house and live outside.

Karen could not stand the thought of Kasey being outside — even if it was in a big yard with shade trees. After a week, she brought Kasey home to live with her forever. Kasey loved their new routine of rides to the bank (for dog treats), the groomer's, coffee-shop patios. Kasey grew into a beautiful dog who never exhibited annoying behaviors; she never even barked.

Except that night. As they ate dinner and talked about their day at work, Kasey kept coming up to them and staring right into their eyes. "Go lie down," Paul said. "I'm trying to eat." Kasey turned away and put her chin on Karen's lap, staring.

"What do you want? More food?" Karen asked, getting up to pour more kibble in the metal dish. Kasey sniffed, and then walked away.

"Kasey, no! Stop scratching your toenails on the brand-new hardwood floor!" Karen groaned from the couch after dinner. Paul and Karen turned their heads to Kasey, who was digging at the floor. Kasey ran to the garage door, whimpering.

"What does she want? She always goes out the front door," Paul mused, flipping the newspaper.

"I have no clue. I'll let her out the front. Come on, Kasey!" Karen exclaimed with her hands up. As soon as she let Kasey out and was back on the couch, Kasey started scratching on the front door. "She is driving me insane!"

Kasey's strange (and annoying) behavior continued all the way to bedtime. As they crawled into bed, Kasey started barking hysterically. At that moment, they knew something was up, since she normally never barked. So, they crawled out of bed and followed Kasey, still barking, down the stairs, across the kitchen and to the garage door. They opened the door, flipped on the lights, and gasped. Their hybrid car was still on, leaking extremely dangerous carbon monoxide!

They hurried to turn off the car, and then opened the garage doors and windows to air it out. Paul had thought the car was off because of the quiet motor. This car just so happened to have the new key technology in which if the keys were near the car, the car stayed on. When he drove their old car, Paul had made it a habit to put the keys on the windshield when the car was parked in the garage so he wouldn't lose them. When he pulled in earlier that evening, he had tossed his keys up on the windshield as he had with the old car.

After everyone was safe, Kasey finally fell asleep, satisfied that her job was done well.

Now, fifteen years later, as Paul and Karen's granddaughter, I think about what could have happened. I am certain that Kasey saved their lives and impacted generations to come, like me.

Because of Kasey, this story has a happy ending.

~Emily Huseman, age 13

Micah Is My Hero

Fun fact: Like people, guide dogs have specific times
when they're on and off the job. Usually, when they're
at home and off their harness, they can relax and
just be a dog.

One lunch hour, I told my secretary I was leaving for lunch and would be going to the bank on my way back. The day was grey, drizzly and cold.

I grumbled under my breath about the weather, but I was grateful because Micah, my constant and loyal companion, was by my side. Micah is my Leader Dog for the Blind; he is excellent in leading me, staying focused, and guiding me with the directions I give to him.

But Micah is no ordinary Leader Dog. He is a Royal Standard Poodle and extremely intelligent. That also means he is a thinker, and sometimes very stubborn. Poodles are not usually used as guide dogs, but my husband has asthma and allergies, so a non-shedding poodle was the best choice.

On the way back to work, the weather turned worse. The wind had picked up and the drizzle turned into a cold rain. Micah and I picked up our pace in order to get back into the warm shelter of our building.

I pulled the hood strings a little tighter around my neck and the top of my hood fell down over my eyes. Not being able to see anyway, I didn't mind, and I gave Micah the command to proceed straight ahead. We arrived at the corner. Micah halted, and then took one step back. I knew we needed to be cautious because we were at a very busy intersection. I stretched one foot forward, located the curb, and tapped it confidently (which indicates to Micah that I am safe and understand his movement). Together, we stood at the curb, ready to continue our journey. Micah and I communicate well with one another, both verbally and with little body movements and gestures, which gives me the self-confidence I need to live an independent lifestyle. I love Micah, and I felt proud to have him standing at my side as we waited for the light to change.

I began to listen to the traffic to determine the direction in which it was moving and to judge the status of the traffic light. When I gave Micah the signal, he would move forward.

As I waited, Micah became restless at my side. Noises in the surrounding area and the voices in my head began to crowd my brain, lulling me into a weary, tired state as the rain continued to fall. I felt Micah's body pulling slightly forward, and I instinctively allowed him to take one step forward as I followed in a state of semi-consciousness. We stepped out into the familiar street to cross to the other side. But Micah pushed me more to the right, and sleepily, I moved right.

With the noise and voices fading in my brain but still lulling me into a semi-conscious state of obedience, I continued to walk across the street with Micah as my guide. Somehow, I began to realize that I should have come to the opposite corner sooner. I raised my foot a little higher so as not to trip on the curb. Micah then pulled me a little left, stopped, and then pulled back. I stopped, put out my foot, and felt something I thought was the curb, so I began to step up onto the sidewalk. But, to my surprise, I found it to be some kind of hard object I needed to step over.

Stumbling a bit, my senses awakened. Micah gave me a slight pull again, and we continued to advance more slowly as he felt my nervousness in each step. Finally, Micah pulled back hard and I stopped, sticking out my foot to find a higher-than-usual curb. Micah inched forward and up against my hip, and I stepped up onto the sidewalk, which was not level at all! Micah stepped up and stood quietly beside me with no movement. I urged him forward. Nothing! In a louder and more demanding voice, I said, "Okay, Micah, turn, find the street, and let's get back to work. Come on, let's go!" Nothing!

Micah sat down and refused to move in any direction. By this point, I was completely confused and had nowhere to go.

Within a few moments, a man's voice cut through the silence. "Madam, can I approach you?"

I answered, "Yes, please do! Micah will not hurt you; he is my Leader Dog."

The man stood beside me, urging me to move back slightly. He explained that the whole area was under construction, and the road was all torn up. Instead of taking me from one corner across to the other corner, then turning and going across the street to the other corner where we needed to be, Micah took me diagonally straight through the middle of the intersection, around a deep, huge hole, over a big pipe and safely to the corner where we needed to end up.

The man's voice was soft and kind, but had a bit of a laugh in it. "Your dog is amazing! He knew exactly how to manipulate you through, around, and over the many dangerous obstacles that were in your path. Watching you both was an eye-opening experience for all of us!" Several individuals started to talk to me and ask all kind of questions.

I could not be angry or upset with Micah because he thought he was doing what he was supposed to do. He did do an amazing job of taking care of me and guiding me through the construction site. I was the one not paying attention to keep him on the right track. We both have to work together to make a great team. Micah remains my hero — he loves me unconditionally, he keeps me safe, and he gives me the freedom and independence to do what I want to do on my own.

~Lynn Fitzsimmons

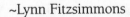

Wonder Puppy

*Fun fact: For dogs that don't fear umbrellas, people
can purchase a wearable "pet umbrella" to keep Fido
dry when he's outside.*

Young and just married, we'd moved into our first home. It
was small, run-down, and in a marginal neighborhood, but
it was close to where I attended graduate school and an easy
commute to my husband's job. It boasted a patch of green
yard that we called the "back forty." Now all we needed was a dog.

At the Humane Society, we picked out the one puppy that seemed
"mellow" to us, as we weren't sure how well we'd cope with "rambunctious." We took her home to our bungalow and put her in the tiny
garden amid the lavender and nasturtiums. There she sat, and then
she lay down. Mellow didn't begin to cover it. Unaware that this was
not normal puppy behavior, we thought she was lovely. We debated
various names, and decided that "Hot Tub" best reflected our puppy's
zen-like vibe.

Of course, when I took Hot Tub for her first veterinary check-up,
the kind doctor explained why our pet had such low energy: worms,
infections, and some other disease… I don't remember the exact diagnosis, but I remember the bill. We were appalled. But we paid the vet
and bought the medications, and before long, Hot Tub was wearing
her moniker with a big dose of irony. We were learning to cope with
rambunctious after all.

We knew nothing of Hot Tub's genetic heritage, but it was soon apparent that she had descended from a line of vigilant watchdogs. She leapt onto the couch to keep watch out the big front window and barked at every person who walked by. She barked extra for people with strollers. Or hats. She barked at dogs, bikes, motorcycles and birds. She even barked at moths. We tried to quiet her because we were worried she'd bother our neighbors.

Her worst enemy was Umbrella. The first rainy day when I tried to walk Hot Tub while holding an umbrella, I thought she'd lost her mind. She barked, ran in circles at the end of her leash, and charged at me. Finally, I realized she was attacking my umbrella. She didn't stop until I closed it. We finished our walk with rain pelting my head.

Each time I left for classes, I assured Hot Tub I'd return soon. I made sure she had her comfy bed, plenty of water and her favorite rope chew toy. Then I closed the kitchen door to keep her in the linoleum-floored room where she'd be safe and quiet.

One afternoon about a month after Hot Tub had moved in, a secretary from the registrar's office hurried over as I was leaving class.

"There was a 9-1-1 call at your house," she said. "Some kind of emergency."

I jumped on my bike and sped down the hill, tearing through intersections and passing cars in my rush to get home.

A police cruiser sat in our driveway, lights blinking blue. I raced up the front steps, unlocked the door and rushed straight for the kitchen.

Hot Tub greeted me there with gleeful wiggling. She wagged. She squealed. She whined. She squirmed. She rolled over for a belly rub. She barked.

Next to her on the kitchen floor was our fancy new landline phone with a big red button that had been pre-programmed for making emergency calls.

BEEP-BEEP-BEEP-BEEP, it was now shrilling.

I hung up the phone and carried happy Hot Tub outside. Our neighbors had gathered, and together with the bemused cop, we pieced the story together. The police dispatcher had received a 9-1-1 call from our phone. She could hear only agitated breathing, and believing it was someone in distress, she sent out the patrol car.

Hot Tub—bored, anxious, curious, or all three—had gotten hold of the dangling phone cord, pulled the phone off the kitchen counter, and stepped on that big 9-1-1 button. She appeared quite pleased that she'd succeeded in summoning assistance and companionship.

We had tried to keep Hot Tub out of our neighbors' way, figuring that we needed to train her to be presentable first. Now, here were the neighbors, cooing and fussing over the adorable puppy. They dubbed her "Wonder Puppy" for her ability to use the latest technology to call help.

The police recommended we move our telephone. They were understanding, but said that if we had another false alarm they'd have to charge us for the cost of responding.

Hot Tub had been with us only a month and already we were in trouble with the law. Maybe we weren't meant to have a dog. She wouldn't let me use an umbrella. She barked at our neighbors. She chewed our furniture. She puked on our rugs.

She summoned the police.

How could we keep her out of trouble? What other mess would she get us into? Should we reconsider the whole thing?

The next day, when I bought dog kibble, I chose the small bag.

But we'd underestimated our dog.

Just three nights later, in the middle of the night, a low growl woke me up. I had never heard that sound before, from either the mellow Hot Tub we'd once known, or from Hot Tub the Wonder Puppy.

"Do you hear that?" I hissed to my husband. The growl grew louder. We got out of bed and crept toward the disturbing noise.

As soon as Hot Tub saw us, she started barking her familiar high-pitched puppy bark. But beneath it, she was still growling. Her tail stood out behind her at an angle, like a flagpole. The hairs on the back of her neck were raised.

Hot Tub was staring straight at the closed laundry-room door. On the other side of that door sat our compact washer/dryer, and beyond that, the back door. Was that a rattling sound coming from our back door?

My husband flung open the laundry-room door.

AAACK!

I couldn't help the scream. In the window of the back door, I saw the dim outline of a face, peering in at us.

I shrieked again, this time with more feeling. The intruder fled, disappearing into the darkness.

For the second time in three days, the police visited our house. They inspected our back door and concluded we'd interrupted somebody breaking in. They said an armed intruder had been reported in the area. He had vanished, and they didn't expect him to return to our house. We were lucky to have such an alert dog, the police told us.

Needless to say, Hot Tub the Wonder Puppy, stayed.

For the next fifteen years, Hot Tub taught us what we needed to know about living with a dog. She graduated from obedience school, helped us make friends with the neighbors, survived multiple emergency veterinary visits and one serious illness, traveled with us to parts near and far, and in the end, trusted us to know when her time had come. And during all that time, in Hot Tub's home, no neighbor passed by unnoticed, no nighttime intruder entered, and not a single umbrella was allowed to unfurl.

~Christy Mihaly

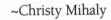

Quiet Devotion

*Fun fact: Helen Keller was the first American known
to have an Akita, which was given to her when she was
on a speaking tour in Japan.*

I look at my grandchildren laughing and playing, and I think of Nago, our first dog. These precious children might not be here, playing on the floor, if the 150-pound Akita had died at puppyhood of parvovirus like the veterinarian expected. If Nago hadn't survived that ailment, I might not know the darlings who bounce about me with enthusiasm. But he didn't die. He grew into the great beast that watched over my own toddlers twenty-some years ago.

I could never say that Nago was an affectionate dog — not like those smaller creatures that dance about one's feet and nestle onto laps like an extension of their human companions. He was aloof — content to lie on the mat by the door and study my offspring through their seasons of growth and development. He was certainly alert — ever ready to put another dog in its place if it drew too near to his charges — but he wasn't one to seek out the nuzzling and stroking and petting of the human hand. If my children overstepped protocol and reached for a shaggy hug, Nago simply relocated to another part of the house.

My children grew, and Nago's sense of responsibility to them deepened. He joined in their backyard play as much as he was able — chasing a ball and then trotting off to watch from a vantage point. He joined us on our walks to the bus stop each morning and waited with me in the afternoons as the long yellow vehicle disgorged its occupants. In the hours between watching our children, he slept. His internal clock seemed to be set to the school-bus schedule and minutes before we would leave for the bus stop, he would rouse himself, give a good shake and meet me at the door. It was as though his heart beat to the piping voices of the three little girls in his care. It shouldn't have surprised me that he would put his own life on the line for them.

I remember the March morning well that Nago showed the full extent of his devotion. The day had dawned frosty. The previous day's spring melt had hardened into sheets of thin ice, hidden in the dark hues of the gravel road. We left for the bus stop, our breaths steaming the air and our children's chatter cutting into the stillness. Nago trotted alongside me, his eyes scanning the ditches and returning to the children every so often. We crossed the main intersection and settled at our station fifteen feet west of the stop sign.

I never noticed my middle daughter's gradual meander to the dust and gravel at the roadside by the stop sign where she decided to draw in the dirt. I was intent on looking to the west to see if the bus was on its way. I didn't notice the pickup truck and its cargo charging up the hill behind me. I hadn't seen the black ice on the crest of that hill. But I did see Nago leave my side and bolt for the road's edge.

Some say that emergencies happen in slow motion. Others say they flash by in brief seconds. I can't begin to place what happened next into either category other than to say that while the events unfolded with lightning speed, my reflexes locked as though mired in molasses. Nago, however, seemed to move with the fluid grace and speed of a wolf.

A local farmer, preparing for the upcoming season, had decided to move some of his equipment from one property to the other. Hitched firmly to the back of his pickup truck was an aging fertilizer spreader. I assume he wanted to get the thing moved before the traffic began to clog the town's main corridors and he chose that early hour to do so. As his truck crested the hill toward the intersection, he began to brake — and discovered the black ice locked into the pitted surface of the road. In my frozen state, I watched the towed piece of machinery jackknife, swinging around toward the stooped form of my daughter, who was still drawing her masterpieces in the dirt.

And then Nago was there, slamming against her six-year-old body, shoving her out of the path of the truck and into the ditch. My daughter clung to his fur, her legs making twin tracks through hoary grass as he dragged her. The dog that lived his life shunning the hands of children now offered his back and side as a lifeline while he did what came naturally to him.

The sounds of gravel churning, brakes screeching and a motor groaning silenced in the aftermath of the moment. There was a brief hesitation as we stood there in shock, and then we all moved fast. I bolted for my daughter, wrapping her in a hug and pulling her back with her sisters. Nago trotted at my side again as though nothing had happened. The truck driver pulled into the parking lot next to us and dropped his forehead to the steering wheel while a bus driver from another district school looked on — horror and relief clearly etched across her face.

We gathered around Nago and petted him as much as he would allow, and I wondered if he understood what he had done for our family. The moment of electric excitement that could have ended in tragedy rolled past, and I watched my children step up onto their bus. Nago and I meandered home, I walking slowly, absorbing all that had been and could have been, while Nago chased imaginary rabbits in and out of the ditches.

Nago died two years later, on the anniversary of his heroic rescue. It was as though he wanted me to know that he understood what he'd given me. I still tear up when I think of what could have been. My children raise questioning eyes, and I can only shrug or pretend the tears are not there. And when I look at them and my grandchildren, I remember that heroic dog who avoided too much human contact but went full force into action when required.

~Donna Fawcett

48

The Biggest Dog on the Mountain

*Fun fact: Dogs are social animals. Wild dogs live
in family groups of dogs called packs, but pet dogs
consider their humans part of their pack!*

We liked hiking together. Today, we were looking for a trail over Wallace Mountain in northern Georgia's Chattahoochee National Forest.

"It's been over an hour," said Jesse, my nineteen-year-old son. "Do you think the trail still exists?"

We had explored several paths in the new terrain with no luck. We pushed through weeds mid-calf high for us, but neck-high for our rusty-brown dog, Shadow, as she scrambled through the brush.

"Hang in there," I responded. "It's easier to find an old trail now in the wintertime with so many leaves down. It hasn't been rough so far. Okay to keep going?"

Jesse nodded, and we continued. Once in a while, he would call Shadow back when she veered off after a scent. She was the size of a large housecat, her face shaped liked a Beagle but with small, floppy ears inviting a gentle scratch. Always content to curl up on the couch beside one of us, she had the build of a boxcar, no longer slim and bouncing with energy. Outside, though, she came alive and raced circles around us, always returning when commanded, wagging her tail like a feather duster. We carried her red leash with us but seldom had to use it.

Suddenly, we heard what sounded like many dogs barking in the distance, an unusual sound in the wilderness around us. Curious, we climbed the ridge, which provided a view down into the valley and to the opposite hillside, dotted with farmhouses.

"Oh, no. Look, that front door is opening...." Jesse said as he pointed to the nearest house.

His words stopped as we watched the farmhouse transform into a dog factory, spewing first a German Shepherd, then a black Lab. Small dogs, big dogs, brown dogs, and dogs I can't even describe poured out as if on an invisible high-speed conveyer belt. The hounds hit the ground, sniffing the air and turning to face us. Their barking rose to a frenzy. With menace in their tones and unity in their strides, they descended down their side of the mountain. Jesse shot an alarmed glance at me before turning to call in a firm voice, "Shadow, come here; stay."

I patted the pockets of my flannel shirt, feeling for the pepper spray, so small it would never work against so many animals. Grim now, I turned, surveying the nearby brush for a potential weapon. I grabbed for a branch, but as I tightened my grip, the rotten limb crumbled, useless. I heard Jesse scrambling through the dry leaves on his own search for protection. With the help of adrenaline, I broke off a decent-sized bough from a nearby tree.

"I've got one. Did you get one?" I rushed to Jesse's side.

"Almost," he said as he pulled and twisted. "Yes," he said, staggering backward with a broken branch.

"Dad, where's the leash?"

The barking intensified. My mouth went dry. Instead of answering, my brain was scrambling to remember how to survive a dog attack. Was it "make yourself big and loud"? No, that was for a black bear. Maybe it was "don't look them in the eye"? I glanced over at Jesse, his lips pinched tight. Our eyes met fearfully and then there was a mutual nod of resolve.

The pack emerged from the dell, still at a distance, but barreling straight toward us. Shadow stood at Jesse's side on alert. She began to growl. I juggled my weapons and worried about Shadow, wondering why I hadn't put her on the leash at the sound of that first bark.

But it was too late. The dogs in the lead were now close enough for us to see that most of them were three times larger than Shadow. Their deep growls rumbling, they ran straight for us. Jesse swallowed hard and looked at me.

Shadow's back fur rose and she started to walk straight toward them, her low serious growl growing, reverberating from the back of her throat.

"No, Shadow, no," I commanded. The three of us could face them together, but she would be no match for even one attacker. What had I gotten us into? My stomach clenched tight in fear. I could taste the bile in the back of my throat. How could we possibly save ourselves and our beloved dog from this enormous pack?

Our usually obedient dog took the time to turn her head my way one last time, as if to shrug and say, "Well, yes, you're my master, but…"

And she continued to advance toward danger, stopping directly in front of the team of angry dogs. They halted in their tracks.

Jesse whispered, "Oh, no, standoff time."

Shadow bolted toward the largest snarling mongrel. Jesse inhaled loudly, and I clutched my tree branch. Ready to step forward into the fray, we froze, astounded, as the entire mass of dogs turned tail and fled.

Amazed, we kept pace as our twenty-five-pound pet followed the bunch back to the edge of their homestead. Still on guard, I worried the dogs might turn on Shadow when we got to their home turf. Oddly, the dogs had already disappeared.

"Maybe they're embarrassed," Jesse said, with a huge sigh of relief. "Come on, Shadow, let's go."

The three of us climbed back to the crest, through stubborn laurel thickets and dense brush. I felt almost shaky with relief. We chose to hike a dirt road back to the cabin and soon came across a man trimming trees. He waved as we cut through his private homestead. It seemed so calm and neighborly, so normal and peaceful after our harrowing brush with the horde of mountain dogs.

Back at the cabin, Jesse and I couldn't stop petting Shadow as we told Mom and Tricia about our miraculous and brave dog.

Jesse said, "You just can't imagine how Shadow stood them down. She went right for the leader of the pack. And to think we were worried about protecting her!"

Tricia patted the new loveseat. "I guess you're allowed up here now, Shadow."

Nobody said a word about her shedding hair where it didn't belong. In fact, we all crowded around and petted her, while Jesse and I kept repeating the mind-boggling story over and over, adding more details with each round. With each telling, I realized how incredible the encounter had been, and how fortunate we were to be home safe and sound.

"Oh, I need to get something for her." I went to the kitchen to get her a heaping plate of dog cookies with her favorite topping of peanut butter, plus a fresh bowl of water.

I like to think I saw a gleam in Shadow's eye as she ate the peanut butter. Her status of loyal family hero went down in history forever. And Shadow's photo remains front and center on the living room wall to this day.

~Dale Keppley

49

Dynamic Duo

Fun fact: In 1876, the Great Dane was named the national breed of Germany, where it was developed in the 16th century.

Courage comes in all shapes and sizes. I'd always known that, but I'd never thought of my skinny, sleepy dog or my lovely, unpretentious, multi-talented wife in terms of life-saving bravery. So I was amazed at the story this stranger was recounting.

"Is that your dog?" the gray-haired, middle-aged lady asked, as I answered her knock on my screen door. Komomai ("come here" in Hawaiian), our shiny-black, floppy-eared Great Dane, lay reclining in the sun. He lifted a lazy head, managed a sniff, and returned to sleep mode.

"I wanted to come by your house and thank you because that dog and the lady with him saved my life yesterday. I was snorkeling at Mahaulepu Beach, and without them I would have drowned."

The azure waters that look so appealing along the secluded beach have strong currents. On Kauai, we know that swimmers can be carried beyond the reef and out to sea before they know it.

"I asked around at the Big Save in town, 'Anybody know who has a giant black dog?' and everybody knew the dog and where you live," my visitor said.

We were a common sight while driving around our country town with Komomai riding shotgun, head sticking out above the top of my little Datsun.

As she continued, I remembered my wife Sandy saying something about swimming with the dog and helping a lady while at the beach.

"I'm a missionary to Japan back home on furlough. I had forgotten how strong the current is at the beach and I'm out of shape. I should have known better, but I was snorkeling by myself, got tired, and realized I was too far out. I tried to swim back and got a cramp. I started floating on my back, calling and waving for help and praying. I thought I was going to drown.

"Then I heard a holler: 'Just grab his collar, and he'll pull you in.' I saw this lady swimming toward me, pushing through the surf, with a giant dog at her side."

The grateful woman recounted how she grabbed hold of the dog's collar as he swam with powerful strokes, towing her to shore. After hugs and tears of gratitude, she departed.

"Sandy's not trained for lifesaving. Great Danes aren't really known as water dogs," I puzzled to myself. "How did she get the nerve to pull off a dangerous open-ocean rescue?"

Upon her return from work, I exclaimed to my wife, "Some lady came by today and told me to tell you 'thank you for saving my life.' I didn't realize you are a hero. What happened?"

"It was mostly Komomai," Sandy explained modestly. "I was at the beach by myself with the dog. I saw this lady snorkeling and heard her calling for help.

"I looked up and down the deserted beach and realized I was the only one who could help. I was scared and couldn't decide what to do. I can swim, but you know I don't have any lifesaving training. I know how easy it is for a panicked person to drown or drag down any would-be rescuer.

"In a flash of inspiration, I remembered how we played with the dog in the water as a puppy and how you taught him to tow you in while you floated on your back holding his collar.

"I called Komomai and got him to swim with me out to the lady. I could tell he knew what to do and wanted to go. His eagerness gave me the courage to try the rescue.

"As we pushed through the surge and current to approach the floundering lady, I remember thinking, 'Lucky I brought Komomai; he's a better swimmer than I am.'

"When we reached the lady, she was in a panic, so I didn't want to get close enough for her to grab me. But I knew Komomai could handle it. Treading water just out of her reach, I calmed her down and told her to trust the dog to pull her in. She grabbed the collar and didn't let go. The rest was easy."

Sandy looked at the sleeping dog thoughtfully: "I've never thought of myself as a particularly courageous person, but with him pulling her, it was easy for me to swim next to her and reassure her all the way to shore. We made a perfect team."

~David S. Milotta

The Night Coffee Woke Up

Fun fact: Black Labradors, rather than yellow or chocolate Labs, are favored among hunters because they blend well into the scenery, making them less noticeable to prey.

I didn't know I wanted a dog until we got one. Shortly after we bought our home, my husband, EW, secretly perused the classifieds seeking a black Labrador puppy. When caught, he began to list his reasons: "She would be a good watchdog. Mo (his son, who lived with us part-time) needs a dog. A home isn't a home without a dog. Did I say that it would be good to have a watchdog?" I was not convinced, but still we drove to a nearby small Maine town with a blank check and returned with the cutest puppy in the world. She had a short puppy nose, a fat puppy belly, lively black eyes, and a livelier tongue. I admit that I carried her home in my arms and was smitten.

We named her Morrison's Midwatch Coffee. She was a pedigreed black Labrador. Morrison was our son's name, Midwatch had been a name on her sire's side, and Coffee was the name we would use for her. We drink our coffee black and we sail, so it all fit. Our home was an old four-square on a large city lot, just a block back from the water of the Fore River in Casco Bay. During the three cooler seasons, she went to work every day with EW, riding in the back seat, taking swim breaks and coffee breaks that often included a game of fetch with a tennis ball. EW sold marine supplies, and many of his customers had dog-friendly shops, with dog biscuits in jars for visitors. Coffee was living the good life.

She had chores to do at home. She greeted neighbors on three sides, played T-ball with the little girl next door, and gave unconditional love to everyone. While she would bark whenever someone pulled into the driveway, she wasn't the best guard dog. When EW's cousin Jeffrey and two friends delivered a sailboat to Maine from the Caribbean, they showed up looking and smelling like three guys who've been on a boat for three weeks. We'd told Jeff where to find the key, and he'd asked us about the "guard dog." Upon our advice, Jeff simply unlocked the back door, put his hand out to a madly barking sixty-pound dog, and said, "Hey, Coffee. Good girl." She totally caved.

"Yep, glad we got a guard dog," I scoffed that night.

Jeffrey laughed and looked at EW. "That's how you got Barb to agree to a dog?"

EW smiled. "It worked. Even if Coffee doesn't."

She slept in our room at night. Every so often, she would find something disturbing outside and wake us. Actually, she would wake me. Every time. While EW slumbered peacefully next to me, Coffee would stand at the window on my side of the bed and growl... at something. Perhaps a neighbor was getting home late, or a squirrel had run from treetop to roof, or a raccoon was looking for an open garbage can. Coffee would hear it, decide I needed to know, and growl — starting softly and getting progressively louder until I rolled out of bed, identified the threat, patted her on the head and fell back onto my pillows.

Early one spring morning, her growls began louder and quickly escalated to short barks. Still, EW slept (or pretended to) while I jumped out of bed and ran to the window. Down below, three men were dragging a large inflatable dinghy with attached motor past our home, keeping to the grass as much as possible. Like Coffee, I knew this was suspicious. First, this was a nice dinghy, and no one who owned it would drag it without a trailer. Second, they were heading away from the river and ocean. I made the call.

"South Portland Police Department, what is your emergency?"

"I'm calling from North Marriner Street, and there are three men who I believe are stealing a dinghy."

"Why do you think they are stealing it? Is it your dinghy?"

"No. It's a very large inflatable. They are dragging it into the field away from the water, and they don't have a trailer."

"Stay inside, Ma'am. We have officers on the way. Can you describe these men for me?"

So I did, guessing at their height, describing their build, noting their hair color and clothing, while Coffee ran from window to window on the first floor, barking and keeping them in sight for as long as possible. By now, EW had gotten up and also kept a lookout. Two police cars passed our home, heading toward the field where our street ended.

Since the dispatcher had asked me to remain available, EW took Coffee for her morning constitutional and "business" trip, while I made coffee. They had returned and we'd all had breakfast by the time a police car pulled into the driveway and a uniformed officer knocked at the front door. Coffee, as she always did, made a good effort to act like a real guard dog, but the wagging tail didn't go with the fierce bark, and he wasn't fooled. "Good dog," he said as he smoothed her head and fondled her ears. "Good morning, Ma'am. Is this the dog that caught our crooks?"

"Really?" I asked. "I was right?"

"Oh, yes. You sure were." Turned out that these hapless fools were part of a gang formed to steal as many large inflatables as they could during one night. They had a panel truck into which they had hidden all but one inflatable — this last, irresistible one they didn't want to leave behind. So the truck driver agreed to meet them in the field, and all these guys had to do was get that boat to the truck. The South Portland Police Department had taken my call seriously, blocked the three streets that had access to the field, arrested the gang and recovered all of the boats.

The officer in our living room patted Coffee again and offered her a large dog biscuit. As Coffee trotted off to her bed to enjoy her treat, the officer took my formal statement. The next day, a very small article appeared in the paper, and then we heard nothing about the case for weeks until Coffee once again alerted us one morning that a police car had pulled into the driveway. She was delighted and clearly remembered the officer (or at least the large biscuit).

She was not disappointed. Not only did she get another biscuit, she was presented with a police department citation, suitable for framing, declaring her to be an outstanding watchdog and a hero to the community. She may not have been the best guard dog ever, but she was smart enough to know when to kick into gear for the important stuff, and that's what mattered.

~Barbara J. Hart

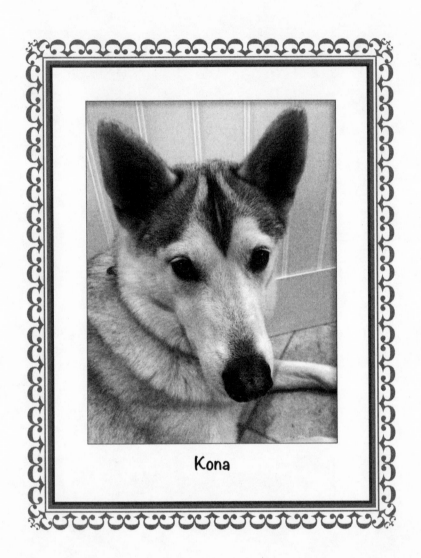

Kona

My Very Good, Very Bad Dog

My Inspiring Dog

Fun fact: The American Humane Association Hero Dog Awards are an annual, national competition, with eight categories: Law Enforcement Dogs, Arson Dogs, Service Dogs, Therapy Dogs, Military Dogs, Search and Rescue Dogs, Guide and Hearing Dogs, and Emerging Hero Dogs (the category for "ordinary" dogs who do extraordinary things).

A Message from Morton

Fun fact: A study published in the American Journal
of Cardiology *found that pet owners had a much
greater survival rate than those without pets one year
after a heart attack.*

T he dogs that need me always seem to find me. I don't look for them but somehow I know, as if they are sending me messages telepathically. This was the case three months after both of our beloved Shih Tzus died suddenly.

I was working at my computer when I was hit with the familiar yet indescribable knowledge that another dog needed me. The sensation was so strong that even though I knew my husband Dave didn't want one, I started searching online to find the dog that needed me. No pictures spoke to me until I came across the Humane Society's website.

Sure enough, there was Morton. He was ugly enough to be cute and he needed an owner who had experience with special-needs dogs. In my mind, we were a perfect match. I expected resistance when I broached the subject of Morton with Dave, but he simply said, "If the dog needs us, let's go get him." I called the Humane Society to make an appointment, but they couldn't fit us in until three days later due to the intake of a large number of dogs.

I found it odd when we finally did meet Morton that he was much larger than I expected, and I didn't feel any special connection to him. Even though I was a bit disconcerted, we went ahead and met with Jennifer, an adoption specialist. The Humane Society cares deeply about their animals, and the screening process is thorough. To my surprise, at the end of our interview, Jennifer talked us out of adopting Morton. She didn't think we were a good fit because of my health issues. I'd had a heart attack two years before, and my energy levels hadn't returned to normal and were not expected to do so. She felt Morton would be too much work for me, and Dave agreed with her.

However, Jennifer thought we'd be ideal for one of the dogs they'd just rescued from a puppy mill where they'd been forced to live in cages for their entire lives. They did not know how to be dogs. They needed the love, patience and experience she felt we had. She took us to an area that was not open to the public where we saw some of the saddest, most scared and timid dogs we'd ever seen. I was overwhelmed with compassion.

They'd all been shaved down to their skin. I'd walked past the first cage thinking it was empty. As we started to make a second walk past the cages, I realized there was a dog in the first cage. "Gaston" was written on the label on his cage. I hadn't noticed him before because he was so little. Actually, with his shaved body and pointy nose, he looked like an oversized white rat, but the moment I looked into his eyes, I realized that Morton had just been the messenger. This was the dog that needed me.

Gaston was only seven and a half pounds. When I picked him up, he pressed his tiny head into my chest and wrapped his little paws around my hand with a determination and strength that belied his size. There was no doubt we were meant to be together. We continued to bond while Jennifer gave us what little information she had on the dog: He was a Maltese, approximately five years old, and Gaston was just a name the staff had given him. Technically, because he had not been seen by the vet, he was not available for adoption, but we could pre-adopt him. As long as everything went okay, he would be ours in about a week. I hated putting him back in his cage, but we had no choice.

We filled out the necessary paperwork, and toyed with different names on the drive home, as Gaston didn't suit him or us. Ultimately, we settled on Gus, a little name for a little dog.

Exactly one week later, we brought Gus home. He'd been neutered and had half of his teeth removed because they were rotten. His liver enzymes were elevated, his back leg was stiff from inactivity, and his coat had a yellow tinge from poor diet. We didn't care. We happily signed the release documents and were thrilled that he was ours.

We'd never had cages for our other dogs, but Jennifer had told us it would be important at first for Gus to have one. A neighbour lent us a cage, and I placed a small soft-sided dog bed on top of a comfy red plaid blanket inside it. Every day while I waited for Gus to be ready, I bought toys, new dog bowls, a sweater, a toy pup tent, soft dog treats and really small chew bones.

At first, life outside the puppy mill was very traumatic for Gus. He was terrified of everything and everybody, including Dave, who is the most caring animal person I have ever known. Understandably, Gus operated on a fear-based assumption that anything new was a threat that needed to be run away from. He wouldn't take food from our hands, and he did not know how to play. He was afraid of dogs that wanted to sniff him and people who wanted to pet him. And he certainly wasn't house-trained.

Every day we share with Gus is a lesson in miracles and gratitude. We have watched him advance from hiding when Dave entered a room, to taking his first piece of food from Dave's hand, to now barking confidently at Dave's heels when he is too slow to give him his morning treat. As for play, he's progressed from shredding paper towels on his own to playing fetch the ball with me. While he still doesn't like to be touched by people, he lets our neighbour Jon pet him and initiates sniffing opportunities with the dogs he knows. The first time he ran freely and fast around our yard was to watch pure joy in motion.

Gus is a happy little soul who appreciates everything in his world. He has gained a full pound, has a shiny white coat, and there's not a trace of stiffness in his leg. While he sleeps tucked into me at night, we ended up buying his cage because he loves it so much. It is located five feet from my desk where I work from home, and it's his safe place where he sleeps and keeps his growing number of possessions during the day.

I was, and continue to be, the center of his universe, but he doesn't panic if he loses sight of me anymore because he knows I always come back and pick him up so he can snuggle with me. I often think of Morton and hope he has found his safe place in the world. I thank him for sending me a message that there was a dog that needed me and, as it turns out, a dog that I needed more than I could ever have imagined.

~Laura Snell

The Dog that Lives under the Table

Fun fact: Most dogs need to be "socialized" — have positive experiences with humans — before fourteen weeks of age, or they may always feel shy or afraid around people.

I was just going to look when I went to the animal shelter. I had lost my best friend, a Jack Russell named Katie, to kidney disease. I knew we could never replace her, but I felt a new dog with its own personality would help fill the emptiness in my heart and home.

The dogs were excited to see visitors and vied for attention, barking and jumping up on the viewing glass. But one dog sat in the far corner, head down, ears drooping, tail tucked, and body shaking. The longing in his soft brown eyes drew me to him. The shelter volunteer said he had been in an animal hoarding situation with forty-seven other dogs. Being invisible was his way of surviving.

I went home without him but I was back the next day. I named him Gibbs after the character Leroy Jethro Gibbs on *NCIS*, my favorite TV show.

The moment I put Gibbs down, he raced around the den looking for a way out. He dove under the dining table, ignoring his carrier and the bed we had so carefully placed in a corner of the room.

We finally put the dog bed under the table, complete with a soft worn towel and a small teddy bear for company.

Gibbs was skin and bones. My husband tried all types of commercial dog food, but finally resorted to home cooking. He made a great meatloaf with beef, rice and cheese. Gibbs loved it. We learned to place the food on the floor. Gibbs would grab a bite and head back under the table. I guess the big dogs wouldn't let the small ones near the food dish.

My husband calls him feral. He grew up ignored, a puppy that never learned to play. Scared of people. Gibbs flinched at any sudden movement, afraid to trust, but most of all, never knowing affection.

My daughter Kathy and granddaughter Kelly came over to meet the new member of the family a few weeks later. "Where is he?" Kelly asked, looking around.

"Under the dining table," I replied.

The three of us got on our hands and knees, peering under the table as we struggled to get a glimpse of my new pet.

"Why is he under the table?" Kelly asked.

"He lives there and won't come out while we're here," I explained. "He's terrified of everything."

"He doesn't look very happy," she said. "You know, Gram, when I was collecting supplies for the shelter, there were all these puppies, jumping around, giving kisses, wanting to play. Were they all adopted when you got there? This one is so sad."

My daughter crawled under the table, trying to pet the timid, quivering dog. "He won't even let you touch him." Kathy shook her head in disbelief. " If it was me, I would take him back."

"I can't do that. I don't think anyone else would have him. Everyone, even animals, deserves a chance."

"What's his name, Gram?"

"Gibbs."

Not making eye contact, Gibbs drew farther back under the table, putting as much distance as possible between himself and us.

"Why did you pick this one?" friends and family asked. "He needed me" was the only answer I could come with. "Look into those eyes. He wants to communicate. He just doesn't know how."

My son-in-law said to think of Gibbs as a fuzzy fish. "You feed him and watch him. That's it."

My friend Kwan said that God sent me Gibbs to teach me patience.

It's been more than two years. What others consider small steps, my husband and I consider major victories. Gibbs still doesn't eat out of a dish, but he will eat off the placemat — no more hiding under the table to eat. While he won't take food from my hand, there are times he will run up and snatch string cheese dangling from the tips of my fingers.

He has found a second haven, a spot wedged between the wall and the end of the couch, close to us, but not too close.

Gibbs's day is spent running from the table to the hidey-hole, dodging anyone standing in his way, still sleeping under the table at night.

When it's just my husband and me in the evening, sitting in our chairs and watching TV, Gibbs will come and lie down on the carpet. Not next to us, but near enough to be a part of the family — as long as no one moves, that is.

Some days when he's comfortable and feeling secure under the table, we can scratch his head. Of course, we have to move slowly and only for an instant.

Gibbs's saving grace is being housebroken. "Outside" is the magic word. Ask if he wants to go outside and then get out of the way. He races around the room, comes to a screeching halt at the back door and does what we call the "potty dance," jumping into the air and spinning around in circles until we open the door. He's still not sure if the yard is a safe place, so either my husband or I have to go outside with him. While sniffing and inspecting, looking for that perfect spot, he keeps a watchful eye on us, making sure we're still there.

The sounds of dogs barking in the distance, neighbors mowing grass, kids at play, or cars driving by send him running back to us. While we can't touch him, Gibbs will softy touch our legs, letting us know it's time to go in.

I hope someday Gibbs will jump up on the couch next to me, let me pet him, give me doggy kisses, and even snuggle. I want to go for walks and play fetch.

Until then, a brief tap of a paw on my leg, a soft nose rubbing against my hand, a soulful glance that says "hey, I'm here" will do.

You can't hurry love.

~Jeri McBryde

Golden Oldies

*Fun fact: Dogs are considered "seniors" at different
ages depending on their breed. Generally, bigger dogs
are considered "old" at a younger age than
smaller dogs.*

"We've got the perfect dog for you," the woman from the rescue group said. I knew what that meant. It was the kind of dog I never wanted — the kind I thought I could never let into my heart.

It all started when my husband Mike and I were looking to adopt a dog after losing our faithful old yellow Lab. Although we had an adorable Spaniel mix at home, something nudged us, telling us it was time for another dog in our family. We contacted Peppertree, a local dog rescue group. "What kind of dog are you looking for?" they asked.

"Oh, we'd love any," I answered. Or so I thought.

Before long, they sent us a picture of a large Golden Retriever. "He'd be perfect for you," they wrote. I gasped. Were they serious? This dog was gangly, with crooked teeth and patchy fur. He was so thin that his ribs protruded. Likely he had a bundle of health issues. Then, there was his age — they estimated he was eleven. And every one of those years had taken a hard, miserable toll on him.

"Can we get him?" Mike asked, eyes pleading.

"Oh, Mike!" I said. "Eleven!"

I thought the issue was resolved, but Mike couldn't stop looking at the pathetic picture. Peppertree was holding an adoption event the very next day. I was to be out of town at a conference. I was sure he'd rush over and rescue that old dog.

"Whatever you do, don't get that dog," I said firmly.

"But someone else might adopt him."

"Who'd take an eleven-year-old dog? He's probably got arthritis, heartworm, Lyme disease — who knows what. Besides, how could we take him, knowing we won't have much time together? I couldn't bear it."

When I returned from the conference, Mike told me he'd gone to the event and seen the dog. It took all his resolve not to sign the adoption papers then and there. He begged me to just meet the old boy the next day. He was so sincere, how could I say no?

When we got out of the car, there was the rescue worker with a reddish-blond dog, standing still as a stone. When I looked into his eyes, he averted his gaze. I accepted his leash and took him for a walk. He matched my stride, obedient yet detached. I kept thinking about his age.

"Mike, I don't know…" I said, turning to walk away.

"He needs us," Mike said.

I stopped abruptly. He needs us. I hadn't thought of it that way. Maybe it wasn't about what this dog could do for us. It was about what we could do for him. We could give him a warm, loving home for however long we had together. We could give him the comfort and dignity he deserved in his golden years.

I sighed, and nodded. "Okay." I came back and stroked the scrawny dog's side. "What do you think? Do you want to live with us?" His tail wagged, just a little bit.

Brooks, as we named him, responded immediately to our love. Despite having lived possibly for years on his own, he had no emotional issues or bad habits. He didn't run around or chew on the furniture or cry at night. He napped during the day and was content with a few ambling walks. An older dog, we found, fit perfectly into our lifestyle. He followed Mike around the house, and in the evening he climbed into my big green chair with me and cuddled as I worked on my computer. I hugged him tight. "I love you, Brooks," I said. And I meant it.

It's no surprise, however, that just what I feared came to pass one day. Sadly, we lost Brooks to cancer only a year after he came into our lives. Mike said the reason we grieved so hard was because it was so good while we were together. It was a powerful loss, but we felt better knowing Brooks had had the comfort of a loving home for the last year of his life. Maybe that was just the reason he came to us. Maybe that's what we were meant to do.

Since then, we decided to open our hearts to rescuing senior dogs. So when Peppertree called, telling us they had "the perfect dog for us," I knew what it meant. Another senior was looking for a forever home.

Today, our Spaniel is thirteen years old, and we also have a ten-year-old Golden Retriever, Ike. It's a perfect match. We provide him with the love, comfort and security he deserves in his golden years. He gives us just as much in return. And when the time comes that we'll have to say goodbye, another senior dog will be out there that needs us. And we know we can bear it. Sometimes, we discover things in the most unexpected way — like through a skinny, abandoned, eleven-year-old Golden Retriever that just needed some love.

~Peggy Frezon

54

A Pit Bull Love Story

*Fun fact: Pit Bulls were created by breeding Bulldogs
and Terriers together.*

J uliet is my Pit Bull rescue. She lived in the Humane
Society's shelter for more than eighteen months after
being dropped off in the middle of the night. Abandoned.
I saw her picture featured in a local paper, and something deep inside me told me I had to meet her. Upon arriving at the
shelter, I found her cowering at the back of her kennel. It took a lot
of coaxing to even get her to come close enough for me to reach my
fingers through the chain links and pet her. She licked my hand.

I took her out to play in their meet-and-greet area. She was cute,
but still aloof. I asked a million questions about her. Why had she been
there for more than eighteen months? What was she like with other
dogs? Kids? Cats? They were unsure of her history and gave her a bad
rep at first. One of the volunteers told me she did not do well with
children or dogs, so I left disappointed. I didn't want to risk putting
another animal or child in danger. I was well aware of the reputation
of Pit Bulls.

Later that day, I had several messages and an e-mail about Juliet
from the Humane Society asking me to give her a chance. They asked
me to foster her for one week and see how she did. They sent a video
of her interacting with other dogs, and she seemed okay, so I agreed
and went to pick her up.

The minute she got in the car, I knew she was mine. I read everything

I could about rescues and Pit Bulls. I watched every video I could about dog training. I took owning her very seriously. I asked friends with big rescue dogs about socializing her. I exercised her religiously. I walked her. I ran her. I took her to the park and ran up and down the slides, like an obstacle course. She was happy and loved.

But I watched as people crossed the street to avoid her when we were out for our evening walks. They were afraid to get too close, but she was more afraid of letting them get too close to her. She was the most gentle, loving, sweet dog within the walls of my house. She even learned to interact with my cats without trying to eat them. I was so proud of her accomplishments. She never disappointed me. She never chewed anything she wasn't supposed to. She was perfection, and I loved her wholeheartedly. It was then I realized that all she ever needed was for someone to have faith in her, to give her a chance to prove herself, to be loved.

It occurred to me that Juliet was the perfect metaphor for my life. I had spent many years feeling abandoned by my father, my husband, and at times my family. All I ever wanted was a chance to be loved, but I was always afraid to let someone get too close, always proving myself to others only to be let down and left again. I understood now her initial reaction to meeting me. Why would she extend herself to me and trust me when I was just going to walk past that cage as others before me did for eighteen months?

We have spent the last four years together, rehabilitating each other and learning to trust. I cannot imagine my life without her.

Juliet does not have a tragic ending. She is my best friend, companion and soul mate. Because of her, I have learned to love unconditionally, and so has she.

~Christie Page

55

Healing Oreo

Not-so-fun fact: "Kennel cough" (canine infectious tracheobronchitis) is contagious, so infected dogs should be kept away from other dogs.

The phone rang at 11:30 p.m. The young man on the other end was the resident assistant in my daughter Mimi's college dorm. "Your daughter has been rushed to the hospital. She wasn't breathing," he said. I prayed my way to the emergency room. The doctors said Mimi had overdosed on heroin. Miraculously, they were able to revive her.

Mimi's nurse told her she was lucky. She had another patient who hadn't been as fortunate. "Did she die?" Mimi asked.

"No, but she suffered brain damage, and now she can't even feed herself," the nurse said.

Mimi had been struggling with drug addiction for years. She'd tried often to stop on her own but would slide back into drug abuse. This near-death experience convinced her to seek professional help. She checked herself into a residential treatment center. There, she attended 12-step meetings and sessions with a psychologist. When she was released, the psychologist recommended an unconventional aspect to her continuing therapy — a dog.

The dog arrived hidden in Mimi's jacket. "Surprise, Mom," she said. She opened her coat to reveal a palm-sized Poodle puppy. Her psychologist had suggested that the responsibility of caring for a pet might help her maintain her sobriety.

Who could argue with that? And the pup was adorable. His soft, wavy onyx hair was accented with a diamond-shaped mark of white on his chest. My littlest children, who define the world in terms of sweet treats, promptly named him Oreo.

The first days at home, Oreo romped in the kitchen, skidding on the unfamiliar ceramic tiles under his paws. He pranced to investigate his new stainless-steel food dish. We laughed when his dog tags clinked against the dish and he jumped backwards — he'd startled himself. Oreo's favorite toy was a blue octopus the size of his own head. He refused to nap without it, so he'd struggle to drag it into his bed.

Then, the cough started. The veterinarian diagnosed kennel cough. Soon, Oreo stopped romping and prancing. The cough advanced to frequent choking jags. Oreo had developed pneumonia.

Mimi stayed by his side, patting him as he coughed. "You'll be well soon," she'd whisper to him. His only response was an upward gaze of his brown marble eyes. Oreo was too weak to pad over to his food dish, so Mimi handfed him. She gently coaxed him to swallow his antibiotics. At a time when Mimi might have been tempted to party with old associates or visit a bar, her heart and soul were focused on her beloved pup.

Despite the round-the-clock nursing, Oreo worsened. The vet warned that the pneumonia might take Oreo's life.

Mimi had found an out-of-state animal hospital that specialized in treating pneumonia. She was making arrangements to have Oreo admitted when he began to perk up. Day by day, he regained his health.

I could see how grateful Oreo was to be alive. When Mimi scratched behind his ears, his tail wagged so furiously that it would knock him sideways. He loved to play fetch with Mimi. She would throw his octopus, but Oreo would wait for her to crawl across the floor to retrieve the toy. Then, when she came close to him, he would grab the octopus from her hand. Every evening, he would curl up on Mimi's lap with his head resting in the crook of her elbow.

Almost thirteen years have passed since Oreo first joined our family. Mimi has earned her doctorate in psychology and is helping other addicts overcome their drug abuse. While she is at work, Oreo stays at home with me. It is my privilege to rub the underside of his neck and give him tight hugs. I hope he knows how thankful I am that he helped make Mimi healthy.

~Lily Ryan

56

Runt of the Litter

Fun fact: "Dachshund" means "badger dog" in German. Long ago, they were coveted for their digging skills, which enabled them to hunt underground pests such as badgers.

I stepped off the back porch and approached Fritz's house, which was nestled beneath his favorite spot under the shade of my family's sprawling pecan tree. Using our shared German language, I commanded Fritz to dinner: "Fritz! *Kommen Sie hier — Abendessen!*"

Yet, Fritz didn't come when called to dinner. I knelt down and peered inside his doghouse. I caught a glimpse of his shiny dark nose and found him huddled in the back corner of his doghouse, shivering and whining. He tried to stand up, but whimpered and immediately collapsed.

"What's the matter? Why are you shaking?" I reached inside, hoping to pull him into my arms, but he yelped even louder. His doghouse had no floor, so I lifted up the house, placed him in my arms, and wrapped him in the softest blanket I could find. I rocked him back and forth, gently stroking his back. "Just go to sleep. When you wake up, you'll be okay." As I waited for him to drift off to sleep, I remembered the day Fritz had come into my life.

I was just six years old that hot August afternoon when I heard Mr. Davis announce, "Hilda's gone into labor!" I leapt down the back porch steps, ran next door, and watched Hilda strain as five pups slowly wriggled their way from her belly. Fritz was a runt and the first of Hilda's litter of five milk-chocolate-colored Dachshunds.

I giggled as I watched the five bundles of energy squirming beneath their mother's tummy, all begging for lunch at the same time. But the magical moment abruptly ended when Hilda nudged her runt puppy away from her. Although the runt inched his way back to Hilda's stomach, she shoved him away again, growled and then pounced on his tiny back and tail. The runt yelped; I screeched in horror as Mr. Davis—the neighborhood Dachshund aficionado—ran to my side.

"She's hurting him… make her stop!" I waved my hands in front of Hilda's growling face.

Mr. Davis scooped up the injured pup and placed him in my hands. "Run, kiddo. Find a shoebox and put that pup in it! Hurry back!"

I darted for the Davises' house, gingerly holding the wounded pup in my hands. I found a shoebox, placed the pup in it, and then watched it stretch and twist its tiny body ever so slightly. Relieved, I returned to Mr. Davis's side.

"Hilda's a mean dog… I don't like her!" My voice trembled. "Why would a mama dog kill its own puppy?"

"Kiddo, you have to understand that Hilda's not mean; she loves her runt. But her instinct tells her that her puppy is too weak to survive, and she believes that killing it is the strong and merciful thing to do." Mr. Davis patted me on the back. "Hey, kiddo, if you have a doll blanket and baby bottle back home, go get them. I believe we can save this pup."

I dashed home, found the two items, and returned. We put the blanket in the box and placed the runt on it. We heated some milk, added Karo syrup to it, and poured the mixture into the baby bottle. The runt sucked on it and wiggled contentedly. While I caressed its tiny body with my fingers, he fell asleep—serene and out of harm's way.

"You know, kiddo, many runts die before they ever open their eyes. But if we can keep this runt alive until his eyes open, he'll probably survive. If he pulls through, you can have him. I bet he'll be the most loving and energetic pup of the litter."

For fourteen days, we handfed him and waited for his eyes to open. Over the next few weeks, we watched the runt develop into a high-spirited, mischievous but loving Dachshund puppy with a slightly broken tail.

"Hey, kiddo, at some point you have to give your puppy a proper German name," suggested Mr. Davis.

"Well, for some reason I like the name Fritz. It suits him!"

"Fritz is a right and proper name. I like it. So Fritz it is."

Fritz quickly became part of our German family. For the next twelve years, we were inseparable except when I was in school. But immediately after school, I'd run home, throw open the backyard gate, and plop on the back porch steps. Fritz would dart up the steps, jump into my lap, and shower me with love and kisses. Then he'd turn his head from side to side as if to ask, "How was your day at school?"

I always obliged him with some school story. "Today I learned how to write in cursive. I'm not very good at it yet, but do you want to see?" I would open my satchel and pull out my writing tablet.

He'd tug on my school satchel, wag that broken tail of his, and bark as if to say, "Where's my treat?" I'd offer him a cookie or other snack that I'd saved from lunch, and while he munched on his treat, I'd pet his elongated back and belly.

As I grew up, I often shared my deepest thoughts, secrets, and fears with Fritz. "Today I met the cutest boy in my algebra class! Do you think he'll ask me to the dance? I want to go to the dance, but what if he doesn't ask me? You know, Fritz, I'm not very pretty, and I'm not a popular girl. Maybe I should just go by myself." He'd tilt his head side to side as if to nod and look at me with those encouraging doe-like eyes. "What if my acne flares up the day before the dance? What then? Should I go?" He'd lick my face, wag his tail, and bark, leaving me to interpret his advice.

As Fritz matured, he embraced his German heritage, for he loved sausage, sauerkraut, pretzels, and even an occasional beer. At some point, Fritz acquired a bit of wanderlust — escaping from our yard and roaming the neighborhood. I always found Fritz, for he was the only neighborhood Dachshund with a broken tail. As soon as I spotted him, I'd yell in German, "Fritz, *kommen Sie hier. Schlechter Hund!*" As commanded, Fritz came to my side with his head down and his broken tail between his legs, pretending to be my bad dog.

Once inside the house, Fritz sounded like Fred Astaire tap dancing — his little toenails clicking on Mother's linoleum floor. Fritz was half-a-dog high and a dog-and-a-half long with short, stubby legs and tiny feet. As you can imagine, he lacked Astaire's coordination and grace, so he often ran down the hallway and slid out of control, with the back of him always going in front of him.

Today, though, Fritz looked listless, fragile, and feeble. "What do you need, old boy?" I stroked his head. "Please tell me. I'll get you whatever you need."

Mr. Davis must have seen us on the back porch. "Hey, kiddo. Looks as if old Fritz is in some pain. Let's take him to the vet. How does that sound?"

I silently boarded Mr. Davis's truck, resting Fritz comfortably in my lap. When we arrived at the vet's office, he immediately took Fritz from me and disappeared from view. When he reappeared, the vet said, "Fritz has arthritis, and he's also had a severe heart attack. He's an old dog and too weak to survive." He took my hand in his. "The strong and merciful thing to do would be to put Fritz to sleep."

"Are you sure? Maybe all Fritz needs is some rest."

"Yes, I'm sure. I know you love Fritz and letting him go is a hard decision, but…" the vet's voice trailed off.

I gulped hard and nodded. "Okay."

"Would you like to see him one last time?" The vet patted my shoulder.

"Go ahead, kiddo." Mr. Davis squeezed my hand. "I'll wait for you right here."

I entered the back room and approached the examination table. Fritz lifted his head, licked my face, and wagged his broken tail. I stroked Fritz's belly and patted his head, choking back tears. "Fritz, you're weak and sick, and you're not going to get any better. I don't want to see you suffer. So I'm… I'm… putting you to sleep." I hugged Fritz one last time. "I'm going to miss you!"

Fritz looked at me with those familiar doe-like, understanding eyes, and then nodded his head as if to say, "I'll be okay. Thanks for being strong and merciful."

The vet handed me a box of tissues. "Putting Fritz to sleep is safe and harmless. Fritz will receive two shots. The first will render him unconscious. The second will painlessly put him to sleep, usually within about thirty seconds."

After Fritz received the first shot, I waited until unconsciousness washed over him like a soothing rain. Then, with the second shot, Fritz peacefully slipped away. I lingered by Fritz's side for quite some time and remembered what Fritz taught me about tenacity, love, encouragement, and now, death.

The next day, Mr. Davis and I buried Fritz in his favorite spot — beneath the cool shade of the pecan tree. Afterwards, I stood in silence and found myself thinking back to the day Hilda tried to kill her runt puppy. As I did, my perspective shifted, for I now better understood and even respected Hilda's instinct to be strong and merciful.

~Sara Etgen-Baker

57

Meant for Each Other

*Not-so-fun fact: Dogs can develop a disease similar
to Alzheimer's called Canine Cognitive Dysfunction
Syndrome. Symptoms include disorientation, house
soiling, or changes in sleep or interaction.*

Among the many dogs at the Animal Resource Center on that day, the old dog stood out because of his dignity and poise. He did not rush to the front of his cage, or bark madly, or leap about as if to say, "Look at me!" He simply lay quietly near the back of the cage, head raised and bulbous brown eyes fixed on us as we paused just outside his cell.

My son had dragged me there that day. Since my husband had died three years before, my dog-loving son had tried to persuade me to get a dog for company. I was reluctant, not sure I wanted to be responsible again for another creature. I had raised my children and, now that they were all on their own, I was not eager to take on another life. But this afternoon my son and his friend had come by to take action.

"We just came from the pound, Mom," my son said, "and there is a dog there that is perfect for you." Again I said, as I had many times before, "I'm not sure I want a dog, Trey."

"Oh," he said, "but this one is just right for you. Come on, let's go look."

Thinking this would be the only way to get him off my back, I went. We walked the aisles, looking at every dog in every cage. There were Shepherds, Border Collies, Chihuahuas, mutts, and many Pit Bulls.

Some were sad, some hyper, others frightening, but all were appealing and heartwrenching in their way. As we rounded the corner to the last aisle, I saw ahead of me a little black-and-white ball of energy. He was in a topless cage, leaping straight into the air and down again, barking like a seal with each jump. I asked that he be taken out and brought into the visitors' enclosure. I quickly realized that, although he was adorable, he was way too high-energy for me. I was looking for a dog with a laidback temperament to match my own.

Next we went to the dog my son had picked for me — a little Chihuahua with big ears. She pranced like a circus pony and was indeed charming. Once in the enclosure, however, she showed no interest at all in any of us, and simply ran about, dashing from point to point with no apparent purpose. I shook my head at my son.

"I need to think about it. Nothing here really grabs me."

We retraced our steps, looking again at each animal as we passed. One of the last cages was the one with the old Boxer, and I noted the sign that said, "A Senior Dog for a Senior." He was very big, however, and I wanted a smaller dog for my small house. We got in the car and headed home. A short distance away, I opened my mouth.

"I'm just thinking about the old dog," I said.

I surprised even myself because I had not been thinking of him — not consciously, anyway. The words had simply come without warning or forethought.

"You want to go back?" my son asked. I agreed.

Once there, we went directly to the cage. Crouching to look at the dog, I could see the gray hairs in his muzzle. He got up and walked slowly to the front of the cage, but did not make any overtures or appear particularly excited. My son read the card at the top of his cage. He was owner-surrendered, seven years old, and had been there five weeks.

"Does he have a name?" I asked.

"Yes, his name is Tater."

"And I'm from Idaho," I said. "I think this is my dog."

We found a staff member and asked that he be brought out for us. She tied a light rope around his neck and brought him out, handing the end of the rope to me. He walked sedately beside me as we left the cage area and exited to the outside exercise pen. I sat on a bench, and the dog sat quietly beside me. After just a few minutes, he stood up, put his front legs and his big barrel chest onto my lap, and settled in. His big head was now level with my face. At regular intervals, he would turn his head, look into my eyes, and lick my face with his wet, warm tongue. Oh, yes, he was playing me. After a few minutes, we took him back inside, turned him over to the staff member, and went out to the front desk.

"I want the big Boxer, Tater," I said to the young woman behind the desk.

I learned that Tater had been a companion dog, but no record existed of why he had been surrendered. I paid the fees and was told that I could pick him up on Saturday, after he had had his neutering surgery on Friday.

Immediately after arriving at my home on Saturday, Tater explored the house. He then settled down on the living room floor to sleep. Later, alone with him, I had some anxious moments. At one point, Tater stood in front of me and made a low, growling sound, a little like an engine trying to turn over. The sound increased in volume and urgency. It was clear he was trying to tell me something, but I had no idea what. When he began barking in his deep, loud voice, the thought crossed my mind, "He could rip out my throat!" We had a few days of muddled communications, puddles on the floor, and getting-to-know-you moments, but eventually settled into a routine.

Tater has been with me almost a year. We take walks together, and he is content to stay on the leash, ambling along slowly and sniffing at points of interest along the trail. Wherever I am, he is sleeping nearby. He will not stay in the fenced yard alone. It is clear that he likes people but has little use for other dogs. I have learned to put food away or beyond his reach — and his reach is long. He likes to ride in the car, in the back seat, with the windows cracked. He likes to sleep on the beds, and his choice of bed varies from day to day.

Most people choose young dogs when they go to the shelter, just as most adults want babies when they adopt. There is little interest in an old dog whose functions are slowing and whose life is nearing its end.

Who knows what would have happened to Tater if I had not taken him home? I feel certain that the words that came from my mouth as we drove away from the shelter that day were put there by a caring Power, and did not come from my own mind. As a result, I have a sweet companion for my last years, and Tater does not have to live out his life in a cement-floored cage.

~Twilla Estes

58

Chicken Soup for the Soul

My Social Butterfly

Fun fact: Dogs are naturally social, but when they first meet, they need to figure out which one is "top dog" in their social ranking.

"Do you know the names of all the dogs in the neighborhood?" my friend Becky asked me during an evening walk.

"Yes, I guess I do since I am the mother of a four-legged social butterfly."

Our rescue puppy, Cornbread, a yellow Lab–Spaniel mix, loves to be around other dogs. Her temperament is very different from our beloved Catfish, a yellow Lab that passed away two years earlier. He was the exact opposite; he loved people, but he did not like other dogs. On walks with him, I constantly had to avoid other dogs.

It is quite a different story with Cornbread. Whenever we meet another dog, we have to stop and visit. It is just the polite thing to do, according to Cornbread. She pulls on her leash and whimpers until we stop to visit and say hello. So, yes, I do know the names of all the fellow canines in our neighborhood. We must always stop and visit Maggie, Sandy, Oreo, or Sika, the cute Husky with the crystal-blue eyes.

When we are not walking, Cornbread roams our yard within the confines of an electric fence. However, sometimes electric fences do not work. When this happens, Cornbread usually makes a run for it. I am never concerned because I can usually find her visiting one of her friends nearby.

On one such occasion, she got out, and we received a call from our neighbors that she was over at their house visiting Sandy. I quickly went to pick up my social butterfly and take her home. Days later on our walk, we stopped at Sandy's house to say hello. Looking down, I noticed one of Cornbread's toys lying outside Sandy's fence. Why, she must have brought it when she came to see Sandy the other day. Bending over, I picked it up and handed it to her. "Cornbread, you left your toy here. We need to take it home."

She quickly took it from my hand, dropped it on the ground, and looked up at me. I picked it up a second time and, once again, she took it from my hand and dropped it. After repeating this for the third time, I finally understood what she wanted to do with her toy: She wanted to give it to Sandy.

In Cornbread's mind, you show your friends that you care by taking the time to stop and visit and occasionally bring them a gift. She had brought her toy as a gift for Sandy on her previous visit.

"Do you want to give your toy to Sandy?" Cornbread patiently sat, waiting for me to understand. Realizing her intent, I threw her toy over the fence into Sandy's yard. It was then that she happily wagged her tail, pleased that she had been able to give her friend a gift.

~Tanya Shearer

How Stella Got Her Groove Back

*Not-so-fun fact: An estimated 4–6 million dogs
are euthanized in the United States every year
because they aren't adopted and animal shelters are
overcrowded.*

I was making one of my all too frequent stops at the large veterinary hospital I've been taking my pets to for the past two decades. This time none of my pets were in tow as it was just a med pick-up run. I'm such a frequent flyer I know just about everyone who works there. Lisa, who has managed the pharmacy as long as I've been a client, is one of my favorite people. We always chat about our pets and this time I got to meet Stella, who was spending the day in Lisa's office.

Stella is an adorable Pit Bull mix with an engagingly uneven grin. Her thin tail wagged at warp speed and all I could think was, "What a happy dog!" Little did I know that Lisa was about to reveal Stella's secret life before her adoption. I would soon learn that any luck in Stella's early life had been bad.

"Working in this large veterinary hospital, I've seen a number of throwaway animals with injuries or a disease and no one to pay for the procedures and medications that will save their lives," Lisa began. "Often they're euthanized for lack of a responsible owner willing to make them whole again.

"About twice a week Animal Control brings in an injured, neglected, abused or sick animal. Many can be saved but they need a home and someone to care for them once treatment is given. Veterinary workers who see these animals often throw the needed lifeline.

"One hot summer day, an Animal Control officer brought in a young, female Pit Bull mix. She'd been used as a bait dog for a dog-fighting ring. A neighbor's complaint led officers to her, chained to a pole along with purebred Pit Bulls.

"The fight dogs were taken directly to Animal Control, presumably to be euthanized. The injured mix was brought in with a suspected gunshot wound to her right shoulder. She was limping without a whimper. X-rays revealed that her wound was actually a deep, infected dog bite. She was covered with other bite marks in various stages of healing.

"The bones of her rib cage stood out prominently, as she weighed only nineteen of the thirty pounds that are healthy for her breed and size. A collar, obviously put on her as a young pup, was embedded in the flesh around her neck. It was apparent that her previous owners had no concern about her outgrowing it; perhaps they never expected her to survive in the deplorably violent world they'd placed her in.

"She was anemic from the fleas and ticks that covered her body and swarmed in her ears, under her legs and in her groin. To make her more comfortable, the fleas and ticks were treated immediately. With antibiotics and two to three weeks of crate rest, her shoulder would recover. Her chance for a better life was contingent upon someone adopting her."

I'd remained speechless throughout Lisa's vivid description of Stella's arrival at the clinic. Throughout it, I glanced down at Stella and noticed her unwavering focus on her human mom. I saw adoration in those soulful eyes. I waited to learn how Stella evolved from being a friendless victim to a cherished family member. Lisa didn't disappoint me.

"Most of our animals have come from this veterinary clinic. My husband Kevin has always been a pretty good sport when I've wanted to bring another sad luck case home from the hospital. We had two cats and a dog already when I told him about the sweet bait dog. He said we had enough animals and he was reluctant to add another, especially one with all the issues this one had.

"I knew he'd change his mind when he saw her, because, despite the abuse she had suffered, she was friendly and offered a toothy grin and gentle tail wag whenever any hospital workers approached her. As predicted, Kevin took one look at the half starved, much scarred dog and was impressed by her desire to befriend everyone she met. He looked from her to me and said, 'I guess we've got a new dog, Lisa.'"

I was transfixed and would have stood there all morning petting Stella's head as she leaned against my leg. Only the growing line of clients waiting to receive their pet medications could interrupt this fascinating tale.

"I've got to get back to work," Lisa sighed.

I didn't want it to end like this. I had to hear the details about Stella's recovery. "Sure, but can we meet sometime soon to finish Stella's story? Maybe Kevin can join us."

Several days later Kevin and Lisa met me at a diner. Between bites of their roast beef sandwich, I learned about the highs and lows of Stella's baby steps toward health and happiness.

Kevin covered her transition to indoor living. "It was obvious she'd never been under a roof and was spooked by the confinement. Since she had to be crated to rest her leg and shoulder, we kept her in our bedroom. She soon adapted to her kennel and sought it as a safe spot.

"The ceiling fan frightened her. If it was on, she'd stare at it and quiver. She wouldn't pass through doorways or walk down the hallway. We had to carry her outside to go to the bathroom. Loud sounds made her shake with fear."

"Her adjustments were so subtle and came in such tiny baby steps that we sometimes wondered if she'd ever adapt to her new life," Lisa added. "We had to repeatedly show her how to do everything and her progress was so very slow. Our vet, Dr. Porte, counseled me to have patience and assured me that everything would work out.

"Just when I thought she'd never leave our bedroom, she observed Puck, our nine-year-old Rottweiler, playing with his ball. She just walked out our door to retrieve it. After that Puck befriended Stella, showing her she needn't fear him as she had the other dogs in her life."

Both Lisa and Kevin marveled that the attacks Stella endured never made her aggressive. "She loves to socialize with our neighbors' kids, my niece and anyone willing to pet her," Lisa said.

Kevin's mom, who considers Stella her grandchild, lives 141 miles away but manages to spoil Stella anyway by mailing her squeaky toys and dog cookies. "We take Stella with us every Thanksgiving. She stays with Grandma while we stay at a "no pets" hotel. Grandma makes her scrambled eggs and rack of lamb, her favorites. When we travel, Stella also stays with Grandma. Her Doberman, Toby, taught Stella how to use stairs, a feat she seemed too terrified to attempt at home. The first time she saw Toby trotting down the stairs, she just followed suit."

Though Stella managed to conquer her fear of things inside the house, she was still timid around the swimming pool. Kevin helped her overcome her fear of water. "I used to bring her into the pool and helped her paddle near the steps. Now she swims in the shallow end and uses the steps to climb out. If we take a walk near the river, she wades in on her own."

A quiet dog, Stella rarely barks or whines. "Our new neighbor didn't even realize we had her because he'd never heard her. She just stands near the door or in the kitchen when she wants something. We're so well trained that we respond quickly and correctly every time," Lisa giggled, "and Stella is pleased with our progress."

TV time is a shared event with Stella, Kevin, and their cat Guinness lounging comfortably on an oversized sofa. "When it's time to sleep, Stella hops onto our bed and dives under the covers. She's definitely overcome her fear of enclosed places," Kevin boasts.

Lisa reached over to hug Kevin. "He's made a complete reversal since that first day I asked to bring Stella home. Now he adores Stella and the unconditional, childlike affection she offers us."

Rhetorically, since Lisa clearly adores her unstoppable Stella, I asked, "How about you, Lisa?"

"As for me, I thought I was just helping another victim, never guessing that she was so much more than a survivor. I hadn't imagined the positive changes in store for me. Watching Stella open her heart to us and learn to trust humans, despite her early treatment, was inspirational. If she can take another chance on life, I can live mine fuller as well. Moving on is a wonderful form of liberation."

Our meal finished, Lisa and I dabbed away a few tears and hugged at the diner door. I remain in awe of the connection between man and his best friend.

~Marsha Porter

60

One-Eyed Lily

Fun fact: Many dogs lift their legs to pee higher
because urine scent sprayed above the ground, such
as on a fire hydrant or pole, carries farther, better
marking their territory.

I arrived one morning at the Humane Society where I volunteered as a dog walker. An old black German Shepherd lay on the office floor, curled up on an old blanket. She'd been brought in as a stray and put in the office to spare her the stress of the chaos of the kennels.

Her information sheet really didn't say much, other than the name they'd given her, Lily; her age, just "senior"; and her status "stray." Only she knew where she'd come from, but she looked like it had been a long, hard road.

"Can I walk her?" I eyed her uncertainly.

"Sure, go ahead," the desk clerk said. "We've had her out a few times."

I grabbed a leash and signed her out. "Come on, Lily!" I said in my most cheerful, happy-dog voice. "We're going for a walk."

Of course, she didn't know her name yet, but she knew I was talking to her and struggled to her feet. Most German Shepherds ride low in the back, but Lily looked as if her hips could go out at any moment.

When she looked at me, I gasped. "Oh, my gosh! She's only got one eye."

But when I looked more closely, I realized her second eye was there. It was just very small and sunken. The vet said it was probably the way she'd been born.

Lily slowly followed me outside. We plodded up the hill to the free-run pens, where I turned her loose. For a moment, she stood there, back end drooping, with no life in her face. Finally, after a few moments, she wandered off and stood with her nose in a corner.

I tried to toss a ball for her, but she just stood, head down, and watched it roll away. "Oh, Lily, what are we going to do with you?"

I clipped the leash back on, and we took a little walk, shuffling along so she could sniff the bushes. Finally, I brought her back to her blanket in the office. "See you in a couple days, Lily," I told her, but her head was already down on her paws again.

For the next couple weeks, I made a point to stop and see Lily, and take her out for a bit. She started to make the effort to stand when she saw me. She walked a bit stronger, it seemed, and I thought I saw some glimmer of interest in what we were doing.

But nobody seemed interested in her.

With so many healthy young dogs and puppies needing homes, few people stopped to look at a broken-down, old, one-eyed dog. After a while, it became clear she was not going to be adopted.

The Humane Society dog trainer had spent his career training German Shepherds for police work. Lily was breaking his heart. He'd noticed my bond with her. "She can't live on the office floor forever," he told me. "Would you maybe be interested in fostering her?"

I wasn't even an approved foster home, but my heart said "yes" before my brain had time to kick in. Twenty-four hours later, I had myself an ancient, one-eyed foster dog.

My daughter Kika went with me to pick her up. I put a blanket down on the back seat, and together we hoisted Lily up onto it.

Kika laughed. "Look at her! She knows she's going home."

Lily lay across the seat, tongue lolling, grinning from ear to ear. Her one good eye was bright. For the first time, she seemed like a happy, optimistic dog.

Kika and I drove home in high spirits, laughing and feeling good about our rescue mission.

We pulled into our driveway about twenty minutes later, and I opened the back door to let Lily out. That's when we realized she'd soaked the blanket — and the car seat, too. It was an omen of things to come....

When we got into the house, I expected Lily to explore, but she went no farther than the kitchen and adjoining family room. She didn't sniff, like most dogs in a new place would. She just walked in circles, wearing a big smile.

"Look how happy she is!" Kika said.

I'd have thought she was appreciating her new surroundings in her own way if she hadn't walked right into a corner and stood smiling at it until we finally pulled her out and turned her around.

Okay, so she had some dementia, along with her one eye, sinking back end, and maybe incontinence. We were in for good times.

But Lily smiled — oh, how she smiled. And we just had to smile back.

We set up a crate in the family room for her, lined with soft blankets. She went right in, beaming like a proud new homeowner.

From then on, that crate was Lily's home base. She divided her time between curling up there, walking in circles... and smiling radiantly at the corner.

Lily had been billed as house-trained, but we never saw any evidence of it. In fact, she seemed determined to "hold it" anytime we took her outside or tried to walk with her — only to let it fly as soon as we stepped back inside.

All I could figure was that Lily was — literally — *house*-trained. She only wanted to pee in the house.

Nor did she respect her own crate, as any dog expert will tell you dogs naturally do. Every morning, I pulled soaked bedding from the crate and threw it in the washer. Every day, I treated stains in the area rug (and finally gave up and hauled it out to the curb).

After several weeks, I had gotten no calls about possible adopters for Lily, so I went online and looked at her listing. There was my one-eyed girl — with a banner across the photo that said: "Adopted!"

Kika thought that was hysterical. "They got you, Mama! They

really saw you coming!"

The shelter later explained that's what they mark on unadoptable animals in hospice foster. After that, when anyone asked about our "new dog," my insistence she was "just a foster" rang a bit hollow.

"How long are you fostering her for?" a friend asked.

I hesitated, lips twitching at the joke on me. "Till she dies."

Lily's tongue hung out in a wide, panting grin. She got the joke, too.

We had Lily eight months, until her back end sank so low she could no longer get up and down the steps to our back yard without a boost. And she was much too heavy for me to do that, especially several times a day. Lily never lost her smile, but her body was quitting on her.

The day she left us, my daughter Maria and I sat and petted her while the drug took effect, and she slipped away. In that moment, eight months of soggy bedding and destroyed carpeting didn't even come to mind. All I saw was her happy smile. It had blossomed from the moment she'd left the shelter, seemingly knowing she'd be safe, fed, and loved, with a roof over her head, a corner to stand in, and blankets to pee on.

The vet tech held me while I sobbed. When I left, I told the shelter, "No more fosters."

A month later, I got a call. "What if it's a very little foster…?"

And that is how we got Spike.

~Susan Kimmel Wright

61

The Crate Escape

Fun fact: The term "dog days of summer" was coined by the ancient Greeks and Romans to describe the hottest days of summer, coinciding with the rising of the Dog Star, Sirius.

The cruiser slows as it rounds the bend, the policeman looking across the street in amazement. The construction workers on the corner drop their shovels and stare. The neighbors watch from their windows and doors, mouths hanging open.

What they're looking at isn't a fender bender, or a tsunami, or a Sasquatch. It's my sister Brittany "Rollerblading" her dogs.

Clad in a helmet, elbow pads, and Rollerblades, fourteen-year-old Brittany careens down the street, pulled by Georgia, Sadie and Tucker, three energetic dogs sprinting as fast as their legs can go. My brother Zac follows, Rollerblading behind a large Boxer named Digsby. As neighbors gawk and stop to watch, the humans and dogs finish their last twenty-mile-per-hour loop around the neighborhood and slow to a halt in front of our house. Inside, five more canines — two Portuguese Water Dogs, two Cockapoos, and a Golden Retriever — wait eagerly to walk at their own slower pace.

"How many dogs do you take care of?" people often ask incredulously. When Brittany was ten, she started a home boarding business called The Crate Escape, turning her love of dogs into a way to earn money for horseback riding lessons. She started out with a dozen dogs that visited throughout the year, but word spread quickly, and she got more e-mails and calls every week. Now, she cares for more than seventy dogs on a regular basis.

Most kennels keep dogs in cages, but in Brittany's care, a dog's day couldn't be more different. Visiting pups nap in front of our fireplace, chase tennis balls in our back yard, and join the family on hiking and kayaking adventures. Brittany brushes them, gives them baths, removes wax from their ears, and clips their nails, all free for the owners. Many dogs sleep in her bed at night, often four or five at once. Depending on the size of the puppy pile, sometimes there's barely enough room for Brittany.

When they're not staying at The Crate Escape, our neighborhood dogs pull at their leashes when their owners walk by, trying to turn in to our driveway. Georgia, a Boxer who lives a few houses down the road, runs over whenever her owners let her outside. She trots up our steps and "knocks" on the front door with her paw, waiting for Brittany to come out and play.

But it's not all tennis balls, treats, and wagging tails for Brittany. Taking care of dogs is a lot of work. They all have their own foods, medications, quirks and routines. Some have hip or heart problems and need special care. Some are afraid of thunder or bicycles, and others wake up at 4:00 every morning, barking to be let outside. But no matter how complicated or exhausting, Brittany takes care of all her charges' needs.

Brittany has read the entire Dog Training section of our library, and it's not uncommon for owners to be shocked at how well behaved their dogs are after spending time with her.

Recently, Brittany boarded two Labs named Trixie and Muffins. When their owner dropped them off, she warned that the two were uncontrollable, and often jumped on the dinner table and took food. Brittany knew her work was cut out for her as she watched the frantic dogs tearing around the kitchen, barking and jumping on people. But as soon as the owner left, Brittany got to work re-training Trixie and Muffins. First, she took both dogs for a long walk to get rid of all their pent-up energy. To teach them that she was the leader, she made them walk slightly behind her. When they got home, she went through the door before them. Trixie and Muffins were used to going wild at dinnertime, but she waited for them to sit quietly before putting the bowls of kibble down.

At first, the dogs seemed uncertain about the new way to behave that Brittany was showing them. But within half a day, the change was unbelievable. The Labs followed Brittany around like shadows, obedient and relaxed. If they started jumping up or barking again, it only took one stern look from Brittany for them to stop, sit, and wait for her to tell them what to do. Needless to say, the owners were dumbstruck when Trixie and Muffins came home one week later — calm, polite and happy. In the months since, people who have had dogs for years have started coming to Brittany for advice.

Our brothers joke that Brittany spends so much time around dogs, she's starting to sprout a tail. Nobody is ever surprised to hear that she wants to become a veterinarian. For Brittany, running The Crate Escape isn't about making a profit, or impressing people with how much she's accomplished. It's about the 280 muddy paws that she's constantly wiping, the hundreds of Milk-Bones she hands out while teaching new tricks, and the blankets that will never, ever be fur-free again — no matter how many times they're put through the wash.

Big or small, purebred or mutt, well behaved or a diamond in the "ruff," each dog is special to Brittany. She gives a piece of her heart to every four-legged fur ball that comes into her life. When people remark on how lucky all the dogs are, Brittany has a thoughtful reply. "It's true, I scoop a lot of kibble, and go on more walks than I can count," she says, "but there's nothing quite like being woken up by three wet noses on your face, or having a caring paw placed on your arm when you sneeze. There's no doubt about it — I'm the lucky one."

~Caitlin Brown

Kineo

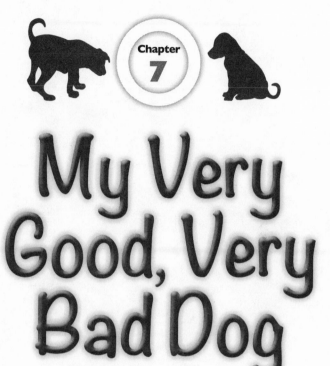

My Very Good, Very Bad Dog

My Clever Dog

Fun fact: For his book The Intelligence of Dogs *Stanley Coren contacted all of the dog obedience judges registered with the AKC and the Canadian Kennel Club. According to the judges' rankings, the top ten dogs in terms of working and obedience intelligence are, in order: Border Collie, Poodle, German Shepherd, Golden Retriever, Doberman Pinscher, Shetland Sheepdog, Labrador Retriever, Papillon, Rottweiler, and Australian Cattle Dog.*

62

Precious Punishes Herself

Fun fact: Dogs can understand, on average, up to sixty words or phrases, although some can understand up to 300 words.

Precious, our black Lab-Shepherd-Chow mix, showed us early on that she was oozing with personality and intelligence. As a puppy, she figured out how to unzip her bed and how to drop a ball down the stairs to play fetch with herself. She recognized the need to make noise (drop-catching a ball, continually squeaking a toy) to get attention, and seemingly understood more than basic commands and words.

She knew that if she was a "good girl" while we were at work, she would get a special treat when "Mommy" came home. One day, I came home, and noting the trashcan was still in its usual position, assumed she had been good. I promptly handed her a treat. I was a little surprised that she initially wouldn't take it, and then did so only with my encouragement. Then she lay down uncharacteristically in the hall with the treat in front of her. I remember thinking that perhaps she wasn't feeling well and figured I'd keep an eye on her.

I headed out the other side of the kitchen and found trash strewn about the dining room. I couldn't help but shake my head in disgust, and said, "Oh-ho... so somebody really wasn't a good girl after all." I thought, too late now, she already has the treat, and went to change clothes after picking up the mess.

After changing, I sat down on the couch to begin grading papers. A few moments later, Precious came into the living room, walked up to me, and placed her uneaten treat on my lap. Then she backed away and sat with her head down in shame. I sat there stunned—I couldn't believe it! She knew she didn't deserve the treat, and so she returned it.

Of course, with that demonstration of shame, I had to let her have the treat, though it took quite a bit of coaxing and letting her know I forgave her. After that, I don't think she ever bothered the trash again!

~Catherine D. Crocker

63

The Timeshare

Fun fact: Three types of identification are often used for dogs: tags, microchips, and tattoos. Identification greatly improves the chances you'll find your dog if she gets loose.

he black-and-white-spotted, mixed-breed dog had been spending a lot of time around our house for the past week. "It says her name is Boones, and there's a phone number," my son Chris confirmed after checking the small ID tag hanging from the dog's collar. "I'll give them a call to let them know where she is in case they're worried about her."

I stayed with the dog while Chris went in the house to make the call. I didn't want her to run off should the owners wish to come and get her.

Chris returned looking disheartened. "I see why Boones has been spending so much time here. That guy's a total jerk! He says to do what we want with her — but if she returns to his house, he'll shoot her."

When I asked if the man explained why he didn't like her, Chris replied, "No, but he sounded pretty adamant about shooting her."

"Let's keep her here for a while. Maybe he's just having a bad day and will have a change of heart." I tried to remain positive.

"I wouldn't count on it," Chris chuckled. "I doubt he even has a heart."

Food worked wonders for keeping Boones at our house. Although she had to share the cat's food on the first night, we made certain to buy her some food of her own early the following morning.

After a couple of weeks, we assumed we had a new dog. We hadn't encountered any problems with her, nor had we heard from her owner.

Chris decided to give him another call to ask if he wanted us to return his dog. His response in not-so-kind words was that she was all ours, and we were never to call again.

That was fine with us.

Boones seemed to thrive with our love and care. However, after several weeks, we began to notice that she was a little heavier than what would be an ideal weight for her. Since we knew she was getting plenty of exercise chasing butterflies, jumping for the Frisbee, and retrieving her ball, which the grandkids loved throwing for her, we decided to cut down on her food.

Although she spent most of her time at the house, she was free to come and go as she wished. She was a good dog, and we hadn't had a single complaint from the neighbors. She slept in the doghouse we put on the front porch and seemed to be very content.

One sunny afternoon, I decided to walk the half-mile or so down our gravel road to the mailbox—something I hadn't done in a while, since I'd been getting enough exercise trying to keep up with Boones.

As I approached our nearest neighbor's house, I was surprised to see Boones sitting on the front porch looking very much at home. She came running out to greet me, and Tim stopped his riding lawnmower to walk over and join us. Tim was a middle-aged, divorced father of four, and although we didn't visit often, we got along very well.

"What do you think of our newest family member?" Tim asked with a proud smile.

As I looked around, expecting to see another child or maybe a new wife, he nodded toward Boones, who was nestled up against my legs.

"Our new dog, Bones," he explained, to my surprise.

Caught off guard, I blurted out rather abruptly, "This is my dog, and her name is Boones, not Bones!"

I'm not sure who was more stunned, Tim or me. But after exchanging very similar stories about our conversations with the fellow across the acres, it was easy to see why we both claimed ownership.

Since Tim worked during the day, he had no idea that Boones was spending the entire day at our home. And while I was busy with my family in the evenings, I assumed she was sleeping in her doghouse.

The reason for her quick weight gain suddenly came to light as well. She had been milking her good fortune for all its worth, eating at both houses twice daily.

"Why do you call her Bones?" I questioned.

"Because that's the name on her tag."

"Tim, it's Boones, not Bones," I giggled.

"Guess I need to see an eye doctor," Tim laughed as he checked her tag to make sure.

We decided that I would continue to feed her every morning, and Tim would feed her at night. That way she'd still know she belonged to both families, but would hopefully lose a little of that excess weight.

We ended our conversation by congratulating each other on our newest family member and agreed to keep in better contact. Then I continued my walk to the mailbox with "my" dog by my side.

Our dog-sharing arrangement presented no problems other than a little bump along the way when we noticed Boones was beginning to gain weight again. This time, however, it was not from overeating — it was quite obvious that she was going to be a momma.

Tim and I acted like proud, expectant grandparents. We were confident that we could find good homes for all her pups, but after seeing them, neither of us could resist our picks of the litter. My family chose an adorable little black-and-white male, and Tim's family decided on a beautiful beige-and-white female. We named them Tucker and Lucy.

To this day, we still share Boones, but we also share the two pups. Since they grew up following their mom back and forth across the field between our houses, they've always assumed they have two homes.

We call their momma Boones at our house, Tim still calls her Bones at his, and she's clever enough to answer to both.

~Connie Kaseweter Pullen

Seeing Red

Fun fact: The way a dog's tail is wagging can help people determine his mood.

Our Beagle, Red, stood guard as he and I watched my new husband's vintage Naugahyde furniture get carried into the house. Everything about it was wrong — wrong size, wrong style, wrong color. It was squeezed into our family room like a sumo wrestler in Spandex.

"Honey," I prodded. "We should start fresh. Why don't we get new furniture that we pick out together? Something a little smaller and darker so it won't show dog prints." My husband looked hurt and perplexed. "You don't like it? My stepfather gave this to me. It has sentimental value."

Sentimental value? Who gets sentimental over light tan Naugahyde and a forged-iron coffee table? For better, for worse. I had said these words just two weeks earlier. Is this what they meant? I looked down at Red. "What do you think, pal?

It did not take long for Red to claim one end of the sofa as his resting place. Terrified of thunderstorms, it became his go-to spot whenever the skies rumbled and lightning flashed. There he would tremble and whine until the storm passed. A Beagle-shaped indent formed in the cushion, and scratches marred the surface, the result of Red's attempts to fluff up the spot in preparation for his numerous naps. In time, the dirt he dragged in from the yard, coupled with the oil from his coat, created a dark stain. No amount of scrubbing with detergents and upholstery cleaner would remove it.

Six months after our wedding, I broached the subject again. "Sweetheart," I cooed as I inched sideways along the infinitesimally narrow space between the love seat and coffee table in order to sit next to my husband. "I think it's time we decorate this room in a more adult style. You know, something that says, 'We're married.'"

He looked at me sideways. "Why do we need new furniture to prove we're married? We have a marriage license for that. Besides, Red seems to like it." From the end of the sofa, Red lifted his head. His soulful brown eyes seemed to say, "Give it a rest, Mom."

I tried for the next four years. When a local furniture store advertised a ONE DAY ONLY sale, I propped the flyer against the coffeemaker. When a Craigslist ad shouted "MOVING! MUST SELL DESIGNER FURNITURE FOR A FRACTION OF THE COST!" I forwarded the link to my husband's e-mail. When a flea market displayed a chair-and-a-half that would not usurp the entire family room, I texted a photo with the word "PLEASE?" Nothing worked. Finally, I decided to give it a rest.

One June morning, the kind of intensely hot and humid day that typically spawns thunderstorms, I prepared to go out for a while. Red was curled up on his end of the sofa, basking in the breeze of the air conditioner and oblivious to the heat. I patted him on the head. "I'm going out, Red. You be a good boy while I'm gone, okay?" He thumped his tail against the Naugahyde. He really didn't need a reminder. Red was the quintessential "good dog" that could be left alone for hours without getting into mischief. I never worried about chewed-up shoes or trash strewn about the house.

My errands took about four hours and then I began the drive home. It was only then that I noticed black clouds in the distance. In a matter of seconds, they were on me, spilling their contents in such a torrent it was almost impossible to see. The wind pushed against the trees, bending the limbs at dangerously low angles. An alarm sounded from the car radio, followed by a weather alert: "TORNADO WARNING! SEEK COVER IMMEDIATELY! DO NOT STAY IN YOUR CAR!" I pulled into the nearest parking lot and ran toward the supermarket. I was drenched but safe. Then I remembered: Red! He hates storms!

He must be frantic!

As soon as the rain subsided and all danger was past, I jumped in my car and quickly headed home. As I opened the front door, I yelled, "Red! Red, where are you? Are you okay?" I entered the family room and, to my great relief, Red was calmly sitting on his end of the sofa. I wrapped my arms around him. "I was so worried about you! I know how frightened you are of thunderstorms!" As I held him close, my eyes moved to the corner of the sofa… and I beheld one of the most beautiful sights I had ever seen: a hole. A large, gaping, conspicuous, irreparable, beautiful HOLE! Sofa stuffing was all over the floor, along with torn bits of Naugahyde, but they may as well have been diamonds to me. I took a picture and sent it in a text to my husband. "Please don't be mad at Red. He freaked out during the storm. It wasn't his fault!" I was so thankful he couldn't see me grinning.

When my husband arrived, he surveyed the damage. "Can it be fixed?" he asked.

"I'm afraid not, sweetie. Once Naugahyde is torn, it can't be sewn up." I honestly didn't know if this was true or not, but it sounded plausible. "It looks as if we'll have to get rid of it. And since the love seat and coffee table are hard to match, we'll have to get rid of those, too."

My husband looked crestfallen. "Fine!" he barked. "Call someone to get it out of here!" Really? Finally? Oh, what sweet music to my ears!

It did not take long to find an organization that would take the stuff. Red and I stood on the front lawn and watched the last vestiges of bachelorhood get loaded onto a truck and taken to Naugahyde Hell, or wherever Naugahyde goes when it dies. I looked down into Red's face. "Ya' did good, pal. Thanks." Red's tail waved in reply. I'm not certain, but I could almost swear I saw him wink.

~Laurel Vaccaro Hausman

Well Trained

*Fun fact: If your dog urinates in the house, it's
important to give the spot a thorough cleaning or he
may use the same place as a toilet again.*

Olivia was hard to house-train. Having grown up with Golden Retrievers, I was used to dogs that pretty much trained themselves and usually did so within a day of arriving at our house.

Not so with our darling Terrier-Hound mix. Olivia came to us from a rescue. She and the rest of her litter were abandoned in a drainpipe, and she had a stomach infection, mange and worms, so she didn't have an easy start.

But even after she became healthy, she was reluctant to go outside. She would look up at me with her big, long-lashed brown eyes as if to say, "Why do you want me to go there when there are perfectly good spots inside?" I learned, from our trainer, that Terriers have a bit of a stubborn streak, but once they learn something, they learn it well.

Finally, I resorted to umbilical-cording her, or rather, tying her leash around my waist so that wherever I went, she went. If I caught her crouching, I would rush her outside to the designated spot and praise her for doing such a good job. Once she got the motions of going outside, I had to learn to recognize her cues.

Some dogs bark or scratch or ring a bell by the door. I had to catch Olivia's almost disdainful glance at the door. But I am a quick learner, and she is a solid, though slow learner. Eventually, we got the hang of things — so much so that my husband and I prided ourselves that she would only go in one section of the yard. It was a very tough, but valuable trick for her to learn, but learn it, she did.

It was all well and good until we decided to throw a party one summer, and my husband wanted to build a bar right on the edge of her spot. "What about Olivia's spot?" I asked.

"Oh, we'll just walk her these two days before the party, and I'll take it right down afterward," he assured me.

I thought that was it.

Olivia thought otherwise.

That night, she — who hadn't had a single accident since she learned how to go outside — left a present for my husband under his favorite chair in the living room. "I'm sure it's just a coincidence," my husband told me. "After all, we were out late getting ready for the party."

Another day passed in a flurry of party preparations. Olivia was watching. When the bar remained in her spot, she left another present for him.

But this time, it was smack-dab in the middle of his pillow. She had to have really worked at delivering this directly to him, and I'm pretty sure it was quite deliberate since I had a bunch of clothes tossed on my side of the bed, and not an item of mine was touched.

The next year, my husband set up the bar in a different part of the yard.

The moral? Don't ever mess with a dog's special spot.

~Jeanette Hurt

Reprinted by permission of Jonny Hawkins

The Boxer Rebellion

Fun fact: Boxers got their name because they often use their front legs when they fight, so they look like human boxers in the ring!

"**M**a'am, there is a dog on your roof!" I turned from my flowerbed to the bug-eyed driver and sighed.

"I know — I'll get him down. Thank you." I dropped my shovel and headed to the porch where my Boxer hung his head over the ledge to taunt me. "Yogi, get down. Off!"

His jowls were in a full smile, and I heard the patter of four more paws on the shingles. The two Boxers bounced from roof peak to peak like they had conquered the world. My shouting wasn't working, so it was time for Plan B… bacon. Despite their happiness about being on the roof, Yogi always got a little scared on the way down. If the bacon failed today, I would be forced to crawl up to reach him. The only thing more humbling than climbing on your roof to corral two happy dogs is scooping poop at that altitude.

The recipe to have dogs on your roof is simple: Mix a full-time job and evening graduate school with two smart and ornery Boxers. Add in an exterior stairway covered by shingles that ramps up toward your roof, and simply wait a few months. The garage roof was four feet higher than the stairway roof, so the gap was too high for a creature to cross, right? Not for Yogi.

Yogi was special from the time I got him. After getting my first dog, I started volunteering as a foster mom for the local Boxer rescue. I thought it would be nice for my puppy to have some company during my long workdays.

"Sharla, guess what I have?" The rescue coordinator barely paused on the other end of the line. "It is a three-month-old Boxer that was abused and turned into the pound. The family bought him from a breeder, but they are going through a divorce. He is so malnourished that his wrist bones are soft, and he's kind of walking on them. It might be permanent, but we have some vitamins that may help. And his feet are raw. We have no idea what happened to them. They will need to be soaked and wrapped regularly for a while. Can you foster him?"

After nursing the squirmy, bony, cuddly, little puppy back to health, I knew he wouldn't be leaving my home. With a full belly, his wrists firmed up so that he walked correctly, and his paws healed over time. But some emotional scars remained. Yogi would get very anxious if I was home and he was not with me. Anytime I was in the house, I had a shadow.

I would no more put the dogs outside in the fenced yard, put up my feet and crack a book when Yogi's whining would start. When I ignored his cries to come immediately back inside, he decided that the outside stairway roof could help. Yogi would climb the ramp, stand on the window air-conditioning unit, smoosh his face against the window and fuss at me as I glared back from the couch.

As with any other mischief, I suspect that a cat was to blame for the eventual leap to the roof. My neighbor fed stray cats and my two dogs loved chasing the cats that didn't respect the boundaries. Whatever the cause, once the roof gap was conquered by one dog, the other quickly followed suit. Instead of staring through the slats of a privacy fence, the dogs had full view of the entire neighborhood from the roof. This was perfect for barking at cats and neighbors.

Because the situation seemed equally unsafe and embarrassing, I quickly constructed a barrier. I started at the bottom. I built a barrier with lattice and painted it red to match the fence. Yogi jumped over it. I doubled its height. Yogi got around it. When I reinforced it, the wind repeatedly brought it down.

So I abandoned the bottom barrier and went to work on the top with a spare piece of lattice. Yogi the magician would somehow jump an even larger gap to get around that, too. I wondered if his new maneuvers were even less safe than what I was preventing. After each failed attempt, the dogs would become more excited about the roof, and more courageous in defeating every barrier I tried. I'm not sure what looked more ridiculous — the dogs on the roof or the barriers.

I tried to think like a dog. The problem with my barriers was that the dogs could still see the temptation — the alluring roof. I needed to block their view with a wall. I hunted at Walmart for a solution.

What I found was a folding table. I lugged the table onto the roof. I opened the legs and set it on its side at the top of the ramp to look like a wall. It worked! The dogs saw the barrier and didn't try to jump on the roof. At last, I found peace. My dogs were safe, the neighbors stopped taking pictures of my roof climbers, and all was well. Then it stormed. My table came hurtling off the roof, denting the drain spouts on its way to the ground. The following day, I dragged my wet table back onto the roof. I reinforced the legs with five-pound dumbbells. It was a sight to behold.

With every storm, I became more proficient in knowing precisely where weights needed to be placed on the table legs. The table corners were busted and the inside filled with water, but the barrier remained successful. Each time the table blew down, the dogs would resume their roof escapades until I got it readjusted. After five years, the circus finally ended when I moved to the country, where the house didn't come complete with a rooftop ramp.

Yogi is twelve now and has settled into a more relaxed pace of life. I wonder if he sometimes dreams of being back on that roof, surveying the whole community and barking at invaders.

~Sharla Elton

Encountering the Beast

Fun fact: Great Danes, Mastiffs, Irish Wolfhounds, St. Bernards, and Newfoundlands top most lists of the world's largest dog breeds.

had been walking most of the morning through the Spanish countryside, in my third week of a hike to Santiago. Before leaving home, I had attended a talk on the trip I was about to take. The most important warning was about the wild dogs I would encounter on my trip. Being a cat person, I had never really understood dogs, and so I accepted that there would be feral animals lying in wait for unsuspecting hikers like me. I made up my mind that I would avoid contact with them at all costs.

That had not been difficult so far. Most of the dogs I had encountered had displayed the predicted ferocious traits, but all of them were chained up in the front yards of houses and farms. I was able to pass unmolested.

This day, I was in the process of looking for a place to stop for a sandwich and *café con leche*. The town I saw up ahead looked like it might have a café.

The odd thing about walking into many Spanish villages near midday is that they are often deserted, as everyone is at lunch. This one was no exception.

As I approached, I saw a very large animal standing squarely in the middle of the deserted road, right in my path. In Spain, there has always been a tradition of using very large herd dogs to deal with cow control. The animal I found blocking my way was a prime example of these creatures. It was huge. No wonder they were able to control cows; this dog could have intimidated a rhino. His huge eyes were focused directly on mine as I approached. I looked around, hoping perhaps to see a man in a top hat carrying a chair and whip who could control this beast and allow me to pass! But I was alone, and so I advanced slowly, making myself as large as possible so as not to look like a small, tasty morsel.

The dog's gaze never faltered, and he stood his ground. I moved off onto the grassy edge of the road, and he positioned himself very purposely to counter my move. There was no alternative for me but to pass closely by his salivating jaws. Carefully, I sidled past him, hoping not to touch him or to make eye contact. To say that I was terrified would have been an understatement. Up close, he was way bigger than from a distance; he came halfway up to my chest. I had never seen such a big dog.

When at last I had slunk past him, I was aware that he had turned and was now following close behind me in my walk into the village. Relieved, I made it to the safety of the café where I ordered up my café and *bocadillo* sandwich. As I was hoping to eat my lunch at an outdoor table, I looked out the front window and was glad to see that my tormentor was not visible.

Once back outside, I had no sooner sat down at the table when the dog reappeared, looking even more menacing, if that was possible. Just as I was about to retreat back into the café, he sat at my feet and stared up at me with huge, sad-looking eyes. At that point, I realised that it might be my sandwich that had his hungry attention and not me. The drool coming from the side of his mouth was one of the clues. I broke off a piece of my snack and proffered it in his general direction. It disappeared as if by magic. There was not a lot of chewing done as far as I could see; he just seemed to inhale it. In the end, he got more of my sandwich than I did. At least my coffee didn't hold any attraction for him, so I was allowed to have that for myself. Leaving my backpack in the dog's care, I went back to the café and bought another two sandwiches — one for him and one for me. We sat together in the sun and enjoyed each other's company for the short time available.

With a long walk ahead of me, I got to my feet and pulled on my backpack. The giant dog also rose to his feet, stretched and fell in behind me as I made my way out of the village. I was escorted to the village limits where he stopped, sat down and yawned. I came back and stroked his ears. He stood up, rubbed his huge body against me, and licked my hand as if in gratitude. As I climbed a hill leading out of town, I could feel his eyes watching my progress.

Thinking back now, I realise that he had worked out an efficient little scheme. He would sit and wait for hikers passing through town in the hope that they would visit the café and share their snacks with him. Then he would escort them out of town before returning for the next victim/pilgrim. In the short time I spent with him, I could see that he was a smart animal and had a friendly disposition in spite of his huge size. From that day on, I never felt intimidated by any dog I met on my journey. I felt I had been privileged to have interaction with a doggie ambassador. I also came to realise that I should never judge a dog by first impressions.

~James A. Gemmell

Bailey's Best Christmas

*Fun fact: Visitors to Kent, England, can visit the Dog
Collar Museum at Leeds Castle, which contains more
than 100 dog collars dating as far back as the
15th century.*

I will never forget our Labrador Retriever's sixth Christmas. Our sweet Bailey was solidly built, with a shiny chocolate-colored coat and a happy smile. Adored by family and friends for his gentle disposition, he was the kind of dog that liked everyone. Useless as a watchdog, we always joked that if a burglar intruded, Bailey would just wag his tail and lead him to the silver.

Like any beloved child, Bailey had his own Christmas stocking. Nothing fancy, but it was always filled with some special treats for Christmas — usually something to chew on and a plush doggy toy, although most of the doggy toys seemed to go missing eventually.

But this particular year, Bailey's nose might have been a bit out of joint, because we had a new baby in the house. Anika was stealing some of the attention away from Bailey, who'd been spending a bit more time in the laundry room than usual, sulking.

My mother had knitted Baby Anika a beautiful Christmas stocking that I'd hung on the mantle with the other hand-knit stockings. But a few days before Christmas, that new stocking was missing. The rest were still in place — but Anika's was mysteriously gone. That's when I remembered that I'd spotted one of Anika's favorite baby toys out in Bailey's dog run a few days earlier. The plush yellow duckling that sang "Singing in the Rain" had been lying beak-down in the snow. I rescued the kidnapped duck to find that it was in good shape and still able to sing.

Curious about the missing stocking, I looked out the kitchen window. There, on the freshly fallen snow, I spotted the red-and-green sock. Relieved to find it was in perfect condition, I gave Bailey a good-natured scolding and then returned it to its hook with the others. That's when I noticed Bailey's stocking hadn't even been hung yet. Was he trying to give me a hint? So before long, Bailey's Christmas stocking was hanging too, and we all had a good laugh over it.

Christmas came and went, and the following weekend I joined my mother and sister for a little getaway. That evening, my sister asked if I had liked my Christmas present from her. Caught off guard, I tried to remember her gift, but came up blank. She described the packaging (she's known for beautiful wrapping) and informed me that it contained a very special handmade bracelet. "And there was something special in there for Bailey, too," she said with concern.

Suddenly, I remembered how Bailey had snatched Anika's duck and Christmas stocking and wondered if he'd taken anything else. It actually seemed out of character since he'd never been that kind of dog before. But having a baby around had been an adjustment for him. So I called home and explained the mystery to my husband. He promised to do some investigating and called me back a few minutes later.

Now, I must explain that Bailey's kennel wasn't just an ordinary kennel. It started with a doggy-door that led from the laundry room out into a pretty nice doghouse (with two rooms). And that led out into a large, fenced dog run that he could freely come and go from. Pretty posh for a dog.

"I found the wrapping paper and ribbon and box outside," my husband told me. "So I could tell Bailey was responsible." But he explained that the items that were supposed to be inside the box were missing. "So I crawled into Bailey's doghouse with my flashlight. I found the bracelet and a leather dog collar with beadwork that says

'Good Dog.'"

Of course, we had a good laugh over that one — the "good dog" that had stolen a present from beneath the Christmas tree. My husband reassured me that both items were in excellent condition. "He didn't chew them or anything. But what surprised me even more was that he'd decorated his doghouse."

"Decorated his doghouse?" I wondered if I'd heard him right.

"Yeah. You know the boxes of Christmas decorations that you'd left in the laundry room?"

"The ones that just had leftover decorations?" I asked.

"It looks like Bailey helped himself to some of those decorations. And he's put them in his doghouse."

"You're kidding!"

He laughed. "No, I'm serious. Bailey decorated his doghouse."

It took a few seconds for this to even register. "So Bailey found his Christmas present under the tree, opened it up, then took it into his doghouse that he'd already decorated?"

"And that's not all," my husband said.

"There's more?"

"Yeah. Bailey's got a collection, too."

"A collection?"

Now my husband laughingly described how Bailey had all his plush doggy toys lined up against one of the walls of his doghouse — all the toys that he'd gotten for previous Christmases that we thought had gone missing.

"They're all clean and in great condition," he said with wonder. "Almost as if Bailey and the toys were having a Christmas party together."

We had a good long laugh over that, and after I hung up, I told my mother and sister the story. We marveled over how Bailey had known which box actually contained a present meant for him and how he'd carefully opened it and taken it into his doghouse. And they could hardly believe that not only had he decorated his doghouse with Christmas things, but he had neatly arranged his stuffed pals against a wall, as if to celebrate together. I'm not sure what motivated him, but I think

Bailey's Christmas was a good one. And the words on his new collar, "Good Boy," couldn't have been more fitting. He truly was a good boy!

~Melody Carlson

On the Furniture

Fun fact: The American Kennel Club (AKC) was founded in 1884 and has the largest registry of purebred dogs in the world.

Furniture is for people, not dogs. This had been my steadfast, non-negotiable rule for three decades. My family knew my rule, and dogs, husband and children obeyed.

This was before Landon came into my family's life as a twelve-week-old Golden Retriever. The no-furniture rule was easily enforced at first because none of Landon's new family used the furniture anymore. My daughter sat on the floor propped up against the sofa to watch TV so she could play with him. I lay down on the floor with a few throw pillows to read so Landon could climb all over me. My son had puppy-wrestling matches on the carpet. I sat cross-legged on the floor to groom him and give puppy massages. Landon didn't care about the furniture because we were always joining him on the floor.

When Landon was six months old, I decided he was big enough to stay in the back yard rather than in his indoor crate when we were not home. But I was concerned that he would be afraid all alone in our private, fenced back yard. One day, I went out to run a few errands. I intended to be gone for a short time, but it took longer than I thought. I hurried home in a panic. Would my poor little puppy be scared, lonely, and quivering at the back door?

I parked the car in the garage. Leaving the groceries, I rushed through the house to the back door. No Landon. I searched the shady side yard. No Landon. I looked to the oak grove that surrounded the deck. On the deck is a two-seater glider. And on it was Landon, sprawled across the full length of the glider gently swaying in the breeze. I called his name. He raised his head in a sleepy greeting and rolled onto his back, making the glider rock even more. He looked content, happy and, of course, adorable. "Well, it is only outdoor furniture," I rationalized. Looking back, I suspect this may have been the exact point in time when Landon determined there was a crack he might slip through in my "no dogs on the furniture" rule.

Landon grew into a handsome young dog. He was a superstar in training classes. He learned many words and commands. He passed the AKC Canine Good Citizen exam. He didn't bark or dig in the back yard. He came when called. He picked up items I dropped. He was delightful to new people. He got along well with other dogs. The staff at the boarding kennel and veterinary office adored him. And every chance he got, he made himself comfortable on the furniture.

All too often, I would walk into the family room unannounced. There would be Landon snuggled at one end of the sofa with his head on the decorative pillow. "Off," I would command. "Now!" He would obediently and with great effort get his legs underneath him. Then he would carefully steady himself. Once positioned, he would contemplate the floor as if it were twenty feet away. Then he would look at me as if questioning my cruelty. Eventually, his front legs would slide to the floor, and his hind legs would clumsily follow. This was painful to watch, and it took a minute. It was hard to believe this was the same dog that hiked rugged trails, nimbly bounded up and over boulders, and swam for hours in the lake.

Years later, Landon would stay alone in the house during inclement weather. When he heard my car pull into the garage, he would come to the door to greet me. I would kneel down and offer hugs and kisses. He would have such a sleepy look on his face and would be so nice and warm. I never thought much of this until one rainy, cold day. Returning home from an exhausting day of work, I greeted Landon as usual, then plopped myself in my husband's chair, resting my legs on the ottoman. Both the chair and the ottoman were all warmed up for me. Landon stood by the chair and put his head on the armrest. I glared at him. He lifted his left eyebrow, then his right, and then his left. He would not meet my gaze. No words were spoken, but much was said.

My daughter moved back home after completing college. Although she had few belongings, she asked if she could bring just one item of furniture into our home — her antique upholstered chair. We rearranged the furniture in the TV room and found a spot for the chair. Landon, always part of any goings-on, watched with great interest. We positioned the chair. My daughter, satisfied with the location, went to fall back into the chair, but was not fast enough. Landon jumped on to the chair, curled up and gave a sigh of approval. "Landon, you are like having a bratty, little brother," my daughter said. Thereafter, just like siblings, my daughter and Landon grappled over who had first rights to that chair.

It has been nine years since Landon came into my life, and he and I are now in our senior years. We spend much of our time together. We both have agreed that rules, once so important, are no longer necessary. Now, Landon is invited to join me on the sofa when I read. I sit outside on one patio chair drinking my morning coffee, and Landon sits in the other. We somehow both fit, but not comfortably, on the chair and ottoman to watch TV together. We have spent countless hours on the glider made for two — swaying, thinking and being. I have enough wonderful memories of Landon to last a lifetime, but it just may be that the most cherished memories I will have of this dear dog happened on the furniture.

~Elizabeth Greenhill

Posh Poodles

*Fun fact: Poodles have a wide variety of coloring,
including white, black, brown, parti, silver, gray, silver
beige, apricot, red, cream, sable, phantom and brindle.*

Their names were Nicky and Xandie, and they were two of the cutest apricot/white Toy Poodles you ever saw. Littermates, we received them at ten months of age via a rescue site for Poodles. Their owner was forced to move due to her profession and was unable to take her precious babies with her. We had just lost our black Poodle after thirteen wonderful years, and my son's heart was broken. It began to mend the day we brought the puppies home.

Nicky and Xandie became a very integral part of my childcare business. It was up to them to entertain the many children who passed through my care facility during those years, and entertain them they did! The children also learned how to love and care for a pet, which was something their parents appreciated. Some also appreciated that their child could interact with a pet in my home, leaving theirs "pet-free."

Our newfound loves were very particular about their personal appearance and would groom each other daily. Then they would come to me for "inspection" and strut away proudly when I responded with, "Oh, what a pretty good girl (or boy) you are!" This compliment seemed even more important to them than any edible treat I could have offered them.

Nicky wore a blue rhinestone collar and Xandie a red one. If I accidentally placed the red leash on Nicky, he would sit down and refuse to move until I had the blue one secured to his collar.

We lived in Colorado at the time, and winters there can be brutal. Neither dog would go into the yard for their "daily duties" when it was snowy. My husband had to shovel an area just off the patio for their personal use.

Christmas had just passed, and we were in a severe bone-crushing cold snap, with temperatures well below zero. Adults, children, and dogs were confined inside for days on end. Nicky and Xandie were in "dog heaven." They were the center of attention among the children and they loved playing tag and hide-and-seek (yes, they knew how to play both games), with their only reward being the squeals of joy and hugs from the children.

I had the remains of my Christmas prime rib in the refrigerator and one cold day I got it out to make soup. The dogs looked longingly at the bones and tried everything to get me to give them each one. They were begging and standing on their hind feet, twirling like little ballerinas. Finally, I relented, offering them each a bone with quite a bit of meat on it. My only stipulation was that they had to go outside and chew them on the patio. I let them out the French doors leading to the patio but no sooner had I turned around than Nicky knocked loudly on the door. I opened the door and they both ran into the house with their bones.

"We can't eat greasy meat in the house," I told them, opening the door again and letting them out. Immediately, I heard a pounding on the back door. They ran back in with their bones again.

This went on twice more, and I finally had had enough. I made them drop their bones beside the back step before I brought them into the house. They both gave me a scathing look and proudly walked down the hall to my bedroom, where their beds were.

I turned a bit later and saw them coming back down the hallway. I couldn't believe what I was seeing — Nicky carrying his blue sweater and Xandie carrying her red one!

Laughing, I put their sweaters on them and let them out again. This time, they didn't come in until the meat on those delicious prime rib bones was completely gone.

I removed their sweaters, and they once again sauntered down the hallway... to a much-deserved nap.

~Bette Haywood Matero

Don't Ever Do That Again

*Fun fact: A famous Husky named Balto saved
hundreds of Alaskan lives in 1925 by delivering the
diphtheria serum to their remote area in harsh weather.*

The decision was not an easy one — in fact, I agonized over it for days. I had never boarded Bailey, my beautiful Pyrenees-Husky mix. In fact, we were seldom separated. We had travelled together across the vast width and depth of the United States and through a good part of Mexico.

I would pack our lives in the trunk of the car, open the rear door of the old Buick and, with Bailey in charge of the back seat and me at the steering wheel, we'd spend long days together on the road. She rested her white snout and cold black nose on the armrest and watched every truck that passed. Every now and again, she would nuzzle me or I would stroke her as I talked and she listened. We took leisurely walks every few hours, and when we stopped for the night, she would snuggle down on her blanket on the floor, completely trusting that I would always care for her.

And she believed this to be true until I boarded her at a doggy motel.

Bailey and I were wintering in Arizona when my daughter invited me to drive home to Ottawa, Canada, via Michigan, not only to visit her, but to attend the theater performance for which she had designed the sets and lighting.

It was important to both of us that I attend. However, there was one difficulty — her husband was seriously allergic to dogs. Bailey could not stay with me at their home. It was also not feasible to stay at a people hotel because during the four-day visit I would be out and about to places where she couldn't join me. Usually, when I visited Michigan, it was directly from Ottawa, and I would leave Bailey at home with my other daughter, but this time I had her with me. The only possible solution was a doggy motel.

After considerable research online, and having my daughter obtain glowing references from people who had used this specific facility, I finally booked Bailey's stay. After agreeing to pay for extra walks, special treats and broth with her food, I still hesitated to leave her. Sensing my reluctance, my daughter thought I would be happier if I saw her room. It was a large cage! She had never been caged. Reassurances that it was clean, that she would be safe, have two very long walks a day and that the staff would go out of their way to see to her comforts, I left her. I phoned three times that day to make sure she was okay, was eating and wasn't pining. I phoned each day after that to check on her, and when my visit was over, I followed my daughter through the back roads of Michigan to collect her.

When Bailey was ushered into the reception area, she took one look around and headed directly to my daughter, who she hardly knew. I was being deliberately snubbed. I put it down to being in a strange place. Once she was in the car, I reasoned, she wouldn't be confused.

Calling her, I headed for the Buick. She walked right by it. I herded her back and into the back seat, kissed my daughter and headed for the highway to Canada. Bailey immediately sat, turned her rump to me and looked out the back window. No amount of coaxing would entice her to lay her head on the armrest where I could reach her for her regular head scratches and mommy pats. She stayed this way to the Canadian border and beyond. I stopped at a rest area to stretch our legs, for her pit stop and new-place sniffing challenges. Fastening her extendable leash, I stepped aside so she could jump out of the car. Bailey quickly pulled away from me, staying at the end of her long lead, did her business and barely tolerated my forced petting and hugs. Back in the car, she repeated her angry stance and ignored my existence.

Hours later, we stopped in Oshawa to visit relatives. Bailey happily ran in the door, greeted everyone with tail wagging and doggy smiles, then went to my cousin and sat at her feet with her back to me. I was not in her favor, nor did she want any part of me. I was feeling really guilty and somewhat sorry for myself. Would my dog ever love me again?

Back in the car, I pleaded with her, promising to never, ever board her again. I told her how I wasn't happy at having to do it, how I had phoned every day to check on her. I made promise after promise that it would never happen again. I told her she was a good girl and I was a bad mom.

I'm sure I detected a smirk as her big, woolly white head appeared on the armrest, and her wet nose touched my arm. After seven hours of torturing me, I was finally forgiven.

We were companions for fourteen years. True to my promise, I never, ever boarded her again.

~Molly O'Connor

72

Plastered Puppy

Not-so-fun fact: Alcoholic drinks contain many
ingredients that are toxic to dogs.

"There," I said, adding a final toss to the green salad and turning to face our guests. "We can head for the table."

I grinned at the friends milling around the kitchen of our small Japanese house. We were part of a squadron of U.S. Navy pilots and wives stationed at a base in a rural Japanese town on the Inland Sea. Most of us were newly married, some with babies, and all without any family nearby, so we became closer than just friends. We quickly learned to depend on each other for everything and think of each other as family.

We were jammed in our little kitchen, laughing, as one of the guys asked incredulously, "You mean we're going to eat lasagna Japanese-style? Your house smells like an Italian restaurant, not a Japanese tea room!"

"Sure, why not?" I told him. "Pasta or rice, it all tastes good, even when you're sitting on a cushion on the floor." I envisioned his long legs tucked under our Japanese table, which looked like a one-foot-tall coffee table.

He looked doubtful, but finally nodded his head. Good thing, as it was the only table we owned.

Then it hit me. "Where's the dog?" I asked, looking around and through the sea of legs. Then, louder, "THE DOG! OH NO!"

We almost knocked each other down, pushing through the door to the dining room, where the table was set with plates full of lasagna.

Well, some of them were — three were bare, with only remnants of red sauce smeared on the white china. Our one-year-old Cocker Spaniel was finishing off the fourth plate and headed for the fifth.

"NOOOOO!" I screamed.

Buffy shot me a quick look of utter surprise at my ear-splitting scream, then immediately, another one of indecision — should he grab the next plate of lasagna or look contrite? Only a split second passed as he looked longingly at the meat and cheese as well as the next glass of wine before lowering his head and acknowledging his wrongdoing.

I swear he was smiling. And a kind of "triumph no matter what the consequences" gleamed from his eyes when he next glanced at me.

Bill looped his finger beneath Buffy's collar, saying, "Bad dog!" while banning him to our bedroom and slamming the door.

Fortunately, I'd made a second pan of lasagna to freeze and serve another time. Who knew we'd need it that night? Together, we washed and dried the plates and wine glasses, and returned to sit on the floor for our Italian feast.

Our guests laughed as they downed their dinner but I felt guilty for leaving Buffy in such a tempting situation. It was our fault for setting a dog-high table basically under his nose and then leaving it unattended. Never did I imagine everyone would gather in our tiny kitchen while our pup took full advantage of our lack of attention.

Occasionally during dinner, Bill or I would go check to make sure the puppy was all right. He was sprawled out on the floor at the foot of our bed, definitely breathing but not moving much.

Several times during the night, Buffy woke us with whines and rumbles. When we rose in the morning, we had to stifle our laughter. He had his paw over his eyes to block the light in the most human-like manner but it was obvious he was in distress. I made a sarcastic comment about payback for stealing food and wine, and he groaned audibly. We gave him water, and he spent all day outside where he could come to grips with his sour stomach and raging hangover.

In spite of it all, our puppy learned some valuable lessons and even taught us a few.

Never again would he touch Italian food. Never. Not that it's a normal dietary item for dogs anyway, but he turned away from it throughout his thirteen-year life. He remembered too well how it had made him feel afterward.

Even more telling, he would not go near wine, beer, or any other alcoholic beverage again. One sniff and he would back up and shake his head. That one and only hangover forever taught him about the pain of drinking too much.

Clever dog.

~Jean Haynie Stewart

Precious

My Very Good, Very Bad Dog

My Protective Dog

Fun fact: A Newfoundland named Seaman accompanied Lewis and Clark on their historic 8,000-mile trip in 1804, helping to protect them from bears and other dangers in the wild. He even survived a bite from a beaver.

73

A Furry Affair

Not-so-fun fact: If your dog has a high predator instinct, you probably don't want to get a pet rabbit.

"We can't keep this rabbit," I told my husband, as he stood holding a little brown bundle of fur that he'd found outside a medical complex an hour earlier. Obviously, someone had abandoned the rabbit. Our Golden Retriever, Autumn, stretched her neck to inspect the creature cradled in my husband's arms.

We agreed the rabbit could spend the night in our enclosed back yard, and I'd deal with finding a new home for it the next day. Autumn followed me as I put a bowl of water and lettuce near some bushes.

"Don't worry," I told Autumn. "This yard belongs to you, and you don't have to share it with a rabbit." We went back into the house and locked the rabbit outside. My husband stewed all night about the rabbit's safety. I was fine if an owl ate it.

The next morning, Autumn and I checked on the rabbit. Suddenly, the rabbit bolted from under the bushes and charged directly at Autumn. He ran in big circles around my gentle giant of a dog, as if to say, "I'm the boss here. You might be bigger, but you're not going to hurt me."

Autumn looked as if she had no idea what had just happened. Since Golden Retrievers are hunting dogs by nature, I expected her to chase the rabbit, but no, the rabbit chased her.

That evening, I told my husband, "Thumper (the name he'd given his new pet) has got to go. I won't have a rabbit peeing on my dog to mark its territory." Autumn now smelled like rabbit urine, and Thumper was obviously trying to establish dominance over my dog.

One strong shake of the neck from Autumn and that rabbit would have been history. Instead of hurting the rabbit, Autumn made a game of Thumper's attempts to show his power. In retrospect, I realize Thumper was wild with fear and trying to protect himself from this huge animal, but to my eyes, he seemed aggressive.

When Thumper charged, Autumn barked and lunged forward as if playing with a puppy. Then she started running in huge circles while Thumper ran after her. We watched from the kitchen window as an unusual friendship began to blossom.

Thumper quickly realized that Autumn was no threat, although sometimes she grabbed Thumper's ears in her mouth when she got too excited. I'd holler, "No ears!" and Autumn immediately released the ears.

Even with the instinct, power, and size to kill this small rabbit, Autumn allowed Thumper to control their play and backed off when Thumper ran to his safe place under the bushes. After Thumper caught his breath and Autumn had turned away, Thumper would race from his hiding spot, bolt toward a surprised Autumn, and jump in the air like a Teenage Mutant Ninja Turtle — front paws chopping the air and hind legs kicking toward the dog. The game was on! Autumn barked and charged Thumper, all the time using her "gentle retriever mouth" when grabbing Thumper's fur in her mouth.

As this friendship grew, we allowed Thumper to come in the house more. We trained him to use a litter box and created an area in the family room where he could sleep and eat. Every night, I tucked him into his caged area while Autumn followed us upstairs where she slept in our bedroom.

Each morning, I took Thumper outside to stay in the yard for the day, but Autumn had the freedom to come and go through a dog door. Within days of Thumper's arrival, I noticed the rabbit watching Autumn go back and forth through this rectangular hole with a plastic flap. I could almost see the wheels spinning in Thumper's head: "If the dog can do this, why can't I?"

After watching Autumn for a few days, Thumper pushed his front paw against the plastic flap. It moved! He jumped back. Then, very carefully, he poked his head against the flap. It opened ever so slightly. He stood back and seemed to say, "I think I've got this figured out." As I watched, he took one big hop and jumped through the door. Freedom! Just like Autumn.

Now, he could follow Autumn in and out of the house. And he did — and still does. No more would he be confined to his cage or back yard. While I rabbit-proofed the house by moving electrical cords and closing off rooms with our computers, Thumper moved in permanently.

Just like Autumn, Thumper now stretched out on the family room floor in the evenings and watched TV with my husband and me. Quickly, a one-sided love relationship developed. Thumper pressed his tiny body as close as he could to the dog, while Autumn only tolerated his presence. It was obvious Thumper was falling in love with our Golden Retriever, and he couldn't be close enough to her. Autumn resigned herself to the fact a rabbit was now part of our family and sharing her space. But if we gave the rabbit too much affection, Autumn gently pushed Thumper away with her nose.

Since Thumper was now fully trained to use a litter box, we let him stay out of his cage at night. Soon, he was hopping up the stairs after Autumn and stretching out on our bedroom floor. Once Autumn settled on her dog bed, Thumper snuggled as close as he could next to her. Before they fell asleep, Thumper would lick Autumn's head and body, like a cat washing her kitten.

Today, Thumper and Autumn share our home like good friends, but Autumn has set boundaries. Thumper gets a warning growl if he goes near her food dish, but they share the same water bowl. Whenever I leave the house, I remind Autumn that she's in charge and Thumper must obey her. But I never worry that Autumn will harm the rabbit because she's such a trustworthy dog. When I arrive home, Autumn greets me at the door, and Thumper is usually napping under the coffee table.

Sometimes, we catch Autumn snuggling nose-to-nose with Thumper, but the minute she sees us, she moves. Certainly, she doesn't want us thinking she actually likes this rabbit.

We remind Autumn daily that she's a very good dog for sharing her home with a rabbit.

~Jeanne Getz Pallos

74

The Night Watchman

Fun fact: The only dog that doesn't bark is the African Basenji, one of the oldest dog breeds. Paintings of them have even been found in Egyptian pharaohs' tombs.

"He doesn't look like much of a guard dog," my husband said, as he cupped the face of the yellow Lab puppy and looked into Buster's eyes. He ran a hand over Buster's smooth back and picked up one of his large feet. "But if he grows into these feet, he's going to be big."

We had rescued Buster from a shelter. His previous owners had tried to contain his energy, but the fenced back yard of their city home had not provided enough room for exercise. The neighbors had complained about his barking, and Buster had escaped too many times by digging holes under the fence. The shelter staff thought he would be happier on our farm, where he would have room to run.

We put Buster in a large, fenced-in area with a bowl of fresh dog food and a pail of water. He barked all night. Early the next morning, after a night without sleep, my frazzled husband let him out. We worried we'd spend the rest of the day trying to find Buster, but we shouldn't have. He had found a home and didn't intend to leave. He spent the day napping on our deck. We got him a doghouse with a heated mat and gave him easy access to the warm barn where he could sleep with our other animals. We never locked him up again.

Those first months, my husband and I would look at Buster and wonder if we had made the right choice. We had wanted a guard dog, but Buster loved everyone and spent his days sniffing out the squirrels or chasing rabbits. He greeted visitors with a wagging tail and a sloppy grin.

Buster's favorite spot was a rocking chair on the front deck. He nosed the chair next to the picture window and sat upright on the flowered seat cushion. He would rock and doze.

At Buster's mealtime, he walked back and forth across the deck as he watched us prepare his food. He would emit one of his infrequent barks on hot summer days, until I added more cold water to his bucket. In the evenings, after the boys had finished their outdoor chores, he watched while my sons worked on their homework and I swept the kitchen floor. Buster was happy to once again sit in his chair on the deck, rocking contentedly.

As Buster grew to 140 pounds, so did his devotion. Hour after hour, he ran behind the tractor as my husband baled hay. He was a constant companion to our sons and caught countless balls during their frequent baseball games. Quieter moments were spent curled in the hammock with our youngest son, until another burst of energy would hit and they were off on another adventure, Buster always right by his side, never resting until all the boys were safe inside.

During calving season, Buster loved to sleep in the barn, nestled in the hay next to the new mother and calf, keeping them safe. The cattle learned to stay inside their fence and the deer stayed away from the apple trees when Buster was on patrol.

When our boys were outside playing or riding their four-wheeler, Buster would be right by their sides. The kids spent hours playing with him. He grew to be the kind of dog that earned the respect of strangers, who remarked, "That's the biggest Lab I've ever seen."

In his last years, after a dozen good years as a faithful companion, Buster slowed some. But he was still on patrol, his feet following the path he had tread around our house a million times, the trampled grass trail a testament to his vigilance.

After my husband returned home from work, Buster would settle into his warm doghouse for the night, his black nose visible through the opening. He stirred from his bed only if a car turned onto our driveway or a deer ran across the yard. But on evenings when my husband was away on a business trip, Buster didn't sleep in his usual spot. On those rare nights when I was home alone, Buster was on high alert throughout the night, nestled beneath my bedroom window, warning intruders to stay away.

Every few hours, I would hear Buster make his rounds, his feet following the thin dirt trail around the perimeter of our home. After he was assured all was safe, he returned to his spot beneath my bedroom window until the time came to make another round, another patrol.

Like a night watchman, just keeping us safe.

~Angela F. Foster

75

Juneau

*Fun fact: Whole genome sequencing indicates that
domesticated dogs and gray wolves are descended from
a common extinct wolf ancestor 27,000–40,000
years ago.*

first started my wonderfully fulfilling journey into the world of animal rescue eighty-seven years ago, at the age of ten. Although each creature, large or small, was precious, there was one that formed a special bond with me and will remain forever in my heart.

Born in the mountains, Juneau was the descendant of an adventurous Husky that had invaded the wild-wolf gene pool many generations before her birth. While adopting wild animals of any kind into the home as "pets" or companions is not recommended, Juneau's small percentage of dog genes precluded any thought of abandoning her to the wild where, without wolf parents to guide and nurture her, she would soon perish. This little wolf pup needed someone to care for her, and that someone happened to be me.

When I first met Juneau, she was about four weeks old. Her coal-black fur was thick and soft, with a narrow white streak running down her chest, a trait commonly seen in black tundra wolves. Her fat little tummy caused her to waddle, as her long, thickly furred tail helped her maintain her balance. I fell in love with her at first sight, but wondered for a moment if I could give her the kind of home she deserved. What wolf traits lurked inside that sweet, innocent-looking little body? But as I cuddled her, warm and yielding in my arms, all my doubts and fears vanished. She would be raised with my other canine rescues who would welcome this little orphan as one of their own.

After wrapping her in a blanket, I bade farewell to those who cared as deeply about her future as I did, and climbing into my pickup with my precious little bundle, I headed for home.

Our first night was spent in a mountain cabin. I gave her a bottle of prepared formula after which she eagerly chewed on a small amount of ground meat. When she had finished, I lifted her onto the rough-hewn bed. She crept under the blanket, and we fell asleep together.

When we arrived home, the resident dogs crowded around the latest arrival, sniffing her all over with tails wagging as they welcomed her into the pack.

I continued to give Juneau a bottle for as long as she wanted. I also handfed her, and when she snatched morsels of meat, her sharp little teeth bloodying my hands, I wrapped the meat around a spoon. Without harming her, the hard metal taught her to take food gently and with restraint — a habit that remained with her for the rest of her life. To further enhance the bonding process, I "wore" her in a little sling around my neck, breathing into her nostrils as she breathed into mine. She traveled everywhere with me in this fashion until she grew too heavy for comfort. At six months, she could jump like a deer, and all the fences were raised to a height of ten feet. But we needn't have worried, because Juneau had no intention of leaving home.

As she matured, there were times when she was chastised, but she was never physically punished. A stern word of reproof was all it took for the ears to flatten, the head to lower in shame, and the body to roll over in the classical pose of submission. And because she was always treated with gentleness and respect, she learned to be gentle and loving in return. She settled well into family life, and apart from her super-intelligence and obvious wolf appearance, she was just another dog. At no time during her life was she ever a threat to humans, or even to other animals.

This incredible super-intelligence never failed to amaze us. Spontaneously, she learned to point with outstretched paw at a carton of milk on the counter, or anything else she happened to fancy. She learned to open latched gates and turn knobs. She skillfully used paws and teeth to pull the blankets off me when she thought I should be up (which was usually at dawn), rushing at me with teeth bared, uttering fearsome noises. But the prancing gait and furiously wagging tail assured me that it was all a game.

I remember waking from a deep sleep one night to find Juneau standing over me, two feet on either side of my body, frantically trying to rouse me. As I slowly came to my senses, I smelled smoke. A small fire, caused by faulty wiring, had started, and the carpet was already beginning to burn. Sam, my six-year-old Wolfhound, still snoozed by my bedside, oblivious of the danger. Jenny, our Sheepdog, wandered nervously around the room, aware that something was wrong yet not knowing what to do. But Juneau knew.

For years, a nightly ritual unfolded at dusk. As the skies darkened, Juneau started to pace. Her restless wandering persisted until the door was opened, and she disappeared into the night. Through the window, her dark shape could be seen outlined on the grass, silent and still as she listened for sounds of movement among the nocturnal creatures hidden in the undergrowth. True to her Arctic heritage, deep snow and subzero weather only seemed to enhance her desire for the cold outside world. But before midnight, she was at the back door, ready to rejoin the only family she had ever known.

Now she is gone, but I remember Juneau on fall days when the mountain air is cool and crisp, and the aspens turn to brilliant canopies of red-gold. I see her flitting across meadows, joyously free, poetry in motion, but always ready to return to my side at my command. To her, I was always the alpha, the leader of the pack.

One moment remains imprinted on my memory as if it were yesterday. I was walking in the high country with Juneau and two of our other dogs. Sam was trotting ahead, while Jenny was on some special mission of her own. Juneau was exploring a wooded area a hundred yards away. I was bringing up the rear when, stepping on some loose rocks, I lost my balance and headed down a steep incline on my back. At the bottom, I lay motionless, stunned by my fall.

Within moments, Juneau was at my side. As she stood protectively over me, nose scenting the air and eyes scanning for possible danger, I experienced an indescribable sense of safety. Rigid and alert, she stood guard over me until I struggled painfully to my feet. Then she was off again like the wind, happily investigating every little scent that wafted to her keen nostrils. Sam and Jenny stood at the bottom of the incline, gazing in mild surprise as they wondered what had happened. But again, Juneau knew.

Juneau died peacefully in my arms at the age of fourteen years, five months. I still miss her, squeezed between the counter and my knees as I prepare her evening meal; I still miss her warm body pressed against mine at night; I miss the music of her voice — the haunting wolf call that was her only contribution to the wild she never knew. I miss Juneau, my beautiful, gentle wolf dog more than words can tell.

~Monica Agnew-Kinnaman

76

Extended Litter

Fun fact: A pregnant dog will usually lose her appetite
about a day before delivering her puppies.

It was the Fourth of July and my neighbor decided to give the neighborhood its own personal display of loud but beautiful fireworks. Hershey, my four-year-old mixed-breed dog decided that fireworks were too loud and dangerous. As soon as the first blast exploded into the air, leaving brilliant colors in the clear night sky, she began to pace.

Hershey had given birth to eight puppies only a few short weeks before and she perceived the fireworks as a possible danger to her babies. She nervously paced from room to room in the house. Eventually, she decided she wanted a closer look at the fireworks, so I brought her outside.

Once outside, Hershey began pacing all over again. There was a break in the display, and she wasn't sure where to look for the danger. Just as she was calming down, a bright blue firework whizzed through the air and exploded with a bang. Hershey ran straight for the house door. When I let her back inside, I assumed she would go straight to her puppies, but she didn't. I was curious about what she would do next, so I followed her as she began another tour around the house.

To my surprise, her first stop was to the bed where my younger daughter lay under the covers fast asleep. My daughter was curled up facing the wall, and Hershey couldn't see her face very well. Hershey solved the problem by placing her front paws on the bed and leaning over until she could reach close enough to sniff my daughter. I still wasn't sure what she was doing, so I continued to watch.

Hershey checked my older daughter next. She was still awake and on her cell phone like a typical teenager. Hershey sniffed her quickly, but not for long since she could see she was still awake.

Hershey left my daughters' room and headed into the room containing my two sons and their bunk bed. My older son was sitting on the lower bed, awake, which meant he only required a quick sniff.

But my younger son was more of a problem, as he was in the top bunk. Hershey couldn't put her front paws on the bed to give him a quick look and sniff. She also couldn't see him very clearly from her position on the floor. There was no easy way for her to reach him. What she chose to do surprised me.

She sat down on the floor and stared at my son without moving an inch. When my son moved in his sleep, and she was satisfied that all her human babies were okay, she returned to her puppies.

The fireworks continued to entertain the neighborhood outside for another twenty minutes. Hershey paced the house and checked on her litter to make sure they were all right until the last firework. On that Fourth of July night, I realized that as far as Hershey was concerned, my kids were a part of her litter that needed to be watched over. It felt good to know my dog was willing to protect my children as though they belonged to her.

~Keysha G. Cass

77

Oreo

*Fun fact: If you chase your runaway dog, it may cause
him to run more, but if you run away from him, he
may chase you and you can secure him that way.*

hen you live on a farm, people are always dropping off
stray animals. They leave dogs and cats, and once we
even watched someone open a car door and place an
opossum on the road. So we weren't surprised when a
black-and-white Border Collie mix showed up on our porch one day.
Usually, we called the local animal shelter to pick up the strays, but
my young son Alec fell in love with this dog instantly, and within an
hour, he had named him Oreo.

Within a day, I could see how he would cause havoc in a house.
The great outdoors itself barely seemed enough space for him to run.
When he was let out of his pen, he became a black-and-white blur of
fur darting all over the place at breakneck speed. His high energy was
entertaining, but also wearing. He never seemed to tire of running, of
jumping on people, or of barking.

He barked incessantly, not only at strangers or wild animals, but
at wind, leaves, and snowflakes. Sometimes, at 2:00 a.m., I thought
he must be barking at the dark itself. He was also a world-class escape
artist, wriggling loose from every sort of collar ever devised, and jumping
over his enclosure fence with the agility of a white-tailed deer.

In an attempt to rid him of some of his excess energy, I often took
him on long walks. They never seemed to tire him out, and I soon got

tired of releasing him from the leash as soon as we reached the fields, only to have him return covered in the stench of some dead animal. The last straw was the day I reached for his collar to connect the leash and got a handful of stinky, gloppy cow manure. From that day on, it was my husband Gary's job to leash him up for walks.

One day in late summer, Gary, Alec, and I walked with Oreo to the edge of the hayfield and unhooked the leash. He took off on his normal sprint across the lush, green fields and soon disappeared over the crest of a hill. My family walked the tractor path along the fence at a much slower pace, looking for four-leafed clovers and wondering when the sickle pears would be ripe enough to pick when suddenly we heard barking behind us.

We turned to see two unfamiliar dogs speeding toward us, and they did not look friendly. Ears back, teeth bared, they flew toward us over the dirt path. Gary shoved Alec and me toward a tree with some low-hanging branches. "Get Alec in the tree," he ordered as he picked up a heavy stick. Heart pounding, I hoisted Alec onto a limb, and Gary squared off to face the attacking dogs and give us time to get into the tree.

Suddenly, a black-and-white streak shot over the hill and slammed into the bigger of the two dogs with such force that it tumbled into the other stray. The aggressors scrambled to their feet, but before they could get their bearings, Oreo wound in between them, over their backs, and around them in a tight circle, knocking them to the ground again and again. In less than a minute, the invaders had had enough, and they turned tail and ran back in the direction they came from. Oreo was hot on their heels until we couldn't see any of them anymore.

Shaken, I lifted Alec from the tree. "Is Oreo going to be okay?" he asked, turning in my arms, searching the knee-high alfalfa with anxious eyes.

"I hope so," I said, meeting Gary's worried gaze. Our wild, crazy, sometimes infuriating dog had just saved our lives. I only hoped he hadn't paid for ours with his.

We walked back toward the gate. Gary still carried the stick, and I carried Alec. We had almost reached the end of the field when Oreo came trotting up calmly from the opposite direction, his long, pink tongue lolling. He must have chased the interlopers in a giant circle, all the way to the far borders of our land.

"Oreo!" Alec squealed and twisted out of my arms to drop to the ground. He threw his arms around Oreo, and the three of us lavished our proud dog with praises and pats along his soft fur. His tail wagged happily as he soaked up the attention.

Finally, Gary said, "Let's go home. I bet Oreo needs a drink after all that running."

I grabbed his collar to attach his leash for the short walk along the road.

"Oh, Oreo!" I said in dismay as I discovered my fingers covered in manure again.

"Don't yell at him, Mom," Alec said. "He's a good dog."

I smiled and wiped my hands on the grass until I could wash them at home, then gave Oreo a grateful pat on the head, well away from his collar.

"You're absolutely right, Alec," I said. "He's a hero."

~April Serock

A Light in the Heart

*Fun fact: Some animal shelters test how a dog behaves
around cats so they can advise people on whether the
dog they want to adopt is "cat-friendly."*

"Has anyone seen Charge?" I murmured, only half-expecting a reply. The kids were running around the house, each doing their own thing, and my husband was watching the football game. So I made a quick check of the bedrooms and looked out in the back yard. Since she had only been out of sight for a few hours, I wasn't overly concerned. I assumed she must be under one of the kids' beds, hiding from all the chaos that was normal for a Sunday afternoon in our home.

Charge was a homely, mixed-breed canine, to put it kindly. It wasn't her fault; she was simply gifted with the worst appearance traits from each of the breeds in her background. She was about the size of a Cockapoo, with gray-and-black wiry hair, short legs, and a long straggly tail. She constantly cowered when strangers approached, which definitely did not help her appearance. But she had a heart of gold, and we loved her.

My husband had found Charge wandering along the freeway one day on his way home from work. She looked as though she hadn't eaten in weeks, so he stopped and coaxed her into the car with bits of his leftover lunch. Not knowing what to do, he brought her home with the hope of finding her owners or at least a loving family that would take her.

However, once she was in the house, the kids were bound and determined not to let her go. After a day or two of whining and begging, we reluctantly gave in and told them we could keep her — a decision I never regretted.

After observing her actions for a few days, it was obvious that she had been abused. She was extremely untrusting and afraid of everyone. In time, though, she came to love the kids and slept on their beds every night.

Charge was exceptionally nurturing with the children. I wondered if the fact that she had been mistreated had conditioned her to be protective of those who were hurting.

Every time the kids cried, Charge would run to them and tenderly offer her comforting paw. This worked wonders when they were injured, but it more or less defeated the purpose when they were whimpering during a time-out!

Unlike our mamma cat, who had recently given birth to a litter of five, Charge would have been an awesome mother. Sadly, she was never blessed with puppies. We sometimes joked that she was too homely to attract suitors.

When I was finally able to get everyone's attention at the dinner table, I asked again if anyone had seen Charge. After a unanimous "No," I thought it would be a good idea to take a look around the neighborhood.

"Who wants to go look for Charge with me?" I hollered as I opened the door of the hall closet and reached in to get my shoes.

"CHARGE!" I screamed, because there she was in the closet! She looked up at me from inside the kittens' box as if to say, "Shhh, I just got them to sleep!"

We usually kept the closet door open a bit so Mamma Cat could go in and feed her litter, but she always left as soon as they finished nursing. Apparently, Charge knew they needed more Mamma time and was more than willing to help out.

The kids giggled with glee upon seeing the dog in with the kittens. My husband shook his head and quipped, "Only you, Charge. Only you!"

Charge continued to mother the kittens until they were placed in their new homes. She may not have been an attractive dog, but as Kahlil Gibran said, "Beauty is not in the face; beauty is a light in the heart." Charge truly had that inner beauty.

~Connie Kaseweter Pullen

Reprinted by permission of Bruce Robinson

Our Guardian Angel

Fun fact: Put a rescue alert sticker near your front door to alert firefighters that pets are in the home.

I drove the two-thousand-plus miles across country from Detroit to Los Angeles with my two young children in the back seat and all my important worldly possessions stuffed into my old Chevrolet. In other words, I packed sheet music, albums and stacks of writing tablets. As a lyricist/composer, I was arriving in Southern California to join the newly opened Motown Records as a contract songwriter. The first thing I did was rent a small, three-bedroom house in Hollywood, close to the Sunset Boulevard offices of my employer. I rented furniture and an upright piano. After all, I was a songwriter and had to have my writing tools on the premises.

The day after we arrived in California, I ran into an old friend from Detroit who wanted to move closer to town. She suggested we become roommates. I agreed, thinking of it as a blessing because the cost of living in Los Angeles was four times higher than Detroit. Splitting the rent with my friend sounded good to me. Marthea moved in the next day. Between her stuff and my stuff, there were boxes everywhere. We were slowly getting around to unpacking, but between the kids, working and getting adjusted to a new environment, I felt overwhelmed. Marthea hadn't been there a week when one of her brothers came to visit. Bernard arrived with a bright smile, a bandana tied around his head, a free spirit and a German Shepherd on a long leash. The dog was friendly and liked people. My six- and seven-year-old children were thrilled to have an animal visit because we had always had a cat or dog at home in Detroit.

The brown-and-white German Shepherd's name was Mordecai, and he made himself at home, the same way his master did. My friend's brother had dinner with us and then fell asleep on the couch. To my surprise, he was still there the next morning. Another week went by, and Marthea tried to explain why her visiting brother was still sleeping on my couch and why his dog was still begging for table scraps. She promised that he would be gone by the end of that week. Bernard, she explained, was just waiting for an apartment to be painted, and then he was moving into his own spot. Meanwhile, the children had bonded with the delightfully friendly dog. Mordecai loved chasing the children and being chased. Although the large canine was always underfoot, I had also grown to love the animal. He was house-trained and wasn't a noisy, barking dog. I appreciated that.

One hot, summer Saturday, we decided to take my kids to the ocean. We were all pretty amazed at the expansive Santa Monica beach, and the endless blue-green water was inviting. We spent all day racing in and out of the salty sea. As we drove back to Hollywood, we were pretty exhausted. The kids fell asleep five minutes into the forty-minute drive, and my roommate could hardly keep her eyes open. A thick fog rolled in as we drove, and the air suddenly turned cold. After bathing the children and washing the sea out of my hair, I collapsed in my bed. We were all knocked out.

Suddenly, Mordecai's cold nose was nudging my arm. Then he whined and pressed his damp nose against my cheek, resting huge paws on the side of my mattress and standing on his back legs. That got my attention. He'd never done that before. I sat up, disoriented at first, and glanced at my alarm clock. It was 3:00 a.m. "What is it? What do you want at three in the morning? You want to be let out?"

That's when I smelled the smoke. I leaped out of bed and ran to the living room. As usual, Marthea's brother was fast asleep on my couch, snoring loudly, and just five feet away from him sat a stack of still-unpacked cardboard boxes. One of them was sitting on top of the iron grate that covered the heating duct in the floor. The heat had come on automatically and the cardboard had caught on fire.

I raced to the kitchen with Mordecai close behind, watching my every move and whining. I filled the first pot I saw with water and raced back, dousing the fire with the pot of water and pulling the box off the dangerous duct. I started calling out loudly, "Fire! Fire!" to awaken the rest of the family. Mordecai joined in, suddenly barking loudly. Everyone woke up and we opened all the doors and windows to let the smoke escape. We sat huddled together on the couch, shaking from the experience. I felt thankful and blessed. After all, if it hadn't been for Mordecai, we could have burned down the entire house and been killed in the fire.

I will always be grateful for that friendly dog that saved our lives that night. Bernard moved into his new apartment a few days later, and I didn't miss him that much, but I did miss his dog, our guardian angel.

~Dee Dee McNeil

80

Showing the Way

Fun fact: Dogs' hair may turn white as they age,
especially around the eyes and muzzle.

Heidi came into our lives as an abused, frightened Miniature Dachshund who had been born, raised, and used as a "breeder" in a puppy mill. Five years and ten litters later, she and thirty-five other puppy-mill dogs were rescued by the Tri-County Humane Society in Boca Raton, Florida.

From the moment I saw her huddled in the back corner of her cage, I knew I would take her home and give her a new life. But it would be our dog Sheba who showed Heidi how to live.

Heidi had never been potty-trained, and the shelter warned it might never happen. Her life had been spent in a wire cage inside a warehouse. She had never done all the things that puppies and dogs do. While Sheba never had a litter, she seemed to instinctively understand that she needed to train Heidi as if she were a new puppy. Whether she was walking on a leash, doing her "business," riding in the car, or playing outside, she would always turn around to Heidi as if to say, "This is how I do it — you can do it, too!"

Heidi watched and emulated everything Sheba did, and slowly she began to live a normal life — including using the outdoors for elimination. She learned to walk on a leash and even off-leash. She began to play, run after lizards, chase squirrels and even play with toys. There was less timidity and more energy; there was less fear and a lot of love expressed by a sweet, sweet dog. Heidi and Sheba became inseparable. Today, where Sheba goes, Heidi follows as her sidekick.

Seven years have passed since Heidi came into our home. Both dogs are showing signs of age; Sheba, being two years older, has more discernible issues. She is partially deaf, and her vision is going. It is now Heidi that is helping Sheba. While Sheba does not hear us enter a room or come home after being away, Heidi does. She will get up and go over to Sheba and wake her up, as if to say, "Hey, they're home. Let's go say, 'Hello.'" When Sheba's vision prevents her from seeing, Heidi shows her the way.

While people say they are just dogs, I say that Sheba and Heidi have shown us great intelligence, patience and love. As is part of the cycle of life, children often become parents to their parents. This is true for Sheba and Heidi. As my husband and I are sporting a few signs of aging ourselves, seeing Sheba and Heidi care for each other reminds us of what love is all about.

~Loretta Schoen

81

Chicken Soup for the Soul

Suzi Saves the Day

Fun fact: Dogs' exceptional hearing may make them more sensitive to loud noises, like fireworks exploding.

Just four blocks from my house, the Fourth of July parade starts to line up. My dog and I sit down on the grass to watch.

Political candidates straddle the back seat of convertibles. Marching bands step in place aided by the rat-tat-tatting of drums.

Full-grown men decked out in exotic costumes, including tall hats with tassels, push little bumper cars into place and squeeze inside. Engines roar, making loud popping noises. POP. BANG.

At the first BANG, Suzi, my Boxer–Golden Retriever mix, jumps up, eyes dilated, the fur on her back standing straight up. She does an about-face, tugs the leash, drags me up off the grass and starts heading in the opposite direction.

I say "NO," but at sixty-one pounds of determined dog, she out-muscles me.

Every dog obedience command I ever learned comes tumbling out, one after another: "SIT! STAY! DOWN! LEAVE IT! BAD DOG!"

But she has selective deafness. Suzi then does something I've never seen her do before or since. She squares her shoulders, expands her chest, puts her head down and takes one deliberate step away from the parade, then another step.

My dog is an ox dragging a plow behind her. I, the plow, follow, whining, trying to turn back, to no avail.

One block. Two blocks. Three blocks. Then finally home. Suzi places a front paw on the back door and looks at me. The message: "OPEN THE DOOR NOW!"

I open the door. She collapses on the kitchen floor, panting, mission accomplished. My four-legged protector has brought her human out of danger and into the only safe place she knows — home.

Suzi first came into my life quite by chance. Her mom, a purebred Boxer, was destined to mate another Boxer, but along came a Golden Retriever at the right time.

Two friends got three girls from the unwanted litter. I got a dinner invitation. They knew I was looking for a dog but needed help getting there. I'd lived with cats for years. Change is hard. After all, you don't have to walk cats.

All the pups were lively, but Suzi was the one that crawled up into my lap, sighed and went to sleep.

I was a goner.

The day I took her home, she whimpered in the car. I sang lullabies to her, the same ones I sang to my three sons when they were little years ago. She fell asleep.

We bonded big time — playing with toys, exploring the neighborhood. Walking with a dog is so different from walking alone. Dogs I never knew existed came to their fence lines to greet Suzi. I met new people and their dogs. She expands my world, and I am grateful.

After she was grown, about two years old, we started doing 5K races together, and she even became part of newspaper stories I wrote on getting a new dog park in town. A chapter in my gardening book, *Florida Gardens Gone Wild,* tells about the day she danced with a butterfly in the back yard.

Her only phobia is anything that sounds like gunshots — say, fireworks and those little car engines.

While Suzi panted on the kitchen floor after rescuing me on the Fourth of July, I had an "a-ha moment."

All this time, I thought it was my job to take care of her, to keep her safe and happy 24/7. It was all about me being in charge, being the alpha dog. Never once did it occur to me that she has a job, too, and her job is, well, me.

Suzi's 24/7 job — stay close while walking, share snacks in the evening, let me dress her up sometimes, sleep back-to-back, remind me to get going so we have time for her morning walk.

Every day when I come home from work, she turns herself into a pretzel at the front door, twisting in two, so glad to see me. Let the laughter begin.

She takes her job so seriously that she dragged me from danger to safety that Fourth of July. I feel humbled, protected and loved.

Two-legged humans come and go in our lives, but Suzi always has my back. So when people ask me, "Do you live alone?" I answer, "No, there is Suzi. She takes care of me."

~Lucy Beebe Tobias

Chicken Soup for the Soul.

Falling for You

Fun fact: The first guide dog organization in the
United States, The Seeing Eye, was opened in 1929.

M y family had been getting fluffy puppies every year — boundless energy in the form of a German Shepherd, a Golden Retriever, or a Lab — to train them as Seeing Eye dogs. Seven weeks old and curious, each puppy liked to snuffle into the crook of my arm and fall asleep as I watched TV and did my homework. Little did they know they would be evaluated later for a very grown-up responsibility.

We started doing this while I was in middle school, and by the time I was in college, we were on our sixth puppy. "His name is Kramer," Dad said, holding the Golden Retriever up to the camera so I could see him via Skype from my study abroad in London.

All semester, I would Skype my parents and siblings, and Kramer would be lifted to the camera, licking it with a long pink tongue. Later, he'd jump on a desk or an iPad. I'd say hello, and he'd bark. "He's sweet," I'd say, never having touched the dog.

"He'll never pass," my brother said.

The Seeing Eye is an exceptional organization, the oldest guide agency in the United States. We had each puppy for about a year — a foster situation. We were in charge of teaching it basic commands: sit, rest and come. The Seeing Eye did the hard stuff — and the hard stuff included deciding which dogs would continue in the program. We'd only had two out of five dogs pass up to that point, which was about average.

"Why won't he pass?" I asked.

My brother smiled fondly at Kramer, tilting the camera so I could see him resting his head, with his big droopy jowls, on my brother's lap. "He's a lover," my brother said. "Not a fighter."

When I came home for Christmas, I met the famous Kramer. He was sweet, loving to cuddle on the floor to warm us up after being out in the snow. I kissed him goodbye more than I kissed my family. After all, I'd be seeing my siblings and parents again, but I had another nine months abroad and Kramer would go back to The Seeing Eye before I got home.

Or so I thought.

In August, my brother picked me up at the airport, and it was sweltering. "I have a surprise," he'd written in an e-mail just before I boarded the plane out of London. "Don't worry; it's a good one."

I'd spent the flight trying to think of what my brother could possibly tell me. Had he proposed to his girlfriend, the one he'd been dating for a year? But they were only eighteen, and going to different colleges. Did he get us tickets to a New York Giants game? Sign up for the New York Marathon? Cure cancer?

Kramer greeted me in the car, draped across the back seat where my brother shoved my luggage. I squealed at the sight of him. "He failed?"

"I drove all the way up to The Seeing Eye to get him." My brother rubbed Kramer's ears and pressed his forehead against the dog's big, blocky face. They both heaved big sighs of contentment. "Now he's all mine. He's my mascot. Just a warning, though," he pointed at me, emphasizing his point in the airport parking lot, "he's a lover, not a fighter."

"You've told me that before."

"You'll see what I mean."

We drove to our house, a solid two-story in the New Jersey Pine Barrens, where another surprise awaited: a party in full swing. My uncle got up to pat me on the back, and Kramer brushed up beside me as my uncle squeezed and squeezed.

Then I got lifted off the ground. "Uncle John!" I yelled. "Put me down!" I screamed, and everyone laughed even as my uncle dragged me to the pool.

No one moved to help me except for Kramer.

Kramer jumped up and knocked Uncle John away from me. My uncle nearly fell in the pool, and I just stood there, panting, as Kramer licked my hand.

"Good boy," I murmured. Everyone at the party was laughing—everyone except me, my uncle, and Kramer.

That was just the beginning of Kramer showing his "lover" instincts. He would stand over toddlers if they fell down while trying to walk, protecting them until they could get back up again. He'd go from room to room, making sure everyone was safe and accounted for. He'd nudge the new Seeing Eye puppy toward the food bowl first, making sure he had enough to eat before he would eat himself. And he abhorred violence in all forms. Play-fighting, tickling, even raised voices, would make him jump in between whoever was quarreling as if he could bodily stop the madness.

This all culminated in an event that happened right before I left for my sophomore year of college. I'd taken Kramer with me to meet my friends for a picnic.

I was really meeting Lucy, but she'd insisted on bringing her boyfriend, a piece of work I'd never approved of whom we will call Rodney. Rodney was the type of person who tried to control who Lucy talked to and what she wore. He'd told her she shouldn't apply to any college except the one he was going to, and he threatened to kill himself until she complied. He's the type of guy who kicks dogs, and that's all you need to know about him.

We'd set up the picnic on a bank next to a river. Every once in a while, someone would float past in a tube and we'd wave, but mostly it was the four of us: me, Lucy, Rodney, and Kramer. We talked about schoolwork and movies. I didn't say anything about the deep bruises under Lucy's eyes. I'd said it so many times, I was afraid she would stop seeing me for good.

But this was a nice day. Good weather, and Lucy was being funny, and Rodney was being civil. That's when I realized I'd forgotten the tray of brownies in the back of my car.

"Go get them," Lucy said, waving me away. "I'll watch Kramer."

"It'll be tough," Rodney quipped. Kramer hadn't moved for an hour.

The car was only a three-minute walk back through some trees, and those brownies were so good, warm and moist. "I'll be right back," I promised.

Lucy says the fight started because Rodney told her she shouldn't eat brownies because she was getting too fat. Rodney said it started when Lucy pushed against him, and his foot fell in the water. The bottom line is that a fight did start, and it was a loud one.

I was walking through the trees when I heard it—Lucy pleading and screaming. I dropped the brownies and ran, heart pounding.

When I got back to them, Kramer was standing on Rodney's shoulders and hips, teeth bared, while Lucy sobbed. There was a red spot on her cheek that would later turn into a bruise.

"Get this dog off of me!" Rodney yelled. Kramer growled again.

I went over to Lucy and folded her into a hug. "I don't know what you're talking about, Rodney," I said, patting my thigh in a gesture that Kramer knew meant "come." He did, trotting over and plopping down at my feet, keeping his eyes on Rodney. "Everyone knows Kramer's a lover, not a fighter."

~Katie Avagliano

83

Chicken Soup for the Soul

A Good Nanny

*Fun fact: "Nanny dogs," also called "nursemaid dogs,"
are especially fond of children.*

After our dog, named Bear-doggy, died, I had to admit I enjoyed the peace and quiet. There was no more letting him in and out, no feeding and watering, no cleaning up after him. Of course, I missed him terribly, but I did notice the reduction in my workload.

I hoped my husband would notice how nice things were now. The hallway tiles were clear of metal bowls and spongy puddles. There was no giant animal to step around everywhere we walked, and there were no more wee-hour treks outside for a canine gut sickened by sneaking chicken food. I hoped the children would relish the fewer daily chores: no more feeding, watering, or bathroom breaks in the rain or freezing darkness of our Alaskan winter. Maybe we could be done with dogs.

Alas, one Saturday several weeks after poor Bear's death, my husband and eldest son, fifteen at the time, came home with another animal rescued from the shelter—a scary-looking dog with a huge head and lots of muscles. Even his tail was strong. A Staffordshire Bull Terrier. I blanched.

"He's sweet," they said.

"Look at his face," they said.

"All he wanted to do when we took him out was sit next to us," they said.

"They're called nanny dogs in England," they said.

My son named him Hondo after a favorite Louis L'Amour character.

But I didn't trust the dog, and I was mad at my menfolk. I remained tense and constantly on alert for two days while everyone else welcomed him and glared at me.

Then one afternoon, I stretched out on the couch with our baby, both of us exhausted after a poor night's sleep. Hondo, who refused to believe that I didn't like him, marched over and sat right down next to us, facing outward like some sort of protector. I remembered the nanny-dog sobriquet and softened somewhat as I wondered if it was true.

After a minute, my baby, now heavy with sleep, shifted, and his bare arm flopped down to hang over the side of the couch. And the dog noticed. He turned and gently — so very gently — nosed the baby's chubby arm back up and into the crook of my arm. I think I stopped breathing for a few seconds. He lifted his eyes, and we regarded each other for a short time: Hondo calm and serious, and me surprised and contrite. He then turned back around and remained our gentle sentinel for the duration of our twenty-minute rest. I never did sleep that afternoon, but marveled over the unexpected degree of compassion this dog exhibited. I smiled for hours afterward. What a good nanny.

And he remains so, five years later. Where our children gather, there he sits. When someone naps on the couch, there he quietly keeps watch. Whatever the kids want him to do, he complies, from hours hiking on mountain trails to hours lying still if someone thinks his tummy makes a good pillow.

This scary-looking beast has become a cherished watchman. I'm sorry I didn't appreciate Bear-doggy when he was with us. I'm certainly appreciative of the way Hondo, our good nanny, has improved our lives.

~Allison Howell

Maggie

My Very Good, Very Bad Dog

My Working Dog

Fun fact: Laika became the first dog in space when the former Soviet Union sent her up in Sputnik II in 1957.

84

Misty's Tilted Halo

Not-so-fun fact: Distracting a service dog while she's working could be dangerous to her handler, so do not pet or speak to a service dog.

"Oh, I see you've got one of those angels on earth!" exclaimed a woman who saw me at the park with my first guide dog, Misty. Of course, the public has a misconception that guide dogs are flawless. I smiled and nodded. I couldn't tell her that my guide's halo occasionally tilted. In fact, Misty had just been distracted by a duck and almost pulled me into the nearby pond.

When onlookers see a well-behaved guide dog, that's not an accident; it is hard work for the dog handler. Practicing good dog-training skills is a task I work on daily. A blind owner must give the dog constant praise for good behavior or gentle correction when it makes a mistake or becomes distracted. It's a delicate challenge to discipline my best friend, my buddy that I need to trust.

Stepping into busy streets and walking around construction sites are just two of the dangers we overcome together. Being generous with affection and setting limits have positive results with my dog. A friend and fellow student at the Seeing Eye thinks so, too, saying, "I wish I had gotten my guide dog before I raised my kids. I would have used praise and consistency more."

Misty did a great job looking out for my needs, but she also managed to take care of hers. One day, she skillfully navigated me through a bustling store during the holidays. I was distracted by the commotion. Babies cried, cash registers clinked, bags rustled, and Christmas carols blared on a sound system.

"Can I pet your dog?" other shoppers asked me.

"No, I'm sorry, she's working." Misty's beauty and gentle eyes attracted people like a magnet, but she needed to pay attention to me, and all the hazards in our path. Through the harness handle, I felt my dog move more cautiously, so I sensed obstacles and cramped aisles.

We were ready to go home when I realized that I hadn't said "good girl" for keeping me safe. What an oversight on my part, since our shopping trip was without any flaws, not even a stumble or bump. I heard a "whoosh" as the electric doors parted, and I bent down to give her a pat. That was when I felt something clenched in her jaw — a spongy, round object. My good dog had snatched a ball from the toy department. I went back into the store to pay for the ball, which became her holiday bonus.

Despite her training, good manners, and charm, Misty was full of surprises. One evening, we took her to the theater with us. As the house lights were going down we dashed to our seats. My husband helped me peel off my coat, and then I told Misty "sit." A thud and a sigh let me know she was down, but I learned later, not all the way. The man seated in front of her must have been alluring, full of animal magnetism to my dog. Before lying down on the floor, she lunged forward, and I heard her give him a "kiss" on the back of his ear. My husband told me that the man turned to look at his wife with a huge smile on his face.

Misty gave me freedom and dignity and she was a responsible, careful guide dog; but she was still a dog at heart. Once, at our home during one of our yuletide parties, a guest asked, "What's that sticking out of your nativity scene?" I knelt down and felt around under the decorated tree. And there it was — a stash of buried dog biscuits!

~Carol Chiodo Fleischman

Reprinted by permission of www.offthemark.com

85

Working for Cheese

Fun fact: An avalanche search dog is trained to find humans under up to fifteen feet of snow.

Through most of the 1990s, I rode my Morgan horse, Kelly, in the riverbed that ran through the heart of Santa Ana, California. Many strange and wonderful things happened on those rides. I made friends with gang members who were tagging. I prayed at early-morning SWAT raids. I gave horse rides to children playing at a park. Kelly and I dodged balls from not-very-good golfers. I chatted with homeless people, and they petted Kelly.

Then one morning, my life slipped into another gear when I found a starving dog in the middle of the dirt trail along the riverbed. At first, I thought the dog was dead, but he jumped up when he saw the horse coming at him. I couldn't just leave this skinny, half-dead dog on the trail.

I slid off Kelly and tried putting the dog on the saddle. He squirmed too much for me to hold him and swing back up, so I got back off, put Kelly's lead line around him, scrambled back on my patient horse and hauled the dog aboard. He sat quietly in my lap on the flat dressage saddle. Perhaps he was too weak to struggle more. I could feel all his bones under his black fur. We rode back to the stable, and he meekly crouched in my car for the short trip home.

My husband Jeff and I had been married for almost ten years. We hadn't been able to have children, so getting a dog was wonderful for We named our new charge Wolfgang, Wolfie for short, because he looked like a half-sized German Shepherd.

"I think his father is that junkyard dog I see when Kelly and I go north on the riverbed," I said to Jeff. An identical-looking dog barked furiously every time we went by. After a few weeks, Wolfie gained weight and strength, and would follow Kelly and me, so the junkyard dog had to bark at the three of us.

Wolf adored Kelly, perhaps because he saw her as part of the team that saved him, and he loved to go riding. He would carefully watch me in the early morning to determine if I was dressing to go to work or to ride. Once he discerned that I was going to the stables, he'd bark crazily from that moment on, all through the car ride, until we jumped out of the car at the stable. He never chased or nipped at Kelly. He was a gentleman when he was on the trail, even though he was off-leash most of the time. He learned to respond to hand and voice commands to move out of bicyclists' way and leave loose dogs alone.

Wolfie never became a people-person dog. Perhaps he'd been abused. He loved Jeff and me and two other family members unwaveringly, and that was it. He didn't really like people other than his four favorites to touch him. When Jeff and I occasionally argued, Wolfie would pant anxiously, whine, and run from one of us to the other until we stopped fighting. We called him the Counselor Dog.

He learned so many words that we started saying things in Spanish so he wouldn't get his hopes up that he was included in, say, a car ride when he wasn't. Eventually, he became bilingual! Wolfie continued to show he was very smart. I was a volunteer with a search-and-rescue team in Southern California, and I began bringing Wolfie to some of our team drills.

One Saturday, our team went to a regional park with grassy hill steep ravines and miles of trails. Wolfie had been primed to sea after being fed cheese sticks by the three "victims" prior to their hid

My team and I trampled through the hundred-plus degree looking for victims all morning. Two had already been rescued b teams, and we were walking along a high trail looking for th when Wolfie stopped and looked down a ravine choked with o A trained SAR dog will alert to human scent by doing some barking or picking up a stick. Wolfie and I were new at this, so what would he do? Wolfie stayed very still. Could he understand what we were doing? Was he after more cheese from the victim? Finally, I said, "The dog thinks someone is down there."

So we scrambled into the ravine. Sure enough, under the heavy oak limbs of a tree, was the victim, a teen with a "broken leg."

"You guys took long enough. I was bored," he said. My team members were overjoyed. "Good dog!" everyone said over and over to Wolfie, who graciously allowed them to pet him even though they weren't his fab four. The victim fed him his reward: a cheese stick.

After my team packaged the victim, splinting his broken leg and placing him on a backboard, we transported him back up to the trail where a truck was waiting to whisk him away. Finished with my duties, I looked around for Wolfie. He generally didn't stray far from me. I skittered back down to where we had put our backpacks with our gear and lunch. Wolfie was slinking away.

He had something in his mouth. I caught him and grabbed his jaws. I pried them open and out popped a damp cheese ball about the size of a baseball.

While we had been prepping the victim, Wolfie had been conducting a search of our backpacks. When my team members found out, they stopped with the praise and muttered, "Bad dog! Bad dog!"

Of course, who could blame him?

~Marian Flandrick

86

Real Dedication

Fun fact: Border Collies are the most widely utilized stock dog in the world as a result of being selectively bred for their working ability for many generations.

Zac was a working Border Collie. He was also my teacher and partner. Some people would say his life revolved around working livestock, but he loved working with me even more.

I had just started training dogs to work livestock when Zac was born. The minute I looked into his big, brown eyes, I knew he was put on the earth to be mine. The connection was immediate.

He was one of the smaller pups in the litter and not the most athletic of the bunch but he could be downright bossy with livestock. He'd politely "ask" once, maybe even twice, but the third time there were going to be consequences for any animal that didn't obey him.

One day in the prime of Zac's life, a massive fire raged in the buffalo pasture next to one of our summer pastures. My husband was on the fire line and called over the CB radio to ask me to move cows and sheep out of the way of the fire. I quickly saddled a grabbed Zac and my other dog Kat, and loped out across the hustle the livestock to safety.

Several hundred disoriented sheep were pressed up a fence in the middle of a huge cloud of smoke. There wasn't for subtleties. "Get 'em up!" I hollered to the dogs. They past experience and the urgency in my voice that it was and push hard.

The sheep resisted at first and tried to beat the dogs back. The dogs and I won out, however, and over the hill we went with the whole bunch at a high lope. They raced on until we came to a water tank.

The sheep had been standing in the smoke for quite some time, and they hit the tank hard. The lambs were still quite small at the time, and many got shoved right in. They couldn't reach the bottom and were already exhausted, so it didn't take long before several of them were in real trouble. I jumped off my horse and started grabbing the lambs nearest the edge to drag them out.

The tank was both deep and wide, and many lambs were out too far for me to reach them from the edge. I started pulling off my boots and was headed in to pull them out before they drowned. Zac had been watching me the whole time, and before I could even put a foot into the tank myself, he jumped in.

He swam out and grabbed a lamb by the tail, and like any good lifeguard, dragged them one at time to the edge where I could pull them out. He didn't quit until the last one was rescued. I didn't say one word to him during the process. He just knew what needed to be done and shot into action.

As we both stood there trying to catch our breath afterwards, I ꞏched down and stroked his head, reminding him once again how ꞏ I thought of him. He gently wagged his tail and looked deep ꞏoul like he always did.

ꞏvasn't much time for affection or to kick back as we still ꞏve away from the approaching blaze. We hustled off in ꞏusband said he thought they were last seen. As we ꞏhey were already crossing a fence that had been ꞏ the buffalo pasture. The dogs and I worked ꞏck to safety.

ꞏdown the first hill, Kat heeled one cow ꞏnd her. A heavy kick from the cow ꞏflying through the air. After what ꞏraced down to check on him, but ꞏready up and headed back to work. I

ꞏe
ꞏwas
ꞏ our
ꞏorse,
ꞏills to
ꞏgainst the
ꞏt any time
ꞏknew from
ꞏtime to push,

figured he was okay, and we continued moving cows for another hour.

When all the livestock was safely out of the way of the oncoming fire, the dogs and I headed for home. We took a much-needed break and lounged around for a bit. An hour or so later, I walked out to feed the dogs, and Zac couldn't stand up. He tried several times, but despite no yelps of pain, it was evident he was hurting. I quickly set out with him on the hour-long drive to the nearest veterinary clinic.

My vet checked him over and discovered through an X-ray that Zac's hip had been broken. My heart ached for the lousy job I'd done of looking out for my best friend. He never whimpered or cried when the cow kicked him. Not once did he try to quit in the hour of pushing cows after it happened. There never was a growl toward the vet or me as we poked and prodded to fix what must have hurt so badly.

As I fought back tears of regret, Zac lay on the steel table and licked my face, reassuring me everything would be all right. He was right, as usual. He healed, and we had many more years of partnership. Despite some arthritis in his old age, he lived a long, wonderful life, always by my side. I will forever be grateful for the gift of Zac's faithful heart and his dedication to our work together.

~Laura Hicks

87

Creating a Guide Dog

*Fun fact: The use of guide dogs for the blind increased
when World War II veterans began looking into their
use. Guide Dogs for the Blind, Inc. was founded
in 1942.*

When you see a blind person being guided by a dog, do
you ever wonder how that helpful canine came to be
a service animal? Well, I raise puppies that grow up
to become guide dogs. They live with me from about
eight weeks old until age two. During that time, my responsibility is
to get these untrained dogs socialized to the world.

At that point, the pups return to the Guide Dogs for the Blind
school campus. There they spend several months being formally trained
and thoroughly tested. Only then are the dogs matched up with a blind
person. By then, these service animals have been totally prepared for
anything and everything when teamed up with their human companions.

My most recent pup was Leo. I took him many different places
to practice good behavior. We went to buffets and restaurants with all
those wonderful, distracting food aromas, attended parties, and visited
libraries, stores, and amusement parks. My pup accompanied me to
historic events where he heard cannons shooting off, and he even rode
along with me in my 1926 Model T Ford that rumbled and shook as
we drove. Leo went everywhere people buzzed about their business.

My very good dog and I participated in charity walks and city
disaster drills, greeted people for special events, and visited people in

hospitals and rest homes. Everywhere I took him, Leo was the perfect dog. If I gave the command, "Leo, let's go," he was ready and willing. He never resisted, nor was he afraid to do anything I asked of him.

However, there was one time that Leo "had a mind of his own" and shocked me while making others laugh. I had been nominated for an award for my volunteer service work, and I was invited to attend the awards banquet.

When Leo and I arrived, we entered a room full of people from all over the city. I was dressed up in a long, shiny, silver dress and high heels. This was not my normal attire when out with Leo, so he was already a little surprised. Dressed in his usual green guide-dog training vest, my puppy sat patiently and obediently under the table, and was well behaved during both the dinner and the awards ceremony. In fact, most of the attendees did not even know a dog was present.

After two hours, much to my surprise, they announced that I had won the Volunteer of the Year award. Leo and I were seated at a table way in the back, and I was expected to come all the way up on stage. Since guide dogs in training need to accompany their owners everywhere, I quickly pulled Leo from under the table to maneuver through the crowded room to go up front with me.

Music was blaring and balloons were waving around, while the audience was clapping and cheering loudly. I was in shock and Leo could sense how tense I was. When the two of us finally reached the stage steps, flashbulbs were going off, and the large trophy up on the stage was reflecting bright light about the room. Amidst this blaring music, thunderous clapping, cheering, and a flurry of camera flashes, I sensed Leo's tense mood. In the back of my mind, I realized I had not prepared him for this moment.

For the first time ever, Leo put on the skids! It was like he was saying, "No way am I going up on those steps with you!" So I said, "Okay, SIT and STAY!" Leo obeyed.

I continued up the stage steps alone, almost tripping on my dress, but my obedient companion remained in place. He was focused on me, as he was taught. I was proud of him. Then the Master of Ceremonies said, "Will you say a few words?" He handed me the microphone, and in agreement, I said a nice and loud, "Okay!" Besides meaning "yes," this word also happens to be the "release word" for dogs to break from their last command. In the excitement of the moment, I forgot that detail.

Leo looked up at me, and I realized my mistake. He still was not going to come up on the stage. It was the worst, most confusing command for poor Leo. He turned and ran to the mayor and the chief of police in the front row! Everyone in the room exploded with laughter, and the photographers were taking his photo. I began my speech by saying, "I was going to compliment Leo for being so good here tonight, but now…," and everyone burst into laughter again.

When I walked back down from the stage, Leo was once again the perfect, well-behaved dog, posing in the photos with me and the other nominees.

But for that one moment, when he forgot his manners, I had to remember that he was just a puppy in training. Perhaps he thought that if we went on those narrow steps together, with me in my outfit, we could trip. Or maybe he wanted me to have all the attention for myself. His reaction certainly did get me all sorts of attention. For the next several months, people teased the mayor and me about the event. It became the talk of the town and was on all the social-media pages, as well as the local newspaper.

Most of the time, I feel I can read a dog's mind, but not this time. It was a moment I will always remember. In April 2015, I even ended up sharing that story at his graduation ceremony, when Leo did indeed become an official Guide Dog for the Blind.

~Marcia Lee Harris

88

When the Dogs Come

Fun fact: The word "schnauzer" means "walrus moustache" in German.

I adopted Ebony, a black Miniature Schnauzer, from a local shelter. It quickly became obvious her past must have included some sort of trauma. My heart went out to her. She kept her head low and seldom made even the slightest sound. Although she would climb eagerly into my lap, she tucked in her tail when she was around people she didn't know.

The shelter's adoption counselor suggested I take Ebony to obedience classes. It would help her become more confident when she needed to interact with other people and dogs. This didn't sound appealing to me, but for Ebony's sake, I swallowed my own reluctance and signed us up to begin the next course.

At the first class, Ebony and I tangled around each other during every exercise. It seemed we'd never achieve the smooth precision demonstrated by the trainer. But with each passing week, we worked together more efficiently. It wasn't long before I smiled proudly with the other participants when our instructor took a group graduation picture. Best of all, I noticed Ebony had begun to lift her head higher and didn't shy away from strangers. We attended another series of classes. Then we went on to complete a Canine Good Citizen course. When the instructor handed me Ebony's certificate, he had a surprising suggestion.

"Ebony has such a sweet personality. I think she'd be a natural for our pet visiting team. Would you come with us on Saturday when we visit the Twin Oaks assisted-living facility?"

I hesitated before answering. It wasn't that I didn't think Ebony could do it. She'd blossomed during our training classes. Rather, I worried about how I'd handle visiting with the elderly and frail residents who could no longer live in their own homes. I had no clue what I should say to them. But the trainer's hopeful face made me put aside my fears and agree.

On Saturday, I dragged my feet along the sidewalk to Twin Oaks, reminding myself that we had only committed to one visit. Fortunately, my feelings didn't travel down the leash to Ebony. She wore a colorful bandana, and her ears were perked up at attention. She trotted forward as though on a mission.

Inside, a group of people had already gathered in the sun-filled visiting area. Some were seated in chairs and others in wheelchairs. I watched as one of the handlers began talking to a resident. Ebony waited patiently at my feet until I took a deep breath and walked toward a woman in a wheelchair near the back of the group. I smiled at her.

"Hello. Would you like to pet Ebony?"

The woman's faded blue eyes were fixed on my dog. She smiled and patted her lap. Words weren't necessary for me to understand what she wanted. I lifted Ebony and settled her carefully on the woman's thin legs. She smoothed Ebony's fur from head to tail, over and over in a soothing rhythm. The woman's face beamed. She repeated the same words.

"Just like Sadie. Just like Sadie."

A neatly dressed woman appeared beside me. She wore a badge identifying her as Doris, the facility's Activities Director. Doris whispered, "That's Berta. She has trouble remembering things and sometimes is a bit withdrawn. But when the dogs come, it really lifts her spirit."

Berta was completely absorbed with Ebony, sometimes uttering sounds I couldn't fully understand. Ebony lay on Berta's lap without squirming or changing position. It was as though she sensed that now was the time to be still and simply let Berta touch her. I knelt beside the wheelchair and watched Berta's face soften and her eyes begin to sparkle. Suddenly, my worries about how to act or what to say seemed inconsequential.

By the time we left Twin Oaks, I agreed to continue making weekly visits. Ebony's ability to connect with the residents convinced me we had to return. My dog had traveled from fear to confidence and even acquired a job she loved. I only needed to tie a bandana around her neck to see her tail wag.

When the dogs entered the room, they transformed it. Downturned faces and listless arms changed to wide-open eyes and hands outstretched like colorful day lilies unfolding in the morning sun. My own self-doubts disappeared, and strangers turned into friends.

I realized being part of a pet visiting team didn't require extraordinary skill. It only took a smile, an open heart, and the healing power of a dog's love.

~Pat Wahler

89

Service with a Smile

*Fun fact: The first prison-based dog-training program
was established by a nun in the early 1980s in
Washington State. Hundreds of these programs now
exist in the U.S.*

My neighbor arrived at my door eleven years ago, clutching a tiny, skeletal ice cube under her jacket. I turned on the heating pad as she unwrapped a purebred, red-nosed Pit Bull puppy, about ten days old. As I wrapped her in the heating pad, I remembered the promise that I had made to my husband when the last of my Pit Bulls died at the age of sixteen. During our years together, he had asked only one thing of me: that I bring home no more Pit Bulls.

When I heard his car come down the driveway, I dreaded his reaction when he saw what I was holding. But he merely took the dog, about the size of a soda can, from my arms and leaned back in his recliner while she cuddled up beneath his chin. Each time she woke up for feeding and cleaning, he put her back on his chest.

By morning, she had demonstrated her will to live by learning how to slurp up her formula from a shallow bowl. Our Manx kitten, Clyde, happily shared it with her. My husband declared that her name should be Bonnie. I questioned whether we should name her, since I only planned on keeping her until she was old enough to be spayed. He repeated, "Her name is Bonnie."

The deadly duo proved to be well named. Together, they terrorized our other animals, including my retired service dog, a German Shepherd capable of squashing Bonnie with a well-aimed paw. By the time she was a month old, Bonnie was escaping from every enclosure I put her in. It was time for crate training.

In addition to being small for her age, Bonnie suffered from severe separation anxiety. Each time I left home, unless she was held on my husband's lap, she would scream until I returned. My solution was to bring home a big bone that she could only have when she was in her crate. In less than a week, she was sitting in front of the refrigerator when I dressed in my town clothes, and headed straight for her crate when I pulled out her bone.

Bonnie was just four months old when I began retrieval training with my new service-dog prospect. I had great hopes for her, as her leash work was perfect, and she would even pull my wheelchair with me walking behind it.

Armed with a pocket full of dog treats, we went to police and fire stations so she could learn that people in uniform are friends. We went to restaurants, grocery stores, and casinos. Bonnie was a social butterfly. She would sit and politely greet everyone who spoke to us. To this day, more people in town know her name than mine. I remain the woman who comes in with Bonnie.

When my husband passed away in his sleep I woke up to find Bonnie pounding his chest with her front paws and licking his face as hard as she could. It looked exactly like a canine version of CPR. When the funeral home took him away, she expressed her grief loudly with a sound I had never heard a dog make before. It sounded exactly like a human crying.

Five years ago, we left on a five-hundred-mile trip to visit family in north Idaho. About halfway there, an elk jumped in front of my pickup, and I drove off the road to avoid hitting it. My truck rolled, coming to rest on its top in the middle of the road. Both doors were jammed, and my legs were pinned under the steering wheel. Bonnie was safe, as I had thrown myself on top of her, hanging on to the seat rails.

When help arrived, they first tried to force open the doors, and then broke out a window. They pulled Bonnie out and held her out of the way. She was lunging and barking, trying to get back to me. I was actually afraid that she would bite someone in order to get free. The last thing I needed was to have my service dog in quarantine in the middle of Nowhere, Idaho. My rescuers finally turned her loose, and she rushed back to my truck, turning around so I could reach the handle on her harness. She pulled, slowly and steadily, while I worked to free my legs. The ambulance arrived just as she finally pulled me free.

Bonnie stood with her paw on my knee while the EMTs examined me, watching everything that they did. She then stood like a statue while they also gave her a thorough exam. They determined that I needed to be hospitalized and loaded me into the ambulance. Bonnie rode the entire thirty-five miles with her paw on the foot of the gurney, observing everything that was done to me. At the hospital, she heeled beside the gurney and sat by my bed in the emergency room. A CAT scan showed that I had broken my neck and back, but it was determined that I could continue my trip if I wore neck and back braces. I attended the reunion, had a nice visit with family members whom I had not seen for many years, and was driven home by my brother.

I knew that my life would change with the unexpected arrival of the tiny Pit Bull, but had no idea how much until the day she decided to become my new service dog. Somehow, she knows what I need before I know it myself.

The tiny, dying puppy that my neighbor fished out of a dumpster seemed to realize that she had a mission to complete and intended to live to fulfill it — and fulfill it she did. At the age of eleven, Bonnie is ready to retire. Eventually, I will find a dog capable of performing the tasks I need, but there will never be another Bonnie, the dog that changed my world.

~Kathryn Hackett Bales

90

The Reluctant Volunteer

*Fun fact: There are two types of wilderness
search-and-rescue dogs: air scent dogs can pick up the
scent of any human, while trailing dogs pick up the
scent of a specific person.*

When my husband joined the New Mexico Wilderness Search and Rescue team as a communications volunteer, I cheered him on. What better way for him to make good use of his amateur radio license?

Then he started coming home from his training sessions talking about the various dogs in training. Uh-oh. I knew what was coming.

He wanted to train a dog to join him in the woods as they conducted search-and-rescue missions. Please don't get me wrong. I love dogs. I love all animals. But we already had a black Lab, a huge German Shepherd, four cats, countless fish, desert toad guppies, and a turtle... all in a 1,000-square-foot home. Oh, and lest I forget, we had three children under the age of eight.

While my husband would technically be the volunteer who trained her for search and rescue eight hours a week, you-know-who was going to be the reluctant volunteer for the rest of the week.

My suspicions were confirmed. At dinner one night, Paul said, "What do you think about getting another dog?"

Even though I knew what he was getting at, I pretended otherwise. "We already have two."

"Well, I was thinking about training my own search-and-rescue dog."

There it was. Out on the table.

"How will you know a dog is good enough to train?" Yep, I opened that door.

And he was off at a full gallop. "Well, first you look for a dog with a strong play drive. They need to be intelligent, so I'd want a German Shepherd."

"We have one," I pointed out.

"He's a little old. I want a puppy."

Oh, dear. This was worse than I thought. It was one thing to get a dog, but a puppy? I'd already done that, over and over. No thank you. We didn't argue. After that night, we just avoided talking about it. I didn't bring it up because I knew he would see it as tacit permission. He didn't because he didn't want to hear an explicit "no."

Then one day, he phoned from work. "Our team trainer just called. There's a female German Shepherd, six months old, and she needs rescuing." I could hear it in his voice, the cautious enthusiasm.

Darn him. He knew how to get me. But I wasn't going to give in quite that easily. "Why does she need to be rescued?"

"Well, it sounds like she's a busy girl. Um… she chews things."

Like what? Bones? Shoes? Small children?

"And when her owner's away, she tends to damage things."

I cringed at that.

"Then last night she dug up about 100 feet of newly installed television cable and chewed it into one-foot hunks. I guess that was the last straw."

Wasn't this just sounding better and better?

"The owner is going to put her down tonight if someone doesn't take her." I could hear in his voice he wanted this dog. He hadn't seen her. He hadn't evaluated her. But another woman had already stolen his heart.

Because I love my husband, I said, "Go see her. If she has any potential at all, bring her home."

"Thanks, honey."

What had I done? Exactly the opposite of everything I'd intended. But I wouldn't ignore an animal in need.

I got home shortly after sunset and saw my husband was already home. When he opened the front door, the distinctive silhouette of an erect, alert profile with its characteristic pointed ears appeared.

As I came up the walkway, my husband opened the door, and the dog approached.

"Her name's Sadie."

I knelt down and crooned to her, "Aren't you a beauty."

Sadie buried her head in my chest and was still. Silently, she begged me to open my heart and allow her to stay.

"Welcome to the family, you sweet thing."

The next day, after my husband went to work, my true volunteer work began.

Sadie chewed everything. Socks, shoes, the edge of the dog-food bag, raw potatoes, even wallboard. At least she didn't chew the small children.

Every time I left the house for even the shortest of errands, she caused significant damage. Once she pulled down a wall of pegboard that held our pots and pans. Fortunately, they were aluminum and didn't harm her. The next time she knocked an entire Costco-sized box of powdered detergent into a newly opened bag of Science Diet dog food. Neither the detergent nor the dog food was salvageable.

Something had to be done.

I took my volunteer duties seriously. By leashing Sadie to my waist, I encouraged her to bond with me and lose her fear of abandonment. During the day, Sadie and I were constant companions… until my husband came home. I figured my volunteer stint was up in the evenings. Sadie soon bonded with both of us. She loved playing with the kids and seemed to really enjoy playing dress-up.

"You really think she's going to be a good search-and-rescue dog?" I asked. We looked at Sadie, the longest tongue I'd ever seen hanging out the side of her mouth. She wore a gold bolero, a green bandana around her neck, and a green pair of clown-sized sunglasses on her nose. "That's the goofiest-looking dog I've ever seen."

Paul laughed and said, "Well, at least she's socialized and likes kids. That's a good sign." Leave it to him to look on the bright side of things.

The following weekend, Paul took Sadie deep into the wooded mountains that were our home. There he met with the rest of the dog team to do weekend drills. The smile on his face when he came home that night told me all I needed to know. "She's a natural! She figured it out right away. This is going to be wonderful."

Sadie and Paul spent hundreds of hours training together. I even allowed my eight-year-old son to accompany them and be their pretend victim. Sadie found him every time. I know, not every mother would tell her child, "Go get lost in the woods." But that's exactly what we did. It's how the dogs learn.

I continued my role as the off-duty volunteer, conducting obedience training and socialization at home. Eventually, Sadie passed her test and joined the Wilderness Search and Rescue team and went on many missions. Sadie worked hard and played even harder, becoming a beloved member of our family and an asset to the community.

~Kathleen Birmingham

91

The Natural

Fun fact: Therapy dogs at hospices provide comfort not only to dying patients, but also to their families.

After responding to an advertisement for volunteers at the hospice, I sat chatting with the volunteer coordinator. The hospice had been open for about a year, a very welcome addition in our community, and now was looking for special personnel to visit and comfort residents in their waning days. I reached down and unfastened Roxy's leash as she kept her big brown eyes on the coordinator, as if she was taking it all in. "She's not exactly what I was looking for," the coordinator stated. "I was hoping for a lap-sized dog, but she certainly is gentle and talks to you with her eyes."

"No, she's not a lap dog; she's a Lab — a small one as she was the runt of the litter — but she thinks she should be a lap dog, too," I stated. "She also understands grief. She curled up beside her mother when she was dying, and she grieved for several months. So when someone is feeling down or not well, she senses it and tries to offer her empathy and comfort. She works hard at trying to please."

We walked down the hall with the coordinator. Roxy started to enter one of the rooms, but I told her, "No," and she continued to follow. The coordinator took her into the next room where she was fondly greeted. Immediately, Roxy cuddled up to the patient, who was sitting in his wheelchair. "Well, she's winning me over. Let's try her and see how she works out," suggested the coordinator.

As I was a full-time caregiver to my daughter, we arranged for us to drop off Roxy and pick her up again at the end of her shift. Another volunteer would oversee her. And thus Roxy became the first dog volunteer at the new Foothills Country Hospice.

The first few visits, she arrived with her leash on, but after a couple of weeks it was no longer required. Upon entering the facility, she would stop at the door while her feet were wiped and, when given the okay, she would first say "hi" to the volunteer at the front desk and anyone else close by, and then be escorted to a resident's room. Soon, she was also strolling unleashed alongside wheelchairs as residents enjoyed the fresh air and beauty of the pathways and gardens outside. Being on duty, she never took off chasing gophers like she did at home on the farm.

Baths before visits became a regular chore, and Roxy obediently stepped in to the shower even though this was not one of her favourite activities. Rolling in stinky things was more to her liking, but she quickly associated baths with volunteer days.

For weeks, one volunteer helped hoist Roxy up on the bed to lie beside a resident who was extremely weak. Roxy lay quietly beside the resident, soaking up and giving as much attention as she could. Eventually, the volunteer discovered that Roxy didn't need help, just a small invite and she would climb, ever so gently, onto the bed by herself. Before long, she was up on the couch or bed whenever she felt someone wanted her love. She found her way into the fireside room and the chapel area when functions were going on and greeted everyone. One day, she lay unsupervised beside the tea cart during a memorial tea. She did not even try to take a morsel of the tempting goodies for herself. She never barked in the facility and always seemed to be looking for approval that she was doing the right thing. If she wasn't needed, she snoozed by the front desk.

Roxy always arrived for duty with a smile, and as her popularity grew, one shift a week became two. The residents, staff and volunteers looked forward to her company and sought her out. She did, however, seem to have a built-in clock and would often be watching the doorway if we were a little late in picking her up. People would go in and out, but she never tried to escape. She just waited for her family.

We were told stories about how much comfort Roxy was providing. One young woman was losing her husband. When the volunteer came to check on Roxy in that room, the resident was asleep, but Roxy and the young wife were curled up together on the floor as the woman poured her grief into Roxy's fur. One family had the hospice call us when their loved one passed away. They needed Roxy's companionship, so she made her rounds to console the various family members in the fireside room as they grieved and made funeral plans. Another family made special mention of Roxy's care in the loved one's obituary.

People had their pictures taken with Roxy, and one woman had hers enlarged and hung over her bed. Visiting children loved playing with Roxy. Older ones took her for walks. Regardless of how rough some little ones were with her, sometimes pulling her tail or poking her eyes, she never showed any signs of aggression and gave them all the kisses they could want. It gave their parents time to spend with their failing loved ones.

People who saw us downtown began recognizing us as Roxy's family. Knowing that sometimes residents did not have many visitation days left, we were happy to provide this service for them. We felt bad when we had to be away, causing Roxy to miss her visits.

Other dogs have since joined the program to visit different days accompanied by their owners. Having watched how Roxy worked, we decided that even if we were available to accompany her, she worked better without us. She was totally trustworthy and sensed what people needed. As things were, when a volunteer escorted Roxy to a room and left her with the family, they were free to seek her comfort privately, and she would respond unconditionally.

For six years now, we have continued to bathe, groom and transport Roxy to and from the hospice twice weekly as well as to other occasional special events. Roxy, now ten years old, remains top dog — a hospice favourite — and she relishes her time there. Last year, she also began volunteering with the Literacy for Life Foundation, which uses dogs to help reluctant or struggling readers in elementary schools. The kids read to the dogs and feel more enthusiastic and less self-conscious that way. She gives cuddles and kisses there, too.

Roxy is a busy girl, and she keeps us hopping with her volunteer schedule. We are happy to help Roxy, the little yellow Labrador Retriever, make a difference. She gives her heart to everyone who needs it.

~Irene R. Bastian

92

Lead Me Not...

*Fun fact: The Americans with Disabilities Act, passed
in 1990, says that disabled people and their assistance
dogs must have access to public places.*

I was not surprised to see a woman with an old Golden Retriever, her guide dog, asking a couple for directions to one of the smaller restaurants. The Scarborough Town Center in Toronto is such a large shopping plaza that it is easy, even for a sighted person, to become confused. When the couple didn't know where the restaurant was, the blind woman left.

Forty minutes later, after a totally unsuccessful bathing-suit shopping expedition, I passed the restaurant. The same woman was plodding along several stores ahead of me. I knew that she had walked right by her intended destination, probably not for the first time.

I rushed to catch up to her. "Excuse me," I called, "but are you still looking for Moxie's Grill?"

When she said "yes," I put my arm out and suggested that she take it.

"You walked by the front door a few minutes ago," I said. "You are going to have to teach your dog to read," I added jokingly.

"He knows exactly where it is. I meet my friends there every couple of days," she said matter-of-factly. "He's just pissed off because I won't take him for a ride on the escalator."

~Joei Carlton Hossack

Stella

My Very Good, Very Bad Dog

My Intuitive Dog

Fun fact: When a tsunami in the Indian Ocean killed many people in 2004, few animals such as dogs died because their superior intuition told them that they needed to seek higher ground before the tsunami hit.

93

The Strength of Two

*Fun fact: Malamutes were developed by an Inuit tribe
called the Mahlemuts in western Alaska. They were
trained and bred to pull sleds and endure
harsh weather.*

As a professional dog-care provider, I am often delighted by the behavior of my furry clients. I feel pretty lucky to spend my days being greeted with wags, kisses and happy spirits as I go about my job.

I walk a big, beautiful fur ball named Harper three times a week. He is a pure white Malamute-Shepherd mix with piercing yellow eyes. His greatest loves are squirrels, peeing on the world, and impressing the rest of us with his girth. Harper's personality is, thank God, relatively calm. When other dogs yap around him, he merely gazes at them from his height as if to say, "Of course, you're impressed, Little One." He seems to have little need to prove anything further. And he's right. He is mighty, and he owns it.

When I first started this walking job, Harper's parents told me he might be distracted by small furry things running about the streets. They supplied me with little peanut-butter treats to carry in my pocket to distract him from the furry creatures. The snacks actually work well except when Harper hears the bag crumple in my pocket as we walk, and he begins to think about the glories of peanut-butter snacks. Sometimes, just the thought of them makes him crazy, and we have to stop our walk to partake in these tasty Bits of Wonderful, squirrels or no squirrels.

Harper and I had been walking together and munching on peanut-butter snacks three times a week for some time when a relationship I was in ended in a shocking and hurtful way. Though I was very sad, and it was hard for me to find the energy to go to work, I found myself at Harper's door, ready for a walk, the first day immediately after the breakup.

Usually, when I arrive for a walk with one of my furry clients, I greet him or her happily and am greeted happily back. However, this day I was quiet. My energy level was low and sad, and when I let Harper out of his kennel, his intense eyes raised immediately to mine in concern. As I clipped the leash onto his collar, he continued to look into my face intently, but I could only look back wordlessly. And in this fashion, we set off into the snowy, gray day.

Harper's gait is a long trot, and even for me, a woman of five feet, eleven inches, it's hard to keep up with him. It's a half-hour cardiac workout with a dog that weighs very nearly what I do! Naturally, at that pace, when his nose gets to working on something and he decides to stop and take a prolonged sniff, he can yank very hard. I've come down on the ice more than once after he has made a quick U-turn to get a good sniff of something, so I try to walk very mindfully with him, watching his movements so I can preempt sudden jerks in the opposite direction.

This day, however, he walked much more calmly by my side, glancing up at me as we went, as if to make sure I wasn't crumbling before his eyes. Truly, we walked that half-hour together as if in solidarity, the cold Minnesota wind penetrating my winter gear while delighting Harper, who never blinked an eye, even in below-zero weather. We tromped along through snowdrifts and across ice, my boots crunching along and his nails clicking against the frozen streets. And as we walked, he stayed near me, his attention not on the squirrels or the bag of peanut butter treats crinkling in my pocket, but on me. His silent companionship seemed the most real thing in the world at the time, for his sense of animal spirit strength was solid, and I found comfort in his presence and purity.

When we got home, I let Harper off his leash and encouraged him to drink some water while I wrote his parents' daily note to let them know how the walk went. Harper lay down next to me and waited calmly, keeping an eye on me as I moved about. I grabbed a cookie for him and asked him to get in his kennel, as I always did. It was our habit each day, and Harper always went into his kennel without prodding or complaint, focused on his cookie. This day, though, as I stood by the kennel and waited for him, he leaned up against my leg and stood there with me, the pressure of his head against me like a giant, hairy, it's-going-to-be-okay bear hug.

We stood like that for a while, our souls connected. My hand rested in his long and fluffy fur, his warmth against me.

"Thank you, Buddy," I said. I put my arms around his big neck and hugged him. I swear he winked at me before he moved inside his kennel.

The Big Guy got an extra cookie that day.

~Heidi FitzGerald

94

My Advocate

Fun fact: Pugs tend to snore and breathe loudly, so you might want to wear earplugs if your Pug sleeps in your bedroom.

I was counting down the months. I'd been a stay-at-home mom for eleven years, and my youngest son was starting kindergarten that fall. I was going to have some uninterrupted time alone, and I was going to use it to become a writer. As soon as the bus drove away, I would pack up my laptop and head to the coffee shop to pound out a few pages of my novel, maybe do lunch with the girls, and then stop at the farmers' market to pick up something to make for dinner. I'd be home just in time to waltz through the back door, sashay through the house, and be standing out front waiting for the bus when it returned the children.

But my son had started talking about needing a dog in early spring, and he hadn't let up. And it wasn't just a five-year-old chanting, "I want, I want, I want." It was an obsession.

"Mom, I'm going to die if I don't get a dog."

"We're not getting a dog."

"But I need one."

Every Tuesday our local paper featured photos of pets available for adoption, and one day they ran a picture of a dog that looked exactly like the one I had as a kid. So I did the unthinkable. I took the kids to the shelter to meet her.

She was part Miniature Pinscher and part Pug—a Muggin. And she was a troublemaker. Miss Molly was two years old and had already been adopted out and returned three times. She'd also killed a groundhog that had wandered into the yard, and for some reason they didn't share with us, her present keepers felt she would do better with a family that had a stay-at-home parent like me.

My carefully laid out plans evaporated and we adopted her.

Ever see *Gremlins*? There were three rules for keeping one of those as a pet: no water, no food after midnight, and no bright light. When you broke one of those rules, disaster ensued. Well, our Muggin was cute and fuzzy like Gizmo, but we soon learned she had her own set of rules: no crates, no chicken, and no leaving her alone. Ever.

And boy could she bark. She could also jump a four-foot fence, dig a hole the size of a storm sewer, eat her weight in garbage, and Houdini her way out of a harness. This dog had an attitude. And she was my problem now.

People asked me when I was going back to work. Instead of saying I'd decided to give writing a go, I told them I couldn't leave the dog alone. Which was true. It was silly to think I could be a writer anyway. A pipe dream. I came from a long line of clock-punchers with exceptional work ethics. Sitting and making up stories all day? It would have been conceited to call that my job.

Separation anxiety aside, there were good things about Miss Molly. She got me out for a walk every day. She was very loving and affectionate. And she was a great watchdog. But she remained, despite our best efforts, untrainable.

If we said no dogs were allowed on the sofa, she'd jump up on the loveseat. If the vet said to withhold a certain food, she'd just eat it out of the garbage. If we tried to get her in the house so we could leave, she'd wedge herself under the deck. "Sit" meant bark. "Stay" meant run in circles. "Lie down" drew a blank stare. Through it all, she wasn't a bad dog, not in the malicious sense of the word. She just didn't want to be told what to do.

We developed a routine. As soon as the bus left, we headed out for a walk. Then Molly got a treat. Then I was allowed to write. My computer was in a spare bedroom, and she lay on the carpet at my feet while I worked, but only until school was over. Then she'd nudge my leg and make sure I got downstairs in time for the bus.

When summer came, a strange thing started happening. I'd gotten a few rejections, so my confidence was flagging, and the kids were home from school, so my schedule was altered. But Molly's wasn't. After our walk, she'd lead me to the stairs even if I didn't have plans to write. She'd use all eighteen pounds of herself to block my path if I tried to detour around her. Tripping me wasn't out of the question. She insisted I go upstairs and write for a few hours each day, the same way she insisted she be allowed on the furniture. So I did it.

When the kids came upstairs to tell on each other, she stood in the doorway. No admittance. When the doorbell rang, she scared away whoever it was with her ferocious barking. When 2:30 came, she got up, nudged me in the leg, and left the room. Work time was over. My husband and the kids started calling her my secretary. But she was more than that. She was my advocate.

I started looking at her defiance as a positive. I felt a kinship. Wasn't I bucking the "rules," just like her? Most able-bodied people got jobs and worked for others, but I didn't want to; most dogs stayed in crates while their owners were away, but she didn't want to. Was that so different?

We started to compromise. The thing she hated the most was the crate her former keepers insisted we have before they would allow the adoption. They said crates made dogs feel more secure, but that just wasn't the case with Molly. So we got rid of it.

Now, when we want to leave the house, we put up a gate separating the kitchen from the rest of the house. Molly could jump it easily, but she doesn't. She stays in her area while we are gone.

She won't stay off the furniture, but she will lie on her blanket so she's not shedding directly onto the cushions. Even so, she prefers to be on a lap, which is fine — we all prefer it, too. She knows what "sit," "stay," and "lie down" all mean, though she does occasionally give us that "are-you-talking-to-me?" glare before complying with our request.

Now that she has finally trained us all, it's hard to remember the whirling dervish we adopted eight years ago.

She cannot walk as far as she used to, and I sometimes carry her up the stairs to work now, but she is still the happiest and most enthusiastic dog I have ever known. The whole family has learned about perseverance thanks to her indefatigable spirit. Especially me.

My work has been published, and I write full-time now because it's what I love to do. The reason I never gave up on it? Molly wouldn't let me.

It's a good thing my son needed her so badly!

~Tracy Falenwolfe

95

A Familiar Face

*Not-so-fun fact: Theobromine an ingredient in
chocolate, can be toxic to dogs, causing liver failure
or death. It's best not to give your dog chocolate,
especially if it's small.*

When my husband Ron brought home the gregarious, six-week-old yellow Lab pup, I was dismayed. Although I'm as avid a dog fancier as he is, I had two children, ages one and two, and was expecting a third. The idea of a big, full-of-vim-and-vigor puppy thrown into the mix, with Ron frequently away from home taking university courses, was overwhelming. I wanted to tell my spouse to take that toasty-warm, sweet-smelling bundle of buff-colored fur right back to the breeder. I couldn't manage any more responsibilities. Then I saw the look on his face, and the thought melted like ice in a microwave.

This was his dream dog, the one he'd longed for all his life. Okay, I sighed inwardly. I'd give it a try.

"What are you going to name him?" I asked resignedly as the puppy snuggled into my arms and heart.

He shrugged. Then he glanced past me at the television screen where the children were watching cartoons. A forestry commercial had just flashed on featuring Smokey, the big, amiable fire-prevention bear.

"Smokey," he said. "I'm going to call him Smokey."

So Smokey joined the family that cold April afternoon. He loved the big hayfield that was the back yard of our rural home. He housebroke easily and was amazingly gentle with the children. Small hands in his fur or on his ears or tail didn't deter him, although I tried to keep such unfair treatment to a minimum. In fact, he reveled in being with the two little ones, Joan and Carol. Carol learned to walk by pulling herself upright on Smokey's hindquarters.

And that first autumn, as a green pup, Smokey further distinguished himself by proving to be an excellent retriever in the marsh that was only a couple of miles from our back door. Ron was delighted.

But Ron was frequently away from home, and I didn't have the time or stamina to train a pup and work him into a well-socialized companion. As a result, he sometimes left our property and used the neighbor's lawn as a bathroom. This, of course, brought immediate complaints.

In November, our third child, Steven, was born. Three babies and a big, largely untrained puppy were more than I could handle. At Christmas, in a fit of good-natured exuberance, Smokey knocked over the tree and ate an entire box of candy.

When spring arrived, I was rapidly becoming exhausted by the care of three babies and one large, high-spirited yellow Lab. Something had to give.

And it did. Fate stepped in and gave us a shove into the decision we were so reluctant to take.

In May, shortly after Smokey had celebrated his first birthday, Ron's friend Dan and his wife Mary came to visit. They immediately fell in love with the gregarious yellow Lab. A young, childless couple who lived on a farm about fifty miles away, they'd been looking for a dog, a Labrador Retriever, in fact. When they saw our situation, they cautiously suggested that they'd be willing to take Smokey to live with them.

At first, neither Ron nor I was willing to consider the idea. In spite of our problems with children and a young dog, we loved the Lab with the good-natured grin and constantly wagging tail. We'd adopted him as surely as if we'd adopted a child. He was family.

The following week, our minds were changed when Smokey wandered out of the yard and was nearly struck by a car. Lacking supervision and attention, he'd begun to roam.

His brush with death startled us into facing reality. Smokey needed more time and care than we could give him. If we truly loved him, we'd let him go to a place where he'd get just that.

For most people who give up a dog for adoption, the story ends there. But Smokey was to prove to be an exceptional dog when fate once again stepped in.

The rural school where Ron was principal was suddenly slated for permanent closure in June. We'd have to move. Ron looked over the available teaching jobs for which he was qualified. Finally, he decided to accept a position as a chemistry teacher in a city ten miles from the farm that was now Smokey's home. We didn't foresee this proximity as being a problem. We'd never let the Lab know where we were.

September saw us ensconced in our new urban home, a basement apartment in a residential subdivision. After living in the wide-open spaces with an entire house and several acres of farm land at our disposal, it took a good deal of adjusting physically as well as mentally to become accustomed to the restrictions of a small flat and a postage-stamp-sized back yard. Left each day with three preschoolers in a totally foreign environment, I was more than a bit lonely. I knew no one in the community. Sometimes, after the children were asleep and I was alone, tears came. I longed for a familiar face.

Early one October evening, I got my wish. I was watching television alone in our sunken living room (Ron was at a school meeting, the children safely tucked into bed) when I glanced up to see a pair of glowing eyes peering in at me.

My first instinct was to swish the drapes shut and rush to check the locks on the door. Then I recognized the lolling tongue and good-natured canine grin.

"Smokey!" I couldn't believe it.

Hearing his name, sent Smokey's tail into a wild whirl. A welcoming "woof" erupted from his throat.

By the time I got to the door, he was already there and burst in, all his typical joie de vivre fully intact.

"Smokey!" I knelt to take him into my arms, tears of happiness blinding me. Here, at last, was a familiar face — a happy, lovingly reassuring face. I buried my face in his soft, strong neck and cried.

Later, I took him into the kitchen and, even though I knew it was the wrong thing to do, gave him a slice of roast beef from the refrigerator. Then I sat down at the table and tried to decide what to do.

Call Dan and Mary, of course. They must be frantic with worry. Reluctantly, I picked up the phone.

"Smokey!" Three-year-old Carol toddled into the kitchen. She'd been dragging her favorite teddy bear, but the minute she saw her old friend, she dropped it and rushed to hug him. Smokey set to lavishing wet-tongue kisses over her little face as she laughed and pressed herself against him. "Smokey, I lub you!"

I found a Kleenex, blew my nose, and told myself not to let my emotions overcome common sense. I remembered Dan and Mary telling us in telephone conversations that Smokey never left their fenced farmyard even though they knew he could easily have cleared the rail fence if he'd made a decent effort. They'd taken his lack of interest in running away to mean he was completely content.

What, then, had aroused him to action that beautiful October night? Had he somehow sensed our relative nearness? And how had he managed to find us? We'd conscientiously avoided visiting him, and Dan and Mary hadn't been to our apartment since we'd moved.

While I was waiting for Smokey's new family to arrive, Ron came home. I'll never forget the look of utter joy on his face when he saw his hunting buddy.

He must have been feeling the same happiness I felt when I'd first seen Smokey's irresistible, lop-sided grin peering in at me from the window. I knew then and there that we had to find a way to have the Lab back in our lives once more.

"We have to talk to Dan and Mary," I said.

"I know." Ron was down on one knee, ruffling Smokey's neck.

"But how did he ever find us?" I sat down on a chair at the table again. "I can't imagine…"

"I went to see him yesterday." Ron's confession caught me totally off-guard.

"You what? But I thought we agreed…"

"I know, I know." He avoided my eyes and concentrated on straightening Smokey's collar. "But I wanted to see him, just for a few minutes. I never thought he'd try to find me… us."

He looked up at me, and his expression told me what we had to do.

Dan and Mary arrived a few minutes later. And we talked… into the wee hours of the morning, with Smokey lying between his two families, sleeping at times, watching our faces furtively as if he knew it was his future we were discussing.

We knew we couldn't take him back from Dan and Mary. They loved him; he was their baby. We also knew our landlord had a strict no-pets rule. Final conclusion: We'd have visiting rights, and Smokey would be kept under closer supervision at the farm.

When he died, no one mourned his passing more than I did. The dog that had come unwanted into my life had become an integral part of it. I will most certainly never forget that October night when, with a crooked grin and flapping tail, he drove away the loneliness in my heart simply by being a loving, familiar face.

~Gail MacMillan

96

The Dog Who Mourned

Not-so-fun fact: Dogs show their grief not by crying,
but by moping, lying around or not eating well.

It took us several weeks to adjust to living together. The little white dog had been in my house with her original owner, but had never stayed overnight, never stayed alone with me. We liked one another. I walked her when she lived in her original home, and she played with me there. Now things were different: Suddenly, Gretchen had become my dog.

Actually, it was not suddenly. The little curly-haired Cockapoo must have guessed her owner, my friend Hilda, suffered a serious illness. It was clear to me when I walked Gretchen that summer that it was Hilda's last one with us. The dog knew the terrible truth because she wasn't as eager to walk or be away from Hilda.

I always let Gretchen decide where we would walk. Sometimes, she chose a route a few blocks long. Other times, she wanted to travel only around her own block. But as summer wore on and Hilda's cancer sapped her strength, Gretchen wanted to walk only to the nearby corner and then run home. It made Hilda laugh to see me running behind the dog, holding onto the leash and trying to keep up.

Gretchen no longer played with me as she once had done. Instead, she hovered around Hilda, staying as close to her as possible. She ignored her many toys, but not the treats Hilda gave her.

Near the end of the summer, Hilda said she worried about what would become of her little dog.

"I'll take her, Hilda," I said without hesitation.

"You will?" Hilda asked.

"Absolutely," I answered and hugged my dying friend. "This way, I'll always have a part of you with me." We both cried as we held one another.

Two days before her eighty-third birthday, Hilda entered hospice. I was about to leave for a long-planned family reunion. Another friend took in Gretchen until I returned a week later. Gretchen had stayed with other people known to Hilda when she took trips, so I had the feeling her little dog thought the stay with me was only temporary until she could return to Hilda's house. So each time we walked, I referred to my house as Gretchen's when we headed home.

About two and a half weeks after Hilda entered hospice, I took Gretchen to see her. Hilda's daughters wheeled their mother outside on a sun-splashed October day. They cried for joy when they saw each other.

The little dog tried to climb up the wheelchair and couldn't. Obviously, she wanted to get as close to Hilda as she could. I picked her up so she was at the height of my friend's lap. She licked Hilda's face as the dying woman kissed her between sobs.

We stayed for more than a half-hour as Hilda petted Gretchen and talked to her. The dog nearly danced for joy; she couldn't stay still. Finally, we had to leave so Hilda could go in for lunch. Reluctantly, Gretchen allowed me to lead her away. As we walked to the car, she looked back several times.

When we reached my car, I put down her water bowl so she could drink after all that excitement. She ignored the water bowl at first and tried looking under the cars parked near us so she could glimpse Hilda again.

Once we were both in the car, I backed out and pulled near the spot where Hilda still sat in her wheelchair. Gretchen normally lies down on the back seat when we go out in the car. Upon hearing Hilda's voice, the dog stood up at the window as if to say her final "goodbye" to her beloved Hilda.

After that day, Gretchen seemed to settle in with me, but she still didn't want to play and ignored the toys that I had brought from Hilda's house. We established a routine of three walks a day and trips to the local park once a week. Still it seemed as if Gretchen yearned to "go home" to the house where she had been raised and lived for twelve years.

Near the end of October, Hilda lapsed into a coma. I had spent a few hours with her that day, but came home to let Gretchen out. That evening, a friend and I sipped tea at my dining room table. I wrestled with the idea of returning to Hilda's bedside.

Suddenly, Gretchen became very restless. She wandered around and around, unlike her usual calm behavior. I petted her and told her to lie down, but she couldn't relax and seemed uncomfortable.

Then she let out a sound I have never heard from a dog. It was a mixture of a cry and a moan with a little scream in there, too. I rushed to her, wondering if she had somehow injured herself. Obviously, she was hurting. It was as if she sensed Hilda was on her deathbed.

In a few minutes, she settled. I remained puzzled by what I had just seen and heard until my telephone rang. Hilda's daughter called to tell me her mother had died at about the same time Gretchen acted so distressed.

I believe Hilda came to say "goodbye" to her beloved little dog, and Gretchen heard her. I also know that Gretchen mourned.

~Sandy McPherson Carrubba Geary

97

Friends for Life

Fun fact: The Hebrew word for dog is kalev from the
words ka (like) and lev (heart) meaning like a heart.

My mom, Maryanne, had at least one dog in her home
from the time she was born. They were like an extension of her. When my mom was diagnosed with cancer, she could no longer care for herself, let alone a
pet, so her dog ownership days were over.

I had to find a home where my mom could be cared for profes-
sionally. I visited numerous board-and-cares to interview the staff and
make sure they would give my mom the attention she needed. One
of those facilities was All for Seniors, a five-bedroom, private home in
the Mira Mesa community of San Diego, California. When I knocked
on the door, and we were greeted by Sammy and Bella, I knew my
mom was home.

Bella is a beautiful, posh Maltese with long, fluffy-white hair. She
runs around the house in frilly dresses, getting lots of attention, and
is affectionate with anyone and everyone. Sammy is a white Poodle
with brown ears and a large snout. She's a bit standoffish and awkward,
and lives in Bella's shadow. My mom loved them both but Sammy was
her favorite.

When my mom declined suddenly and became bedridden, Sammy
didn't leave her side. Sammy lay at the foot of her bed, resting her
face on her front paws, and watched over my mom while she slept
the days away. If anyone tried to remove Sammy, she growled. When

the caregivers had to make Sammy leave my mom's room, she stayed outside the door like a guard until she could go back in. When the doorbell rang, Sammy didn't budge. When it was mealtime, Sammy stayed with my mom, missing out on all the scraps dropping on the kitchen floor.

Hospice determined that my mom was dying and put her on the imminent list. I wanted to stay and be there when my mother passed, so I had to be sure about the timing.

"How do you know she won't pull through again?" I asked her nurse.

"She's not eating," the nurse said. "She's depressed. She's lost her energy. Just look at her."

She was pointing at Sammy. Hospice based my mom's prognosis on some medical factors, but what really stood out was the sudden change in Sammy. Hospice was right. Sammy knew and was there until the very end. So was I. When the mortuary came, Sammy remained to see my mom off. Then she climbed into my arms and comforted me.

~Adrienne A. Aguirre

98

Chicken Soup for the Soul

At Your Service

*Fun fact: When formal guide dog training began in
Switzerland in the 1920s, all of the dogs trained were
female German Shepherds.*

Recently, I went to the movies with my husband and two
daughters. It was the first time we were able to go on
this kind of seemingly commonplace family outing, and
it was made possible in large part by a sable-colored
German Shepherd named Teddy.

Teddy came into our lives about a year ago at eight weeks old, ready
to be trained as an autism service dog for my nine-year-old daughter.
Training began the first day we brought Teddy home. There were the
basics, of course, with housebreaking, crate training, the good-boy list,
and the no-no list. And then there was the bonding list. Bonding would
involve my daughter interacting with Teddy by feeding, grooming, or
snuggling with him, among other things.

When she allowed Teddy to snuggle contentedly on her lap for an
unheard-of twenty minutes during his first week in our home, we were
amazed and hopeful. Maybe this wouldn't be as hard as we'd thought.

No such luck.

My daughter often struggles with doing anything new. If we had
so much as a different-looking workbook page in homeschool, she
would have a meltdown, and it could take as long as three days to get
her to do it calmly.

So it was with her bonding tasks. Initially, it was a meltdown just waiting to happen. But after a few months, my daughter began to accept the dog. Now she will calmly correct Teddy if he doesn't listen when she tells him to sit. And she can bathe him without gagging at the texture of his soapy fur, laughing as he shakes water all over her. She seems to walk taller and more confidently with Teddy by her side.

The first formal class Teddy attended introduced him to the most important and oftentimes most difficult lesson a service dog can learn: to lie down and wait calmly until released, no matter what. Young as he was, though, Teddy's energy was quickly expended, and soon he began to use class time to take a nap. Many times, he had to be woken to take his turn at a task!

From that point on, obedience and socialization were the name of the game. As Teddy learned a few commands, my daughter gained a greater rapport with him. Puppy nipping had made my daughter wary of much interaction with Teddy for a time, but his new and improving manners did a lot to help restore my daughter's confidence, and she learned how to politely tell him no. My daughter began doing her "reading aloud time" with Teddy snuggling by her on the couch. To further increase their bond, she worked while tethered to him as she sat at the table for school.

Teddy went out with us as much as possible. Now there were new rules for him to obey. No personal grooming, scratching, or shaking in public. No sniffing, particularly at any food. No eating any food from the floor or offered by strangers. Only greet people when given permission. I started with low-traffic stores that had little to no food around to tempt him. From there, we worked our way up to grocery shopping and, finally, restaurants. Although Teddy was not always perfect, his eager-to-please disposition helped us greatly with teaching and correcting him. I was often surprised at how easily he handled new situations and stressors.

I have been amazed at the difference Teddy has made in my daughter's life. One day, while running errands, my daughter was tired and resisted going into a store. She was pulling me toward the door and getting louder by the second. I quickly found an empty aisle and had her sit on the floor with Teddy for a moment. He leaned against her side, their preferred method of deep pressure. After about a minute, she began to calm and pet him. I asked if she was ready to continue, and she said she was. Just like that. Nothing had ever worked so quickly to calm her in the past. What could have become a major meltdown was alleviated in a minute. Not only did she complete the errand after that, but she was laughing and happy.

After this first year in training, my daughter is already so much calmer about dealing with loud noises with Teddy around. In the past, we have barely succeeded in getting my daughter to enter a theater because of the loudness. This time, she went in confidently with no hesitation. Despite this being Teddy's first experience, he didn't hesitate either. At one point during the movie, I moved Teddy down to a lower step from where we were sitting, thinking he was squishing my daughter's legs. My daughter responded to this by moving onto the floor to sit beside him. I got the message. She wanted him touching her. She needed that reassurance. I felt hope blossoming more fully in me as I saw one of my dreams realized in the wonder of having the whole family together at the movies.

For months after the event, my daughter still talked about her experience at the movies, often saying, "What's your favorite movie?" — her way of asking us to guess *her* favorite movie. And what movie did we see that is now her favorite? It is called *Max*, about a boy and a German Shepherd.

~Kristin Stuckmyer

Chicken Soup for the Soul

Our Rescue Dog Rescues My Wife

Fun fact: Seizure alert dogs sense oncoming attacks so people can find a safe place or seek help. Some dogs are even trained to press a button to contact emergency responders.

Our dog jumped on the bed at 4:00 a.m., stepped on me and continued to paw at my face until I woke up. He knows he's not allowed on the bed, but he knew he had to wake me: My wife was having a seizure.

My wife Brandy suffers from lupus, a chronic illness that takes its toll on her body daily. To exacerbate her disease, she was also recently diagnosed with epilepsy. A seventy-two-hour EEG showed she had at least ten seizures within three days, mostly late at night while sleeping. This night, however, the seizure was the most severe.

Porter, our chocolate Labrador Retriever, had been very anxious before we went to bed. He paced the floor, went outside only to come back in moments later, barked at random, licked my wife's hand, and would do pretty much anything for attention. Little did we know, he was trying to warn us.

When Porter woke me, the bed was shaking vigorously. I called Brandy's name repeatedly, with no response from her. I turned on the lights and saw Porter lying across Brandy's lap as she seized, trying to comfort her. I could see a scared look in his deep, golden eyes. He wasn't sure what was wrong, but was trying his best to help her.

When my wife came to, she had a crushing headache and a temperature of 105 degrees. I wasn't sure if it was the epilepsy or the fever that caused the seizure, but we immediately went to the emergency room. Brandy was admitted to the hospital for observation, fluids, and treatment for the flu. After a few days, she was released and sent home. To this day, Porter does not leave her side.

Curious, I did some research on service dogs and how they may benefit epilepsy patients. Surprisingly, about fifteen percent of dogs have an innate ability to predict seizures before they occur. Labradors are a common breed for "seizure alert" animals, in addition to German Shepherds, Setters, and Border Collies. While there isn't really a way to "train" a dog to provide an alert for a seizure, some will warn their owners by pawing, barking, or licking them. This allows the owner to prepare for a seizure by sitting down or getting to a safe place. A few dogs even respond by using their body to brace their owner if he or she falls down.

When we first got Porter, I knew he was special… I just never knew how special he would turn out to be. As a friendly stray, he showed up at our house the evening of an ice storm. He was cold and hungry, so he claimed an old couch in our garage for the night. The next day, I posted his photo on numerous local Facebook groups and Craigslist. He had no collar, no microchip, and, sadly, no owners. I often ask myself how someone could throw away such a beautiful animal.

I had been looking for a dog, and Porter was the perfect fit for us. His presence even helped me work through some anxiety and depression issues I had been suffering for years. His companionship was far greater than any medication the doctors prescribed. In short, he was my new best friend.

He came to us looking for a family, and I am glad he made his way into our garage that night and our hearts forever. I like to tell people that Porter is a rescue animal that decided to adopt us. While I'm away at work and the kids are in school, I know that Porter is on constant watch while my wife is home alone. He alerts us to people at our door and keeps the kids warm at night when he sneaks into their rooms. And now, when he starts acting out of the norm, we pay close attention to my wife for possible signs of an oncoming seizure.

Researchers aren't exactly sure why or how seizure alert animals respond. Some suggest it's a unique smell as the body chemistry changes before a seizure. Others say there are minor changes in a person's mood or body language that dogs can sense. Whatever it is, I'm a believer.

~Sonny Cohrs

Paying Their Respects

*Fun fact: In 1896, a veterinarian allowed a friend to
bury her dog in his apple orchard in Hartsdale, NY.
The Peaceable Kingdom now holds the remains of more
than 80,000 pets.*

If dogs have been an important part of your family as they have
been for my family, then you know some dogs seem to have a
special sixth sense about things. While for the most part they
try to keep their special gifts to themselves, every now and then
they slip up.

That was the case with two of our dogs, Lucky and Lil' Bit. Lucky
was the black sheep of the family, not only in color but also in temperament. She loved to find ways to leave the confines of her indoor living
routine, which made her a masterful escape artist. Lil' Bit, on the other
hand, was a near angel of a dog, doing exactly as she was told, never
straying, always staying close to home… except when she came under
the influence of Lucky, the wandering black sheep.

Whenever the two got out together, they could be seen high-tailing
it out of sight and often staying away for hours. More often than not,
they'd arrive home near suppertime, covered in mud and leaves and
smelling to high heaven from their afternoon jaunt in the woods.

I remember one such occasion when they had once again mysteriously escaped, except this time, they returned clean and no worse for
wear. It wasn't until a few days later that we learned why.

My wife ran into our neighbor Carl, who lived a few houses

down from us.

"Saw your two dogs the other day," Carl said with a smile.

"Oh, yes, I'm so sorry. They had been so good lately, so it was such a surprise when they got out. I sure hope they didn't cause any trouble," my wife replied.

"Oh, no, no trouble at all. Did you have any idea where they went?"

"No," my wife answered.

"They attended my dog's funeral," Carl said sadly.

"What?" Ann exclaimed. "Oh, no. I didn't know Toby had died."

"Yep, died a couple days ago. I was burying him in the back lot when your two dogs came running up. They sat down not far from me while I finished burying him, then they left."

"Wow, that's amazing!" my wife replied. "Toby was Lil' Bit's father, you know."

"No, I didn't know that," Carl replied, "but I guess that explains why she felt like she needed to be there. She had to say her final goodbye."

~W. Bradford Swift

Bella

*Fun fact: Like people, dogs with anxiety may be
treated with behavior modification techniques,
anti-anxiety medication, or both.*

I will never forget the day that our Labradoodle Bella came into
our lives. She was crying, whimpering, and shaking as we took
her home, but now she is an integral part of our family.

Bella was the perfect addition to our family. You see, three
people in my family (including me) have Asperger's syndrome. Two
of my siblings are extremely picky eaters. I struggle with anxieties.

So, which of these qualities do you think our wonderful dog got?
If you guessed all of the above, you'd be right. She's a picky eater, only
eating table scraps that she likes (read: meat products). If she were
human, she would have Asperger's syndrome because she exhibits
almost every single quality of it. And as for anxieties? Well, let's just
say that's where the "very bad" part of my dog comes in. You see, Bella
has separation anxiety. When my mom is gone, she freaks out. She
has done everything — and I mean EVERYTHING — you can imagine,
from getting into brownies and crackers, which she doesn't normally
eat but will when she's frantic, to chewing up my aunt's expensive
shoes, to running straight into our screen door when my mom went
outside and she wanted to follow her.

So why do we keep such a high-maintenance dog? Couldn't we
just drop her off at the shelter or sell her? Well, there's a difference
between "could" and "would." Hypothetically, we *could* sell her, or give

her away, but then her heart would be broken… and so would ours.

Bella may be neurotic, anxiety-ridden, picky, frantic, and just plain psycho, but she's our psycho dog. She's there when someone needs comfort. She's sweet and gentle, and has never bitten anyone. She knows how to make us laugh, even if it's not intentional (it never is). She can be a very good dog. And most of all, she knows that she is a part of our family, just as important as any human member.

And I guess that, at least to me, we're all a little like Bella — we can be anxious and neurotic, sweet and gentle. We all have our very good, very bad moments. But then again, that's an important part of us. After all, that's what makes us human, and I have Bella to thank for teaching me that lesson.

~Megan Yeardley

Meet Our Contributors

Monica Agnew-Kinnaman is ninety-seven years old and a veteran of World War II. She served in the British Army and was stationed in London in an anti-aircraft artillery regiment. She has lived sixty years in Colorado and is the author of two other published short stories and one book, *So This Is Heaven*, about rescuing old dogs. (Editor's note: We've read her book and it's fascinating and beautifully written!)

Adrienne A. Aguirre has a Master of Arts in Theology from Bethel Seminary San Diego, where she works in development. She's also a freelance journalist and volunteer chaplain. Adrienne enjoys playing roller derby with her daughter Desirée and spending time with her rescue cat Kitty. She's also working on her first book.

Carol Andrews is a former television news anchor who has published three books — two for children and one for other authors hoping to turn their passion for writing into a successful business. She lives in North Carolina with, and is inspired by, her husband, son and, of course, Dora!

Katie Avagliano is a master's student in creative writing in Washington, D.C. She loves dogs, reading, the beach, and adding shows she will never have time to watch to her Netflix queue. She and her family raise Seeing Eye puppies, and are currently fostering their ninth dog.

Kathryn Hackett Bales and Bonnie live in Nevada with three dogs and four cats. She spends most of her time writing her *Touring With*

Pit Bull series, with proceeds donated to Pit Bull rescue. E-mail her at kgb@frontiernet.net.

Marie Bast is a retired civil servant and now an award-winning author for her first novel, *The Perfect Client*. She is published in newspapers, two book compilations, periodicals, and in the devotionals *The Upper Room* and *The Cup of Salvation*. E-mail her at crossohope@aol.com or visit mariebast.blogspot.com.

A former English teacher, **Irene R. Bastian** loves to write and paint, and recently began drawing. Gardening and working the family tree nursery near the foothills of Alberta allow her to appreciate the great outdoors. Her two yellow Labradors love keeping her company, especially if she is driving the RTV. E-mail her at ibastian@platinum.ca.

Carole A. Bell is a licensed professional counselor. Her ministry is helping families become what God wants them to be. She writes, speaks, and consults about parenting issues. Since 1999, she has written a weekly Christian parenting column for the *Plainview Herald*. Read her blog at www.ParentingfromtheSource.com.

Kathleen Birmingham is a freelance writer and ghostwriter, and is currently working on a number of children's books. She enjoyed her many years as the "reluctant volunteer" while her husband trained Sadie to be a wilderness search-and-rescue dog. When Sadie was not working, she enjoyed being a beloved member of Kathleen's family.

Caitlin Brown is a senior Cinematography major at Emerson College in Boston. In her free time, Caitlin enjoys reading, writing, watching movies, playing her harp, and paintballing. Caitlin loves hearing from her readers. E-mail her at Caitlin_Brown2@emerson.edu.

Melody Carlson is one of the most prolific novelists of our time. With more than 250 books published and sales topping 6.5 million, she writes primarily for women and teens. And every year she publishes a Christmas novella. She's won numerous awards, including a RITA and Romantic Times Career Achievement.

Keysha Cass is a stay-at-home mother of four. In 2011 she published a children's book titled *A Helping Hand*. She enjoys writing children's stories, and plans to keep writing stories for children to enjoy. Keysha also enjoys spending time with her family playing board games.

Sonny Cohrs recently retired from the U.S. Air Force and settled down in his home state of Georgia with his wife Brandy and their three children. Sonny enjoys kayaking, fishing, camping, and hiking. He has plans to work as a freelance photojournalist and hopes to one day publish a photography travel book.

Karen Cooper lives in rural Missouri. She needs a lot of coffee because she likes to stay up late at night looking at the stars. In her free time during the day she enjoys canning, lotion making, and crochet.

Kimberly Crawford currently resides in Frisco, TX. She is an animal lover who shares her home with three Basset Hounds and two hamsters in addition to her two daughters and husband. Kim enjoys sewing, spending time with her family and snuggling on the couch with her Bassets. This is Kim's first published piece.

Catherine D. Crocker earned a Ph.D in education in 2011. She lives in middle Tennessee with her husband and their two dogs, Precious and Annabelle. She works as an online professional academic editor. She enjoys reading fiction and inspirational books, and writing nonfiction. She has authored one small book available on Kindle.

Tracy Crump enjoys storytelling (the good kind) and has published fifteen stories in the *Chicken Soup for the Soul* series. She encourages others through her Write Life Workshops and webinars, and edits a popular newsletter, *The Write Life*. But her most important job is being Grandma to little Nellie. Visit Tracy at WriteLifeWorkshops.com.

Janice R. Edwards lives with her husband and two dogs on the San Bernard River in Brazoria, TX. She currently writes freelance for *Image Magazine*, showcasing Brazoria County. She has three other dog stories published in the *Chicken Soup for the Soul* series. E-mail her at jredwards@brazoriainet.com.

Christina Eichstedt began writing at fourteen and was first published in *Offerings Magazine* at twenty-one. Christina also wrote three books with her mother, Judy Eichstedt: *Weary Souls, Shattered by Life*; *Whispers of Truth*; and *2012: The Last Entries*. She has also been published in *The Poet's Pen*, *Poetry Motel*, and local newspapers.

Sharla Elton received both her Bachelor of Science degree in Finance and her MBA from the University of Akron. She lives with her husband in Ohio, where she works at a school. Sharla enjoys her many nieces and nephews, traveling, writing, camping and spending time outdoors.

Twilla Estes is the mother of eight children, with numerous grandchildren and one great-grandchild. She received her associate's degree in Nursing at the age of forty-five and worked in that field until her recent retirement. Twilla enjoys reading, writing, traveling, volunteering, and her dog Tater.

Sara Etgen-Baker's love for words began as a young girl when her mother read the dictionary to her every night. A teacher's unexpected whisper, "You've got writing talent," ignited her writing desire. Although she ignored that whisper, she never forgot those words. So, after retirement, she began writing memoirs and narratives.

Sue A. Fairchild is a freelance editor and previous contributor to the *Chicken Soup for the Soul* series. She is currently working on young adult fiction and non-fiction novels. Sue enjoys volunteering in her church, long walks and working with her critique group on a variety of stories.

Tracy Falenwolfe lives in Pennsylvania's Lehigh Valley with her husband

and two sons, where she's currently working on a mystery series. Learn more at www.tracyfalenwolfe.com.

Donna Fawcett is the former creative writing instructor for Fanshawe College in London. Her novels *Rescued* and *Vengeance* (Donna Dawson) won Best Contemporary Novel in Canada's largest Christian writing awards, The Word Awards.

Heidi FitzGerald is a produced playwright, screenwriter and author. She lives in the Minneapolis area where she runs her own pet-sitting business, Let Rover Stay Over. Learn more about her writing projects at www.heidifitzgerald.com.

Lynn Fitzsimmons is a professional speaker, best-selling author, coach and trainer. She touches hearts and ignites the flame of hope in individuals to live their passions and desires. Learn more at www.stepoutforsuccess.ca.

Marian Flandrick has had dogs most of her life. In addition to writing, she also pet sits. Most of her clients have dogs, and she cares for family pets, show dogs, ranch dogs, and even a retired military working dog. Marian lives in the Sierra above Fresno, CA, with her Colonial Spanish Mustang mare, Moony, who was friends with Wolfie.

Carol Fleischman is a freelance writer and author. In spring 2015, Pelican Publishing Company released her first children's picture book, *Nadine, My Funny and Trusty Guide Dog*. She does presentations at schools and libraries to educate children about guide dogs.

Angela Foster lives in Minnesota. She works as a freelance editor and teaches at the Loft Literary Center. In her spare time, she haunts animal shelters in search of a dog to replace Buster. Angela co-authored *Farm Girls*, a book about growing up on a dairy farm. Learn more at angelaffoster.com.

Victoria Franzese has degrees from Smith College and New York University. She owned, operated and wrote for an online travel guide for fifteen years before selling it to a major media outlet. Now she writes on a variety of topics and her travel is for fun. She lives in New York City with her husband, two sons, and a Goldendoodle named Jenkins.

Peggy Frezon is an award-winning writer for *Guideposts* magazine. Her new book, *Faithfully Yours*, shares heartwarming true stories about the amazing bond between us and the animals we love. Peggy and her husband rescue senior dogs, including ten-year-old Golden Retriever Ike and thirteen-year-old Spaniel Kelly. Learn more at www. peggyfrezon.com.

Sandy McPherson Carrubba Geary lives with her new husband and dog, Gretchen, in Buffalo, NY, where they walk three times a day and sometimes run. Sandy, a published poet, helps a group of senior citizens become writers. She has been published in magazines for children and adults as well as other titles in the *Chicken Soup for the Soul* series.

James A. Gemmell is a married father of two grown children. Most summers he can be found walking one of the Caminos de Santiago in Spain. His other hobbies are writing, playing guitar, drawing, painting and collecting art.

Elizabeth Greenhill is a freelance writer of essays and articles about her many interests. She received her B.S. degree in Business from Arizona State University. Elizabeth lives in Northern California with her husband. She has two adult children. E-mail her at elizabeth. greenhill@outlook.com.

Marcia Harris taught school for thirty-five years and now says her life has "gone to the dogs" since she raises puppies for Guide Dogs. She is a mom, author, edu-tainer (her word for educator and magical entertainer combined), historical re-enactor, and active volunteer, who lives by the motto, "aspire to inspire before you expire!"

Barb Hart and her husband, Stew, sold their home in 2002 and moved aboard a forty-seven-foot sailboat, living aboard in Maine for eight years before setting out on a cruise of uncertain length in 2010. Barb writes about their adventures on her blog www.hartsatsea.com, and has been published in a number of sailing magazines.

Laurel Vaccaro Hausman lives in Northern Virginia with her husband and two dogs, Red and Jack. She teaches high school English and Literature. Laurel enjoys quilting, biking, reading, and gardening. She plans to write a memoir about her teaching experiences. E-mail her at laurelhausman@verizon.net.

Jonny Hawkins draws cartoons full-time from his home in Sherwood, MI. His work has been in over 800 publications and he creates five *Cartoon-a-Day* calendars annually, published by Andrews McMeel, including *Dog Cartoon-a-Day*. E-mail him at jonnyhawkins2nz@yahoo.com.

Laura Hicks married her husband Mike right out of high school and they have enjoyed many years of marriage. Together they raise cattle and sheep on their South Dakota ranch. Laura is blessed to be the mother of two wonderful adult sons, Dustin and Brady. She is actively involved in her church and youth ministry.

Joei Carlton Hossack has been a travel writer for over twenty years, specializing in solo RV travel. She is a motivational and inspirational speaker and storyteller. She enjoys photography, teaching and recently discovered her love of beadwork. She lives in Surrey, B.C.

Allison Howell has been previously published in *Chicken Soup for the Soul: The Power of Positive* and in the *Catholic Anchor*. She is a regular columnist for *The Frontiersman* newspaper and keeps a blog about her family's adventures of life in Alaska with children with cystic fibrosis. She loves to read, hike, and pick blueberries.

An award-winning author, **Jeanette Hurt** has penned nine books, including her latest, *Drink Like a Woman*. When she's not writing or spending time with her family, she hangs out with Olivia, who enjoys chasing squirrels along Lake Michigan's shoreline. Visit her at www.jeanettehurt.com or tweet with her @JHurtAuthor.

Emily Huseman wrote two 150-page books by hand when she was nine. Now, at age thirteen, she continues to enjoy writing as well as being homeschooled, reading her Bible, playing with her many rescued animals on her hobby farm, and theater.

Jeffree Wyn Itrich has been writing since the age of six. It has been her lifelong passion, and she earned a graduate degree in journalism at UC Berkeley. She works in academic research by day and in her spare time she sews colorful quilts and writes stories for both children and adults. To date she has four books published.

Debby Johnson is a wife, mother, and dog lover. She lives in Southern California with her husband and youngest son, Christopher. Debby's four other children are grown and have flown the coop. Rounding out their house and hearts are their pups, Coco, Pixel and Sadie. They also make room for Macaroni the cat and Zanshin the turtle.

Ann Denise Karson has an English/Writing degree from the University of Colorado. She lives in the D.C. area, but loves to get back to Colorado when she can. Denise's interests include writing, reading, traveling, cooking, yoga, and she especially loves spending time with her family.

Elizabeth Anne Kennedy received her Bachelor of Science degree from Southern Illinois University and is employed at her local library. Her inspiration comes from everyday beauty and is reflected in her paintings and writings of personal essays, short stories, and poetry. Contact her at kennedyelizabetha@gmail.com.

Cris Kenney lives in rural upstate New York with Lokasteinn Kai, an Icelandic Sheepdog. Cris studies wildlife at Finger Lakes Community

College and hopes to do field work in conservation. Kai trains in agility when his human is not studying, running, gaming, or trying to write novels. E-mail Cris at cskwriting@gmail.com.

Dale Keppley is a Behavior Therapist who works with young children and their families. After graduating from Penn State University, he moved to Florida where he met his wife of thirty years. He enjoys outdoor activities, performing music and writing songs. He plans to write children's books in the near future.

Tina Koenig is a writer and technology entrepreneur. In addition to exploiting her family for fun and profit, Koenig is the author of the historical middle-grade mystery novel, *A Case of Considerable Consequence*. Links to other humorous stories about family, holidays and travel may be found at tinakoenig.com.

Kathleen Kohler writes stories about the ups and downs of family life for numerous magazines and anthologies. She and her husband live in the Pacific Northwest, and have three children and seven grand-children. Read more of her articles and join her e-mail list at www.kathleenkohler.com.

Jennifer Land received her Master of Library and Information Science degree and currently works as a full-time web development manager for her local library system. She also founded and directs Monroe's Mighty Mission, a non-profit focused on keeping pets and families together through difficult times. She enjoys traveling and writing.

Kathryn Lehan is a life and business coach focused on creating fruit-fulness in her clients' businesses and personal lives by teaching heal-ing, prosperity and purpose using practical Biblical principles. She untangles misconceptions about God that keep people stuck in fear, pain, sickness and financial lack.

Susan Lendroth is a communications professional and children's author.

Her recent picture book, *Old Manhattan Has Some Farms* (2014), takes a lighthearted look at urban farming across North America. Previous titles include *Calico Dorsey: Mail Dog of the Mining Camps* and *Maneki Neko, the Tale of the Beckoning Cat*.

Liz Lombard is a married mother of five and a lifelong South Boston, MA resident. She loves God, her family and her country. Animal welfare and advocacy is especially important to her and her family. Working to end animal suffering and raise awareness is near and dear to her heart.

Shawn Lutz lives in Capistrano Beach, CA, with her husband, two children, and their beloved Curley Ace. She enjoys being with her family, baking, writing, and exploring California. She is pleased to be a part of the *Chicken Soup for the Soul* series.

Sylvia Macchia is an RN in Neuro ICU. She enjoys writing poetry in her spare time — poetry that speaks of life's experiences and important lessons she has learned.

A graduate of Queen's University, **Gail MacMillan** is the award-winning author of thirty-five traditionally published books. She lives in New Brunswick, Canada with her husband and Little River Duck Dog named Fancy.

Bette Haywood Matero is a retired childcare professional. She lives in Arizona with her husband of forty-six years, and is the proud mother of two sons and a daughter. She takes great pride in her granddaughter and grandson. In addition to writing, she volunteers at the regional hospital in her community as a chaplain.

Jeri McBryde loves sharing her life experiences in the *Chicken Soup for the Soul* series with the hope of helping others. Jeri lives in a small southern delta town. Retired, she spends her days reading and working on her dream of publishing a novel. A doting grandmother, her world revolves around her faith, family, friends and chocolate.

Courtney McKinney-Whitaker lives with her family, including her dog, Lina, in Illinois. Her debut novel, *The Last Sister* (2014), received the IPPY Silver Medal for Historical Fiction. She is currently at work on another novel.

Dee Dee McNeil is a singer/songwriter/freelance journalist. She has been writing a current music column at www.lajazz.com for the past six years. Her songs have been recorded by numerous iconic artists, including Diana Ross, LL Cool J, Edwin Starr, Nancy Wilson, the Four Tops and more. In 2015, McNeil released her own CD titled *Storyteller*.

Christy Mihaly is a lifelong dog lover and writer. She writes nonfiction for children, and also dabbles in poetry and an occasional bit of fiction. Her first book will be published in early 2016. She lives with her family in Vermont. Her current dog is not a wonder puppy, but is an excellent writing companion and mascot.

David S. Milotta has a B.A. degree from Whitworth College, and an M.Div. and D.Min. from Fuller Theological Seminary. Supernatural experiences are his interest. Great Danes, grandchildren, stand up paddle, and windsurfing are his passions.

Beki Muchow lives in Sherwood, OR with family and several pets. Several of her stories can be found in the *Chicken Soup for the Soul* series. She spends her spare time in various Portland-area coffee shops writing short stories found in numerous publications and is working on a novel.

A lifelong dog lover, **Val Muller** is the author of the kidlit mystery series *Corgi Capers*, based on the antics of her two corgis. Learn more at www.ValMuller.com and www.CorgiCapers.com.

Nicole L.V. Mullis is the author of the novel *A Teacher Named Faith* (Cairn Press 2015). Her work has appeared in newspapers, literary magazines and anthologies, including the *Chicken Soup for the Soul* series. Her plays have been produced in New York, California and Michigan. She lives with her husband, children and very good dog.

An active senior, **Molly O'Connor** spends her time writing, walking and capturing photos of wild flowers. She is a published author of four books: *Fourteen Cups* (collection of short stories), *Wandering Backwards* (creative memoir) *Snow Business* (children's book), and *When Secrets Become Lies* (novel). Learn more at www.mollyoconnor.ca.

Shirley Oakes is a wife, mother of four, grandmother of twelve, and great-grandmother of two. She lives on a mini-farm, where she enjoys the outdoors, especially working in the garden with her husband. Researching her family history is a favorite activity, along with indexing records and writing short stories.

Christie Page is an underachieving superhero who spends her daylight hours in the medical field helping people change their lives. Her experiences have led her down a path of spiritual exploration and awakenings. Christie wishes to share her journey with others in an attempt to come to peace.

Jeanne Pallos is the author of several published stories for adults and children. She lives in Southern California with her husband and their Golden Retriever, Autumn. Sadly, Thumper was killed by a rattlesnake the summer of 2015. The family shared two and a half delightful years with this rabbit.

Nancy Panko has contributed to the *Chicken Soup for the Soul* series three times. Published in *Reader's Digest*, *Guideposts* and *Christian Women's Voice*, she is a member of Cary Senior Writing Circle and The Light of Carolina Christian Writers group. The author of a fictional novel, *Guiding Missal*, she and her husband live in North Carolina.

Mark Parisi's "Off the Mark" comic panel appears in over 100 newspapers worldwide and is distributed by Universal Press Syndicate. Visit www.

offthemark.com to view over 8,000 cartoons. Mark's cartoon feature has won best newspaper cartoon twice and best greeting card once by the National Cartoonists Society. Lynn, his wife/business partner, and their daughter, Jen, contribute with inspiration (as do four cats and a dog).

Tea R. Peronto is the author of two children's books and various other smaller works. She runs an online craft shop from Southern Oregon, where she lives with her husband. Tea enjoys the Oregon coast, Native American culture, gardening, Chinese food and bare feet.

Marsha Porter has written numerous short stories and hundreds of articles. She co-authored a movie review guide for twenty years. She perfected the 500-word essay in grade school when it was the punishment du jour.

Connie Kaseweter Pullen lives in rural Sandy, OR, near her five children and several grandchildren. She earned her Bachelor of Arts degree at the University of Portland in 2006, with a double major in Psychology and Sociology. Connie enjoys writing, photography and exploring nature. E-mail her at MyGrandmaPullen@aol.com.

Mark Rickerby is a writer, screenwriter, singer, voice actor and multiple contributor to the *Chicken Soup for the Soul* series. His proudest achievements are co-authoring his father's memoir, *The Other Belfast*, and releasing a music CD for his daughters, Marli and Emma. He is currently working on a series of children's books.

Stacey Ritz is the Executive Director and Co-Founder of Advocates 4 Animals, Inc., a 501(c)(3) non-profit animal welfare organization. Learn more at www.Advocates4Animals.com.

Bruce Robinson is an award-winning internationally published cartoonist whose work has appeared in many magazines, including *National Enquirer*, *The Saturday Evening Post*, and *Woman's World*. He is also the author of the cartoon books *Good Medicine* and *Bow Wows*

& Meows. Visit him at www.BowWowsAndMeows.net or e-mail him at CartoonsByBruceRobinson@hotmail.com.

Cindy Lou Ruffino is the author of *Out of the Texas Mist* and *Dead Xs in Texas*. She holds a master's degree in Criminal Justice. The Boston Terrier entered her life in 1994 and from that point on she was hooked. Cindy has been active in many Boston Terrier forums and groups as well as several rescues.

Stephen Rusiniak is a former police detective who specialized in juvenile/family matters. Today he shares his thoughts through his writing, including stories in several books in the *Chicken Soup for the Soul* series. Contact him via Facebook, on Twitter @StephenRusiniak or by e-mail at StephenRusiniak@yahoo.com.

Lily Ryan is an English professor and the author of books for middle grade and young adult readers. She and her husband have been blessed with five children who are called to help others.

Loretta Schoen grew up in Brazil and Italy, and now resides in Florida with her husband, a cat and two dogs, all of whom are of retirement age. She enjoys traveling and spending time with her grandson. Loretta conducts workshops on how to survive medical adversity, and is writing a devotional of medical parables.

April Serock earned an M.A. in writing from Seton Hill University. She lives with her husband and son where she can see the sun rise over the Appalachians each morning. She's published romantic short stories in *Woman's World* magazine and writes nonfiction articles for money-saving websites.

Tanya Shearer lives in Alabama with her husband, Clay. Their family includes two wonderful married children, their spouses, granddaughter Zoey Clayre, and Cornbread. She loves writing short stories and walking Cornbread. This is her fourth story published in the *Chicken Soup for the Soul* series. E-mail her at tshearer24@yahoo.com.

Jessica Snell is a writer who lives in sunny Southern California. She's the editor of *Let Us Keep the Feast: Living the Church Year at Home* and *Not Alone: A Literary and Spiritual Companion for Those Confronted with Infertility and Miscarriage*. She blogs about faith, fiction, and family at jessicasnell.com.

Laura Snell, her husband Dave and their dog Gus Gusterson live in Wasaga Beach, Ontario where they operate their web development and online marketing firm, GBSelect.com. Her son Ryan lives in Melbourne, Australia. E-mail her at laura@gbselect.com.

Jean Haynie Stewart has shared her memories in the *Chicken Soup for the Soul* series eighteen times. She edits freelance books and articles from her home in Southern California where she lives with her retired husband of fifty-five years. Their grand-dog and grand-cats are nearby, along with the grandchildren, to bring much joy.

Kristin Stuckmyer is a music therapist who has used therapy animals to assist in her work with children who have special needs. She lives in Wisconsin with her husband, daughters, service dog Teddy, and her cat Crystal. For more about a day in the life of a service dog, check out Teddy's Tales at www.allshewrote.org.

W. Bradford Swift has written several true-life stories for the *Chicken Soup for the Soul* series. He and his wife co-founded Life On Purpose Institute in 1996 (www.lifeonpurpose.com). He also writes speculative fiction under the pen name of Orrin Jason Bradford. Learn more at wbradfordswift.com.

Lisa Timpf is a freelance writer who lives in Simcoe, Ontario. Her creative nonfiction, fiction, and poetry have appeared in a variety of venues, including *More of Our Canada*, *Outposts of Beyond*, *Good Times*, *Chicken Soup for the Soul: Christmas in Canada*, *New Myths*, and *Third Wednesday*.

Lucy Tobias is a former award-winning *New York Times* Regional Group reporter and the author of Florida travel and gardening books plus a children's book about manatees. Lucy writes a popular travel blog called *Saturday Morning Magazine*. Lucy lives in Sarasota, sharing space with one dog and three cats. E-mail her at greatwalks@gmail.com.

Pat Wahler is a retired grant writer and proud contributor to ten previous *Chicken Soup for the Soul* books. Pat resides in Missouri and draws writing inspiration from family, friends, and the critters who tirelessly supervise each moment she spends at the keyboard. Learn more at www.critteralley.blogspot.com.

Jessica A. Walsh lives in New Jersey with her husband and dog. She blogs about her inspiring journey of self-discovery at blog.crackingnut. com. She co-edited *Reading Glasses: Stories Through an Unpredictable Lens*, a fiction collection, including her own story, "Unquiet Mind." She is working on her first novel.

Dallas Woodburn is a writer and teacher living in the San Francisco Bay Area. She is proud to have contributed stories to more than two dozen *Chicken Soup for the Soul* books. Learn more about her youth literacy organization Write On! at www.writeonbooks.org and visit her blog at dallaswoodburn.blogspot.com.

Sandy Wright is a gifted-and-talented teacher who is also a mountain girl who loves to tromp and snowshoe with her dog. Her passion is writing and she is active with the North Texas Christian Writers. Painting, horseback riding, and traveling with her husband are right up there as well. E-mail her at wrightonsandy@yahoo.com.

Susan Kimmel Wright lives and writes in a creaky, old western-Pennsylvania farmhouse with her husband Dave and her animal family and fosters. Her car and clothing are permanently embedded with pet hair, and her heart with love and precious memories. E-mail her at kidsbookwrighter@gmail.com.

After receiving a Master of Education degree at UBC, **Sarah Wun** traveled to the Middle East to begin her career as an ESL teacher. She currently resides in Shanghai, China where she teaches sixth and seventh grade English and Sexual Health Education. She enjoys writing, often about her experiences overseas.

Megan Yeardley is a college dropout who loves spending time with her family, friends, and especially her dog and cat! She would like to give a shout-out to Silver 4 for molding her into the person she is!

Meet Amy Newmark

Amy Newmark was a writer, speaker, Wall Street analyst and business executive in the worlds of finance and telecommunications for thirty years. Today she is author, editor-in-chief and publisher of the *Chicken Soup for the Soul* book series. By curating and editing inspirational true stories from ordinary people who have had extraordinary experiences, Amy has kept the twenty-three-year-old Chicken Soup for the Soul brand fresh and relevant, and still part of the social zeitgeist.

Amy graduated *magna cum laude* from Harvard University where she majored in Portuguese and minored in French. She wrote her thesis about popular, spoken-word poetry in Brazil, which involved traveling throughout Brazil and meeting with poets and writers to collect their stories. She is delighted to have come full circle in her writing career — from collecting poetry "from the people" in Brazil as a twenty-year-old to, decades later, collecting stories and poems "from the people" for Chicken Soup for the Soul.

Amy is a frequent radio and TV guest, passing along the real-life lessons and useful tips she has picked up from reading and editing thousands of Chicken Soup for the Soul stories.

She and her husband are the proud parents of four grown children and in her limited spare time, Amy enjoys visiting them, hiking, and reading books that she did not have to edit.

Follow her on Twitter @amynewmark and @chickensoupsoul.

About Robin Ganzert and American Humane Association

Robin Ganzert has been president and CEO of the American Humane Association since late 2010, leading the nation's oldest organization dedicated to the protection of animals and children. Dr. Ganzert utilizes the insights she gained as deputy director of the prestigious Pew Charitable Trusts and, prior to that, as Wachovia's national director of philanthropic strategies, to bring visionary leadership and a renewed vibrancy to the 134-year-old American Humane Association.

Since 1877 the historic American Humane Association has been at the forefront of every major advancement in protecting children, pets and farm animals from abuse and neglect. AHA also leads the way in understanding human-animal interaction and its role in society. As the nation's voice for the protection of children and animals, American Humane Association reaches millions of people every day through groundbreaking research, education, training and services that span a wide network of organizations, agencies and businesses.

Under Dr. Ganzert's leadership, American Humane Association has been named a "Top-Rated Charity" by CharityWatch and achieved the prestigious "Gold Level" charity designation from GuideStar.

A familiar face to millions of Americans from her frequent TV appearances and the highly-watched Hallmark Channel's *American Humane Association Hero Dog Awards*, she also hosts her own radio show, *Be Humane™ with Dr. Robin Ganzert*, which mixes practical expert pet advice with guest appearances by some of America's best known pet lovers from the movies, music and sports.

She is the author of *Animal Stars: Behind the Scenes with Your Favorite Animal Actors*. She authored the foreword of *Animals and the Kids Who Love Them: Extraordinary True Stories of Hope, Healing and Compassion*.

Meanwhile, the Association's best known program, the "No Animals Were Harmed®" animals in entertainment certification, which appears during the end credits of films and TV shows, today monitors more than 1,000 productions yearly with over 3,400 production days with an outstanding safety record. American Humane Association's farm animal welfare program ensures the humane treatment of over a billion farm animals, the largest animal welfare program of its kind.

Most recently, Dr. Ganzert spearheaded a groundbreaking clinical trial that hopes to provide scientific substantiation for animal-assisted therapy (AAT) in the treatment of children with cancer and their families. The trial is now underway at five pediatric cancer hospitals across the nation.

A graduate of Wake Forest University with undergraduate degrees in business and accounting and a Masters in Business Administration, she served as Assistant Dean for Finance and Administration at the university's Babcock School of Business while pursuing her doctorate in higher education finance.

Robin has appeared on NBC's *Today*, *ABC World News Tonight*, *Fox & Friends*, *On The Record with Greta Van Susteren* as well as other local and national television programs. She has been a guest on *The Diane Rehm Show*, Sean Hannity's radio show and many other radio programs. Robin has written for or been quoted in *The New York Times*, *Chicago Tribune*, *Los Angeles Times*, Foxnews.com, *USA Today*, *Fast Company*, *The Boston Globe*, *The Tennessean* and other news outlets.

Robin and her husband Bart reside in North Carolina and are the proud parents of three human children. Fur children include dogs Gatsby, Daisy and Chas, as well as feline family members Rosebud, Poochie and Cedes.

Thank You

We owe huge thanks to all of our contributors and fans, and to their fascinating, loving, intuitive dogs. We loved your stories about your dogs and how they enrich your lives. We could only publish a small percentage of the stories that were submitted, but we read every single one and even the ones that do not appear in the book had an influence on what went into the final manuscript.

We owe special thanks to Assistant Publisher D'ette Corona, who not only read most of the thousands of stories submitted for this book, but also worked with the contributors on any edits to their stories and ensured that we got a final manuscript on time. She was ably assisted by editors Barbara LoMonaco and Kristiana Pastir, who read hundreds of submissions themselves and proofread the final manuscript. Our outside editor Susan M. Heim deserves all the credit for her fabulous idea of including fun facts about dogs at the beginning of each story instead of our normal quotations. She did an amazing job finding the facts and pairing them with the stories.

The whole publishing team deserves a hand, including our Director of Production, Victor Cataldo, our graphic designer, Daniel Zaccari, who turned our manuscript into this beautiful book, and all our team members who provided photos of their family's rescue dogs for our chapter illustrations.

Sharing Happiness, Inspiration, and Wellness

eal people sharing real stories, every day, all over the world. In 2007, *USA Today* named *Chicken Soup for the Soul* one of the five most memorable books in the last quarter-century. With over 100 million books sold to date in the U.S. and Canada alone, more than 200 titles in print, and translations into more than forty languages, "chicken soup for the soul" is one of the world's best-known phrases.

Today, twenty-three years after we first began sharing happiness, inspiration and wellness through our books, we continue to delight our readers with new titles, but have also evolved beyond the bookstore, with super premium pet food, a line of high quality soups, and a variety of licensed products and digital offerings, all inspired by stories. Chicken Soup for the Soul has recently expanded into visual storytelling through movies and television. Chicken Soup for the Soul is "changing the world one story at a time®." Thanks for reading!

Share with Us

We all have had Chicken Soup for the Soul moments in our lives. If you would like to share your story or poem with millions of people around the world, go to chickensoup.com and click on "Submit Your Story." You may be able to help another reader and become a published author at the same time. Some of our past contributors have launched writing and speaking careers from the publication of their stories in our books!

We only accept story submissions via our website. They are no longer accepted via mail or fax.

To contact us regarding other matters, please send us an e-mail through webmaster@chickensoupforthesoul.com, or fax or write us at:

Chicken Soup for the Soul
P.O. Box 700
Cos Cob, CT 06807-0700
Fax: 203-861-7194

One more note from your friends at Chicken Soup for the Soul: Occasionally, we receive an unsolicited book manuscript from one of our readers, and we would like to respectfully inform you that we do not accept unsolicited manuscripts and we must discard the ones that appear.

Chicken Soup for the Soul.

My Very Good, Very Bad Cat

101 Heartwarming Stories about Our Happy, Heroic & Hilarious Pets

Royalties from this book go to
AMERICAN HUMANE
ASSOCIATION
EST 1877

Amy Newmark
Foreword by Robin Ganzert
President and CEO, American Humane Association

From cats with nine lives to cats that save lives— from cats that wreck houses to cats that repair families—from cats that crack us up to cats that act like therapists—you'll see your own cat with new appreciation for its unique skills and intuition.

978-1-61159-955-8

More Fun and Support for AHA

Chicken Soup for the Soul

for the Soul®

The Cat Did What?

101 Amazing
Stories of
Magical
Moments,
Miracles and...
Mischief

Royalties from
this book
support the
American
Humane
Association

Amy Newmark
foreword by Miranda Lambert

With a special emphasis on the benefits and joys of adopting abandoned and rescue cats, these loving stories will amaze you and put a smile on your face. Most of them will make you laugh out loud, some will make you tear up a little, and others will have you nodding your head in recognition, as you see your own cat in a new light.

978-1-61159-936-7

More Cat and Dog Tales

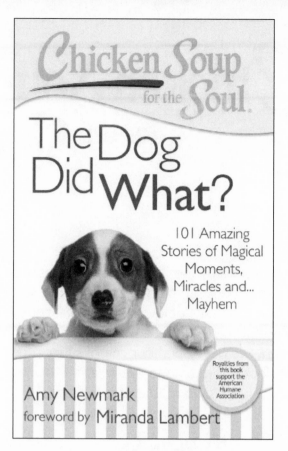

Chicken Soup for the Soul

for the Soul.

The Dog Did What?

101 Amazing
Stories of Magical
Moments,
Miracles and...
Mayhem

Royalties from
this book
support the
American
Humane
Association

Amy Newmark
foreword by Miranda Lambert

With a special emphasis on the benefits and joys of adopting abandoned and rescue dogs, these loving stories will amaze you and put a smile on your face. Most of them will make you laugh out loud, some will make you tear up a little, and others will have you nodding your head in recognition, as you see your own dog in a new light.

978-1-61159-937-4

and Support for AHA

Chicken Soup for the Soul

Brand Pet Food

because Food is more than just Nutrition, it's also about Comfort, Love and Appreciation™

We are inspired by the thousands of stories we receive about the love between pets and people. The stories are of moments... moments of love, gratitude, laughter and even heartache. So many of these stories revolve around food. That is why we developed our line of super premium, all-natural pet food more than ten years ago — to help you turn your own moments into stories.

We believe that all pets deserve to feel loved and appreciated so we proudly feature rescues on our packaging and encourage pet adoption nationwide.

Visit www.chickensoup.com/pets to learn more about our food and how your purchase helps shelter pets in need.